DOSTOEVSKY PORTRAYED BY HIS WIFE

DOSTOEVSKY PORTRAYED BY HIS WIFE

The Diary and Reminiscences of Mme. Dostoevsky

S. S. KOTELIANSKY

Routledge
Taylor & Francis Group

LONDON AND NEW YORK

First published in 1926

This edition first published in 2015
by Routledge
2 Park Square, Milton Park, Abingdon, Oxon, OX14 4RN

and by Routledge
711 Third Avenue, New York, NY 10017, USA

Routledge is an imprint of the Taylor & Francis Group, an informa business

British Library Cataloguing in Publication Data
A catalogue record for this book is available from the British Library

ISBN: 978-1-138-77918-1 (Set)
eISBN: 978-1-315-77147-2 (Set)
ISBN: 978-1-138-78573-1 (Volume 7)
eISBN: 978-1-315-76766-6 (Volume 7)
Pb ISBN: 978-1-138-80338-1 (Volume 7)

Publisher's Note
The publisher has gone to great lengths to ensure the quality of this book but points out that some imperfections from the original may be apparent.

Disclaimer
The publisher has made every effort to trace copyright holders and would welcome correspondence from those they have been unable to trace.

DOSTOEVSKY

PORTRAYED BY HIS WIFE

THE DIARY AND REMINISCENCES
OF MME. DOSTOEVSKY

TRANSLATED FROM THE RUSSIAN AND EDITED
By
S. S. KOTELIANSKY

WITH 4 FULL-PAGE PLATES

LONDON
GEORGE ROUTLEDGE & SONS, LTD.
BROADWAY HOUSE: 68–74, CARTER LANE, E.C.
1926

ANNA GREGOREVNA DOSTOEVSKY

[*front.*

CONTENTS

CONTENTS

PREFATORY NOTE

THE Diary of Mme. Dostoevsky, the rough notes of her
Reminiscences, and copies of her husband's letters to
her from 1866 to 1881, all in her own hand-
writing, were found in August 1922, and delivered by
the representative of the Commissar of Education in
Georgia (in the Caucasus) to the directors of the Moscow
Archives, who published the Diary in 1923.

The first note-book, forming the Diary, contains the
entries made by Mme. Dostoevsky from 14th April to
21st June, 1867. The second note-book contains the
entries from 22nd June to 24th August, 1867. Both
note-books relate to the time when the Dostoevskys
were living abroad—in Berlin, Dresden and Baden.

Mme. Dostoevsky originally made her entries in
shorthand, and the following is her inscription on the
first note-book :

" Diary kept by Anna Gregorevna Dostoevsky during
her travels abroad with her husband, F. M. Dostoevsky ;
begun April, 1867. The Diary was written in shorthand. Deciphered and copied out twenty-seven years
later, in 1894."

From the title of the second note-book we learn that
that part of the Diary " was deciphered and copied out
thirty years later, at the end of 1897 ; copying continued in 1909 and 1912."

The Diary is quite independent of Mme. Dostoevsky's
Reminiscences, which are also kept in the Central
Archives, and the greater part of which has already
been published in Russia.

In one of the rough drafts of her Reminiscences,

Mme. Dostoevsky relates the origin of her Diary as follows :

" As she saw me off on my journey abroad, my mother cried very much. I, too, felt very sad ; indeed, this was my first long parting from my mother, with whom I had lived so well and happily the twenty years of my life. I comforted mother by telling her that I would return in three months, and meanwhile I should be writing to her frequently. I promised her that in the autumn I would give her a most detailed personal account of everything interesting that I might come across abroad. And in order not to forget things I promised her to keep a Diary in which I would record from day to day everything that happened to me. I kept my word, and, in fact, at the railway station I bought a note-book, and began from the very next day entering in shorthand everything that interested me. With that book began my daily shorthand entries, which lasted for a year, until more serious cares interfered, that is, my preparations for my confinement.

At first I wrote down only my impressions of travel and described our daily life. But gradually I wanted to write down everything that interested and fascinated me in my dear husband, his ideas, his talks, his opinions on literature, music, etc. I also recorded our little quarrels, my protests against certain of his views, as, for instance, on the question of women. I could record freely ; for I knew that no one but myself could read what I had put down in shorthand.

Usually in the evenings Fiodor would sit down to work, and I would sit down at another table and write in my Diary. Many times Fiodor would say to me : ' How I should like to know what you are scribbling there with your funny hooks ! You must be scolding me ! '

' Who could help scolding you,' I would reply, answering him with the same phrase which he so often used to me in jest.' "

The background of the Diary is Germany, not Russia. The material supplied by Mme. Dostoevsky's *Diary* and bearing on Dostoevsky is of the highest value.

Mme. Dostoevsky's *Diary* is a large volume of about 400 pages, published in the original Russian by the Central Archives in 1923. We give here only such selections from the entries as we consider valuable for the better understanding of F. M. Dostoevsky.

The rough drafts of Mme. Dostoevsky's Reminiscences consist of over thirty separate note-books of different sizes, and are of varying degrees of literary finish. There is no doubt that these rough drafts served Mme. Dostoevsky as a basis for the final and polished text of her Reminiscences.

The Reminiscences, which begin in 1866, when Mme. Dostoevsky was twenty and first met Dostoevsky, end in 1917, a year before her death.

The Reminiscences give a clear portrait of Dostoevsky's wife during the last fourteen years of his life. Mme. Dostoevsky, with her practical mind, abounding energy, indomitable will and capacity for seeing things through when once a decision was made, is here revealed as the true complement of Dostoevsky, who was rather incompetent in practical affairs.

The first part of the Reminiscences, here published, originally appeared in a Russian literary review in 1923. The rest of the Reminiscences is taken from the Russian volume, *The Reminiscences of Mme. Dostoevsky*, recently published by the State Publishing Company (Moscow and Petersburg, 1925). We give only such selections here as seem to us to throw new light on Dostoevsky.

To understand the important rôle which Anna Gregorevna Snitkin, Dostoevsky's second wife[1] played in his

---

[1] Dostoevsky married his first wife, the widow Marie Dmitrevna Issayev, in February, 1857, at Kuznetsk, while he was still serving his time in Siberia. She died on April 16th, 1864.

later life, a few essential facts must be borne in mind. Anna Gregorevna (born in 1846) was engaged by Dostoevsky as a stenographer in the autumn of 1866. In a very short time he proposed to her, and they were married on 15th February, 1867. (She was twenty-one, he forty-six). All through the fourteen years of their married life Anna Gregorevna was Dostoevsky's stenographer, copyist, secretary, financial adviser, publisher, bookseller and general manager. Those years were the most productive years of Dostoevsky's literary activity, and during that period more than half of his works were written, namely : *The Gambler* (1866) ; *The Idiot* (1867–8) ; *The Eternal Husband* (1870) ; *The Devils*—called *The Possessed* in the existing English translation—(1871–2) ; *The Journal of an Author* (1873–4) ; *The Adolescent*—called *The Raw Youth* in the English translation—(1874–5) ; *The Journal of an Author* (1876–7) ; *The Brothers Karamazov* (1878–1880).

After her husband's death (in 1881) Anna Gregorevna devoted herself exclusively to the service of her husband's works and memory, founding and organising a special department in the Moscow Historical Museum, in which are kept Dostoevsky's numerous manuscripts, note-books, letters, portraits, and nearly everything that has been written on him in Russian and in foreign languages. For the Dostoevsky Department of the Museum Anna Gregorevna prepared a most comprehensive description of all the materials collected there, and published a complete bibliography of her husband's works and of the literature bearing on Dostoevsky. Her Bibliographical Index relating to the life and activities of Fiodor Dostoevsky contains about five thousand entries, and represents a unique achievement in Russian bibliography. The last years of her energetic life Anna Gregorevna devoted to the work of preparing her Reminiscences, to be published after her death.

In the preface to the Russian volume of *Mme. Dostoevsky's Reminiscences* the editor, Leonid Grossman, gives the following account of his meetings with Anna Gregorevna Dostoevsky, about a year before her death :

"I met Anna Gregorevna several times during the winter of 1916–17 in Petersburg, and I also met her in Sestroretsk after the Revolution.

Despite her declining years Mme. Dosteovsky possessed rare freshness and vigour of mind. Her conversation was delightful. For long hours, almost without a break, she could tell of past events, of family traditions, of men of the past, and particularly, of course, of him, who during the last fourteen years of his life was her life companion and who had now more than ever before become the object of her reverent worship.

" I am living not in the twentieth century," she said. " I have remained in the seventies of last century. My people are the friends of Fiodor Mikhailovich, my circle the band of those who are no more, the intimate friends of Dostoevsky. With them I am living. And every one who is studying the life or the works of Dostoevsky is to me as a near relation."

Mme. Dostoevsky considered the work of her life far from being complete. " I am seventy-one," she said, " but I don't yet want to die. And at times I believe I shall, like my mother, live to be ninety. There's still a lot of work to be done, the task and labour of my life are still very far from being achieved."

And the old lady in a lace cap, with a faded, but still charming face, with clear, understanding grey eyes, and with a well-preserved youthful smile, would show everyone interested in Dostoevsky's works the manuscripts of her Reminiscences, the precious relics of her personal archives and the extensive correspondence of her husband.

" I always needed an ' idea ' in life," Anna Gregorevna went on. " I have always been engaged in some work or other which absorbed me completely. Even our estate in the Caucasus I acquired with a special object in view. There are moments in the life of everyone, when one needs to be alone, to tear oneself from the habitual rut, to endure one's sorrow away from the everyday bustle. Well, I thought, let my grandchildren have such a refuge, let it serve them in their adverse moments and be of help to them. And I am deeply convinced that in such a continuous realisation of one's designs is the only road to happiness. No, I cannot complain—I have known happiness. At times, sitting here in the evening stillness of my garden and admiring the sunset, I ask in my mind : ' Lord ! why hast Thou given me such a happy life ? Lord, how shall I thank Thee for it ? ' Of course, I too am familiar with painful shocks. The last one was of a comparatively recent date." Anna Gregorevna's face darkened as she passed to the most painful memory of her old age. " You can imagine," she continued with visible agitation, " what a terrible impression the publication of Strakhov's letter some years ago made on me, the letter in which he calls Fiodor Mikhailovich malicious and debauched. I was staggered by horror and indignation. What an unheard-of calumny ! And from whom does it come ? From our best friend, from our constant guest, from the witness at our wedding—from Nicolay Strakhov, who, after Fiodor's death, asked me to allow him to write Dostoevsky's biography for the posthumous edition of my husband's works. If Strakhov had been alive I would, despite my years, have rushed off to him immediately and smacked his face for this vileness."

Anna Gregorevna's pale cheeks flushed red with indignation, her eyes kindled with a youthful fire, her voice rang with exasperation and pain. And at that moment the face of the lovable old lady clearly recalled the portrait of her as a young woman, done by Victor Bobrov on the margins of the best Dostoevsky engraving ; the same piercing fiery glance kindling under her distinctly outlined brows.

" I decided at that time," she continued, " not to publish a refutation in the press. But my answer to Strakhov I shall give in my Reminiscences, the book which is to be published after my death. That book will explain a great deal in the personality of my late husband. I wish I could repeat to everyone the answer I gave Leo Tolstoy to his question : ' What sort of man was Dostoevsky ? ' ' He was,' I replied, ' the kindest, the gentlest, the wisest and most generous of all the men I have ever known.' "

And Anna Gregorevna told me with a smile of an incident to which she seemed to ascribe some significance.

" You know that the Maryinsky Theatre is going to produce a new opera by a young composer on the subject of one of Dostoevsky's books. The composer had not troubled to make any enquiries about copyright, and we had to put him right on that point. The matter was settled. But last Sunday the composer paid me a visit to apologise in person for the mistake. He brought me the score of his opera autographed by himself. And in return he asked me to write something in his album. It was useless to refuse, I had to yield to his insistence. But when I took the pen, the young composer declared : ' I must tell you, Anna Gregorevna, that this album is dedicated exclusively to the sun. Here you can write only of the sun.' And do you know what I wrote ? . . . ' The Sun of my life—Fiodor Dostoevsky. Anna Dostoevsky.' " . . .

The last time I met Anna Gregorevna was after the Revolution, in March, 1917. In her Sestroretsk retreat she showed me over the room and halls, which also had been the scene of revolutionary events.

" We here knew, of course," she said, " of the events in Petersburg, but we did not expect that they would have reverberations here. Yet on the third or fourth day of the Revolution we saw from the windows of our hotel a huge crowd of workmen from the Sestroretsk arms factory coming in procession to our resort—all armed, carrying flags, as though prepared to besiege us. What their object was we could not make out. To our terror the crowd was coming straight up to our hotel, and in a few minutes we heard a slamming of doors and a tramping of feet which reached us from the ground floor. I locked myself in here, in my room, thinking with terror that all these things so dear to me, all these portraits, heaps of manuscripts, letters and books were doomed to destruction. In a few minutes I hear the noise approaching the first floor, and the crowd rushing past my door, talking aloud, shouting and yelling. Another few minutes and I distinctly hear the noisy and excited crowd gathered outside my door. I catch a fragment of a sentence with the name of Dostoevsky. There is a knock at my door; but to my surprise, a rather gentle and respectful knock. I make the sign of the cross, open the door and address myself to the noisy crew, praying them to treat me, an old woman, with humanity. One of the leaders hastened to reassure me. ' We know who you are,' he said, ' and we shall do you no harm. But we must have a look at your room.' And, indeed, they only examined the room, without making a search.

" It turned out that the workmen were looking for the late Minister Protopopov, who was in hiding. A rumour had spread that he was hiding in Sestroretsk. The rumour turned out to be false. They did not find Protopopov, but unexpectedly they found Makarov here. Here, in the hotel, many persons witnessed that painful scene in which the late Minister Makarov tried to hide himself, while sending out his wife with an icon to face the workmen."

It was strange to hear the quiet and rather favourable account of the remarkable scenes of the days of March,

1917, from the lips of her, who in her time copied Dostoevsky's indignant prophecies of the coming Russian revolution.

Anna Gregorevna's hopes of a life prolonged to ninety were not fulfilled. She died on 9th June, 1918, in Yalta, at the age of seventy-two. The new labours which that indefatigable worker had projected remain unexecuted.

I received the following account of the last year of Anna Gregorevna's life from a lady who is a relation of hers. At the end of May, 1917, Mme. Dostoevsky left Petersburg for her summer residence in the Caucasus, whereto she was soon followed by her nearest relations. " During that year," my correspondent goes on to say, " the work of constructing the railway, connecting Tuapse with Adler (and further down) reached our neighbourhood. The layers of decaying soil and the clouds of mosquitoes poisoned our place, which up till then had been safe from malaria. Almost the whole population, including Anna Gregorevna, fell ill with malaria. At the insistent request of her son, Fiodor Fiodorovich, who was then in another part of the Caucasus, Anna Gregorevna, accompanied by a few relations, left that infected area. Half dead we arrived at Tuapse. The journey was especially hard on Anna Gregorevna : her age, her worries, and certain privations which she had already undergone, broke down her strong constitution ; while the attacks of malaria drove her to loss of consciousness, to a half-paralytic state. Yet in a fortnight she had sufficiently recovered to continue the journey by herself to Yalta (her companions had to go to another place). Later in the winter she even thought of returning to Petersburg. But the fatigue caused by her journey probably had a disastrous effect on her health, and very soon I received a letter from her, telling me she suffered from attacks of malaria and slight strokes. Yet in December,

1917, she had quite recovered. In the spring of 1918 the Germans moved to the South of Russia, and we found ourselves cut off from Moscow, where Fiodor Fiodorovich then lived, who from time to time had been sending small sums of money to his mother. Anna Gregorevna thus found herself by that time absolutely without a penny. Continually going without sufficient food, and almost starving, she bought on 1st June two pounds of bread still hot, and in her hunger she probably ate it. That very evening she suffered most violent pains, and the doctor who was called in diagnosed acute inflammation of the bowels. A friend of hers, a woman doctor, hearing of her state, engaged a nurse for her, who attended her throughout her illness. On 5th June a letter was despatched to Mme. Dostoevsky's nearest relations to say that her condition was becoming critical ; but, through the irregularity of the postal service at that time the letter arrived only after considerable delay. On 7th June Anna Gregorevna lost consciousness, and passed another two days in the most violent pain. On 9th June, at 11 o'clock in the morning, she died. Her body was taken to the crypt under the church, and lay there till the arrival of her son. She was buried not far from the church. So, sadly and in complete loneliness, without her children and relations, almost in poverty, died in the seventy-third year of her life Dostoevsky's most devoted friend, who had done so much for the writer's happiness during his life and for his name after his death."

PART I

THE REMINISCENCES OF MME. DOSTOEVSKY
(1866)

REMINISCENCES
OF MME. DOSTOEVSKY

*THE EVE OF MY ACQUAINTANCE WITH F. M.
DOSTOEVSKY*

ON the 3rd October, 1866, about seven o'clock in
the evening, I arrived at the Sixth Grammar
School (by the Tchernyshev Bridge) to attend Professor
P. M. Olkhin's shorthand class. The lesson had not
yet begun. I sat down in my usual seat, and had just
started arranging my exercise books when our professor
came up, sat down on the bench near me and said :
" Would you like to undertake some shorthand work ?
I have been asked to find a shorthand writer, and it
occurred to me that you might like to take on the
work." I answered him that I was longing to find
work, but doubted if I knew shorthand well enough to
undertake any responsible work. Mr. Olkhin said that
the work in question would not need greater speed than
I possessed (one hundred words a minute), and that
he was sure that I should be able to manage it satisfactorily. Then I asked who was to give me the
work. " Dostoevsky, the author. He is now writing
a new novel and wants to write it with the help of
shorthand. Dostoevsky thinks that the novel will
contain about seven folios of large size, and he offers
fifty roubles for the work." On my expressing my
consent, Mr. Olkhin gave me a folded piece of paper
on which was written Dostoevsky's addresss, and said
to me : " I'll ask you to be at Dostoevsky's to-morrow

at half past eleven sharp, not earlier and not later; that is how he put it to me to-day. I am only afraid that you won't make friends with him : he is such a gloomy, stern man." I gave an involuntary smile, and said to Mr. Olkhin : " But why should we be friends ? I'll try to do my work as well as I can. Dostoevsky, the writer, I respect so much that I am even afraid of him, and this somewhat frightens me."

Mr. Olkhin looked at his watch, went to the chair and began his lecture. I must confess that this time his lecture was wasted on me. My thoughts were occupied with the conversation that had just taken place, and I was filled with happy thoughts. My cherished dream was to be realised : I had got work. If Olkhin, so strict and exacting, found that I knew shorthand and wrote quickly enough, then it must, indeed, be so ; otherwise he would not offer me the work. Olkhin's recognition of the progress I had made delighted me and raised me in my own eyes. I think that to everyone the first independent work in any branch whatever, must have a great, perhaps even an exaggerated importance. Of such importance to me, too, was my first work. I felt as if I were advancing along a new road, that I could earn money with my own labour, that I was becoming quite independent ; and the idea of independence to me, a girl of the 'sixties, was the dearest of all. But still more pleasant and important than the work itself was the chance of working with Dostoevsky, of getting to know the writer personally. Indeed, he was my father's favourite author, and the name of Dostoevsky had been familiar to me from my childhood. I myself was enraptured by his works and had cried over *Memoirs from the Dead House*. And, all at once, the happiness, the great luck—not only of making the acquaintance of the famous novelist, but of actually helping him with his work ! My agitation was intense, I wished to share my joy with someone. I could not help telling it all to my colleague, Alexandra Ivanovna I., who had just come into the class-room. She was much older than myself, quite clever, extraordinarily bold, sharp-tongued and very capable, but she often missed her lessons. Hearing of the work offered to me, she was a bit shocked that Olkhin had offered it to me and not to her ; for she considered herself the best pupil. She congratulated me on the commencement of my shorthand career, and began asking me questions ; but I did not answer them, for I knew that Olkhin did not like the students to talk during the lessons. But when the lesson was over, Mlle. I. had her curiosity satisfied. I walked with her as far as her house, and then took the coach, and in half an hour's time I was at home. I told my mother all the particulars, and she, too, was very glad : we talked for a long time of my luck. From joy and excitement I scarcely slept the whole night, picturing Dostoevsky to myself. Considering him a contemporary of my father, I imagined him as a quite elderly man. Now I imagined him as a stout and bald-headed old man ; now as tall and awfully thin, but always stern and gloomy, as Olkhin had described him. Above all, I was agitated as to what I should say to him. He seemed to me so learned, so wise, that I trembled beforehand for every word I might say. I was also upset by the idea that I did not clearly remember the Christian names and surnames of his characters, and I felt sure that he was bound to talk of them. Never having met authors in my circle I imagined them as different beings, who had to be spoken to in quite a special way. Recalling to my mind those days, I see what a child I was then, in spite of my " respectable " twenty years.

DOSTOEVSKY IN A NEW LIGHT

MY FIRST MEETING WITH F. M. DOSTOEVSKY

On 4th October, the momentous day of my first meeting with my future husband, I awoke cheerfully, happy and excited by the idea that to-day my long-cherished dream was to be realised : from a schoolgirl and undergraduate I was to become an independent worker in the field chosen by myself.

I left the house a little earlier so as to call at the Gostiny Dvor to get a fresh supply of pencils and to buy a little portfolio which, in my opinion, would give my youthful appearance a more businesslike look. By eleven o'clock I completed my purchases and in order to get to Dostoevsky's at the appointed time, " neither earlier nor later "[1] I walked with slow steps along the Bolshaya Meschanskaya and Stoliarny Lane, continually consulting my watch. At twenty-five past eleven I came up to the house, and asked the *concierge*, who stood at the gate, where flat No. 13 was. He pointed to the right, where, by the very gates, was an entrance to a staircase. The house was a large one, with a great number of small flats, inhabited by small shopkeepers and artisans. It at once reminded me of the house in *Crime and Punishment* in which Raskolnikov, the hero of the novel, lived. Flat No. 13 was on the third floor, reached by an ugly staircase, from which at that moment were coming down two or three men of a rather suspicious appearance. I rang the bell, and immediately the door was opened by a middle-aged woman, with a green checkered shawl thrown over her shoulders. I had read *Crime and Punishment* so recently and remembered so well the Marmeladovs' checkered " family " shawl, that the identical shawl on Dostoevsky's servant involuntarily

---

[1] This was Dostoevsky's usual expression. In order not to lose time in waiting for someone he would fix the exact time, always adding " neither earlier, nor later."—A.G.D.

struck my eyes. To her question whom I wanted to see, I said that I came from Mr. Olkhin, and that her master knew that I was coming.

I had not yet had time to undo my scarf when the door into the hall opened wide, and in the background of a bright sunlit room there appeared a young man, quite dark, with dishevelled hair, with an open chest and in slippers. On seeing an unfamiliar face he cried out, and instantly disappeared behind a side door. The woman asked me into a room which was the dining-room. It was quite modestly furnished. Near the walls stood two large trunks covered with carpets. A chest of drawers stood by the window and was covered with a white, knitted cloth. Against the wall stood a sofa and over it a clock. I felt great relief when, at that moment, I saw the clock showing half past eleven. The woman asked me to take a seat, saying that her master would come in presently. Indeed, in a couple of minutes Dostoevsky appeared and asked me to come into his study on the right, and himself went out, as it turned out later, to order tea.

Dostoevsky's study was a large room with two windows, which was very bright that day, but at other times produced a gloomy impression; it was rather dark and still; one felt oppressed by that strange stillness. In a far corner of the room stood a couch covered with a brown cloth, rather worn, and in front of it was a round table, covered with a red cloth; on the table stood a lamp and a couple of albums, and round it were easy chairs and stools. Over the couch in a walnut frame hung a portrait of a very thin lady, in a black dress and a black bonnet. " This is probably his wife," I thought, as I did not know anything about his family life. Between the windows was a large mirror in a black walnut frame. As the space between the windows was much wider than the mirror, the latter was nearer to the right window, which was unsymmetrical and ugly. Two large Chinese vases of a beautiful shape stood on the window sills. Against the wall was a large divan of green morocco leather and near it a little table with a jug of water. Against the back wall, across the room, stood a writing table, at which I always sat afterwards when Dostoevsky dictated to me. The furniture was most ordinary, similar to what I had seen in the houses of not too prosperous people. I sat and listened, thinking that I should presently hear the voices of children, or the noise of a child's drum, or that the door would open and there would come into the study the unusually thin lady whose portrait I had just recently been examining.

But Dostoevsky came in. To start a conversation he asked me how long I had been working at shorthand. I replied that I had been learning it for the last six months. " Has your teacher, Olkhin, many pupils ? " he asked. " At first there came over one hundred and fifty applicants, but there remain now only about twenty-five." " But why so few ? " he asked. " Many of them thought that it was quite easy to learn short-hand ; but when they saw that it could not be done in a few weeks, they gave it up," I said. " With us," he said, " it is always like that in every new thing : many start ardently, but cool down quickly and give it up. They see that application is needed, and who wants to work now ? "

Dostoevsky seemed strange to me.

At the first glance he looks rather old, but presently one can see that he is not more than thirty-seven. He is of middle height, erect. His face is worn, sickly. Bright brown, even slightly reddish hair, well greased and strangely smoothed. His eyes fail to match.[1]

---

[1] During one of his epileptic fits he fell down and stumbled on a sharp object, and so injured his right eye. Professor Yunge, who treated him, prescribed atropine, owing to which the pupil of his eye was dilated.—A.G.D.

One is an ordinary brown eye, the pupil of the other is very much dilated, and the iris cannot be seen. This dissimilarity gives his face a mysterious expression. Dostoevsky's face appeared very familiar to me, probably because I had seen his portraits before. He was dressed in a rather old blue jacket, but his shirt was snow-white. To tell the truth, at first sight I did not at all take to him.

Five minutes after my arrival the woman came in and brought two glasses of very strong, almost black tea. On the tray were two rolls. I took a glass, and although I did not want tea, and even felt hot, I began drinking it so as not to make a fuss. I was sitting by the wall at the little table near the writing desk ; and Dostoevsky was now sitting at his table, now pacing the room, smoking all the time, frequently putting down his cigarette and starting a fresh one. He offered me a cigarette. I refused it. " Perhaps you refuse out of politeness ? " he asked me. I said that I did not smoke, and did not like to see women smoking. A conversation by fits and starts began and Dostoevsky kept on turning from one subject to another. The longer it went on, the stranger he seemed to me : crushed, exhausted, ill. It also appeared strange to me that almost at once he declared that he was ill, that he had epilepsy. Of the work to be done he spoke vaguely. " We shall see how to do it ; we shall try ; we shall see if we can manage it." It seemed to me that our working together would hardly come off. It even occurred to me that Dostoevsky doubted the possibility and convenience of that way of working, and was perhaps going to give it up. To help him out, I said : " Well, let us try ; but if you find it inconvenient, tell me frankly then. Rest assured I shall not regard it as a grievance if our work does not come off." Dostoevsky asked my name. I told him ; but he forgot it immediately, and asked me again. The time was passing in conversation. Finally, Dostoevsky dictated to me from the *Russky Vestnik* and asked me to copy my shorthand into ordinary writing. He began dictating very rapidly ; but I stopped him, and asked him to dictate with the speed of ordinary conversational speech. Then I began translating my shorthand into ordinary writing, and I did it rather quickly ; but he hurried me all the while and was surprised that I copied out so slowly. I observed to him that, as I should be making the copy at home, not there, it ought not to matter to him how long the work took me. Looking through my copy he found that I had omitted a full stop and the hard sign in one word, and he remarked on it, sharply. Altogether he was strange ; either somewhat rude, or evidently too frank and outspoken. He was evidently irritable, too, and could not collect his thoughts. Several times he would ask me something, and then he would pace the room, pace it for quite a long time, as though forgetting my presence ; and I sat without stirring, afraid to disturb his train of thought. At last he said that he could not possibly dictate to me then ; but if I could come to him that evening at eight o'clock he would then start on his novel. Although it was very inconvenient for me to come the second time, I promised to come, as I did not wish to put off the work. When I was leaving he said : " You know I was rather glad when Olkhin proposed sending me a girl shorthand writer, and not a man. You are probably surprised, perhaps it seems strange to you, you may ask why ? " " Why then ? " I asked. " For this reason that a man is sure to have a drinking bout, and you, I hope, will not." The idea of my " having a drinking bout," seemed to me so funny that I burst out laughing and said : " Most certainly I shall not, you may be sure."

When I left Dostoevsky I was in a very depressed

mood. I did not take to him, and he left a painful impression on me ; it also seemed to me that we should not be able to work together and that my ideas of independence would come to nothing. This was the more painful to me because the previous night my mother and I had been so delighted at the starting of my new career. It was about two o'clock when I left Dostoevsky. It was too far away to go home, and I decided to call on my relations, the Snitkins, who lived in the Fonarny Lane, to have dinner there, and to return to Dostoevsky in the evening. Besides, as I was young, I wanted to boast to my relations that I was already beginning " to earn a living." More than once they had let drop a hint that " it was easy for me with my mother behind me," that " it was time I did something." But when I began learning shorthand, they made fun of my " art," and said that I was only wasting my time. My relations were intrigued by my new acquaintance and began asking me about Dostoevsky. The time passed quickly, and by eight o'clock I was at Alonkin House. It was very unpleasant for me to enter that house : there were so many people there in the street and near the gate, and all of them such rough people. The door was opened by Fedosya (she was quite pleased when, leaving in the afternoon, I gave her 20 copecks) and she went to announce me to Dostoevsky. I waited a few minutes in the dining-room, then entered the study and after exchanging greetings with Dostoevsky, I took the same seat as in the morning, at the little table by the wall. Dostoevsky proposed that I should sit at his table, assuring me that it would be more convenient for me to work there. I must say that I felt highly flattered by his suggestion that I should sit at the table at which had been written such an outstanding work as his recent novel, *Crime and Punishment*. We changed seats, and began talking.

He again asked me my name, and my father's name, and enquired if I was a relation of the gifted young writer Snitkin who had died recently. He made further inquiries about my family, of whom it consisted, where I had studied, what had made me learn shorthand, etc., etc., and why had my studies been so successful. In answer to his questions I had to tell him many particulars of which I shall speak later on in my story.

I told him that my father was a civil servant who had died in the spring. My mother was alive ; my sister was married to G. Svatkovsky, the Censor ; and my brother studied at the Petrovsky Agricultural College. I had finished my studies at the Grammar School with honours, and had been awarded a large silver medal. Then I had entered the Teachers' Classes, only just founded by Prince Peter Oldenburgsky. There I had no luck. I took up natural science, but my heart was with literature, and during the hours when, according to the professor, I had to make chemical experiments in crystallising salts, I was so much absorbed in reading my favourite authors (and above all, by the novels of Dostoevsky, which fact, of course, I did not mention to him) that all my tubes and retorts, left unattended, burst, and I myself became the laughing-stock of my sweet colleagues. And when at the lecture of Professor Brandt I saw the dissection of a dead cat, I felt sick with disgust, and decided that a scientific career did not suit me. I left the Classes for good.

To Dostoevsky's question "what made me take up shorthand," I answered that my family was well-off, and that there was no need for me to earn my living. But, like most of the younger generation, I set a great value on complete independence, which could only be achieved by those who have work to do which compels them to rely on their own efforts. Dostoevsky said, seeing that Olkhin had selected me from all his pupils, I must possess brilliant ability. I said it was not a question of brilliant ability, that my success in short-hand was due to a special reason. Dostoevsky wished to know what that reason was, and I had to tell him. The courses commenced in the beginning of April, 1866. I immediately started on them, but after five lessons I was in complete despair : shorthand appeared to me a regular abracadabra, which I could not grasp— so obscure and unintelligible it seemed. I wanted to leave the classes ; but my father, whose days were numbered, persuaded me to give up the idea. He assured me that if I worked hard I should overcome the difficulties. And his words, indeed, came true.

On April 28th, 1866, my father died and I was terribly upset by his death. It was the first real sorrow of my life : I was distressed, I cried and could find no peace. My mother, to distract my thoughts from this great calamity, advised me to work, to stick to my shorthand. I wanted so much to justify my father's belief in my abilities, that I made up my mind to work hard and to achieve my purpose of becoming an efficient shorthand writer. The kind Olkhin came then to my assistance. Learning of my desire to work hard at shorthand, he suggested, for the sake of practice, that I should copy pages of a certain book in shorthand and send him my exercises by post. He corrected them, and sent them back to me. I learnt by my mistakes, and, of course, avoided making similar ones in my subsequent work. The shorthand correspondence with Olkhin made it possible for me to make progress in the practice of shorthand, and a daily two hours' dictation helped me to achieve a speed of one hundred words a minute. When, in the beginning of September, Olkhin's lectures commenced, it was found that the great majority of the pupils, over three-fourths, had given up shorthand altogether. The rest did almost no work during the summer months ; so that it turned out that I was the only one quite prepared for independent work.

To all questions put by Dostoevsky I answered simply and seriously. On the whole, I behaved seriously, almost sternly, as Dostoevsky told me later on. I had made up my mind beforehand that if I had to work for private persons, I would establish my relations with them on a businesslike footing, avoiding any familiarity ; so that no one should dare to address to me an unnecessary word, or to make a joke. It seemed to me that such behaviour on my part would be the best : for surely my object was to work, and not to make acquaintances ; why then take part in trifling conversations ? It would be much more becoming to behave strictly. Dostoevsky told me later on that he had been pleasantly struck by me : I was so young and yet behaved so well. No one who talked to me would think of using an unnecessary word ; such an effect would my reserved manner produce. I believe I did not laugh once as I talked to Dostoevsky. He told me afterwards that my capacity for establishing my relations with people on a cold, respectful footing had pleased him very much. He had been used to meeting many Nihilist women and, from watching their behaviour, he had expected the girl recommended to him to be like them ; therefore he was pleased to find in me the complete opposite of the prevalent type of young girl of that time.

During our conversation Fedosya prepared the tea in the dining-room and brought us two glasses and two rolls ; also a lemon. Dostoevsky asked me again if I wanted to smoke. Then he went to the window and took two pears from a paper bag, and gave me one. Being used at home to good manners, such lack of ceremony on the part of a man who scarcely knew me appeared somewhat strange to me. But Dostoevsky offered the pear so good-naturedly, that the lack of ceremony pleased me ; I took the pear and ate it then and there with my young teeth, which needed no artificial assistance.

We went on talking and, owing to his sincere and good-natured tone, it suddenly seemed to me that I had known him for such a long time, and I felt at ease and happy.

For some reason our conversation turned on the Petrashevsky revolutionary group and on capital punishment, and Dostoevsky told me that when he was standing on the Semionov Drill Ground among the others sentenced to death, he knew, by the preparations which were going on, that he had only five minutes left to live. But it seemed to him that his life would last not five minutes but five years, five centuries. White death shirts were put on them. The group was divided into batches, three men in a batch. Dostoevsky was in the second batch. The first three men had already been conducted to the pillar and tied to it. In a minute they would be shot, and then would come his turn. Oh Lord, how much he wanted to live ! How sweet life seemed to him, what a lot of good he could do ! He remembered then his whole past life, the indifferent use he had made of it, and he wished so vehemently to try again; so strongly did he wish to live, to live long, long. But suddenly the retreat was sounded—and he felt the relief. The first three were untied from the pillar and led back ; and a new sentence was read. Dostoevsky was sentenced to four years' hard labour in the Omsk Fortress. He was happier that day than he had ever been before. He paced his cell all day long (in the Alexeyev Ravelin of the Peter and Paul Fortress) singing all the time, singing loudly, so happy was he that life was given back to him. Then his brother was admitted to see him before his deportation, and on Christmas

Eve he was despatched into that remote region. He told me that he had in his possession the letter[1] written by him to his brother Michael on the day the sentence was pronounced ; that he had recently recovered it from his cousin. He told me a great many things that evening, and I was extremely struck by the fact that he was so deeply and sincerely frank with me, a young girl whom he had seen to-day for the first time in his life, and whom he did not know at all. He seemed so reserved and stern ; and yet he was telling me so much and giving me so many details, all so frankly and sincerely that I could not help being surprised. Only later on, when I got to know him as well as his family relations more closely, I understood the reason of his frankness and confidence. Dostoevsky was at that time spiritually lonely and he felt acutely the need of sharing his thoughts and feelings, even with perfect strangers ; so long as they were not hostile to him, and so long as he could discover in them a sincere and attentive attitude towards him. As for myself, his frankness and confidence pleased me very much, and left a wonderful impression on me.

I was a bit uneasy and annoyed that he did not begin dictating to me. It was getting late, and I had to go home. I had not seen my mother since early morning. I had promised her to come home after my morning interview with Dostoevsky, and now I was afraid that she might worry. I had no wish to spend the night at the Snitkins' house. It would have been awkward to tell this to Dostoevsky ; but, to my great pleasure, he himself said he was going to begin dictating. He started pacing the room with long strides, from the fireplace to the door, and every time he reached the fireplace, he invariably knocked twice on it. He

---

[1] The letter here referred to is included in the volume *Dostoevsky : Letters and Reminiscences*, translated by S. S. Koteliansky and J. M. Murry (Chatto & Windus).

F. M. DOSTOEVSKY
about the time he married his second wife

face p. 16

was smoking cigarettes all the while, taking a fresh one and throwing the unfinished one in the ash tray on the desk. After he had dictated to me for some time, he asked me to read to him what I had written, and at the very first sentences he stopped me. " From Roulettenburg ? Did I say Roulettenburg ? " he asked. " You dictated that name," I answered. " Impossible ! " " But is there a city of that name in your novel ? " I asked. " The action takes place in a city where there is a casino, which I must have called Roulettenburg," he replied. " If there is such a place you must have dictated its name, otherwise how could I have known it ? This geographical term is perfectly new to me," I said. " You are quite right," Dostoevsky admitted. " I must have muddled things up." I must say I was a bit put out, thinking that I had made some mistake. But I was glad that the misunderstanding was cleared up. Dostoevsky was evidently absorbed in thought and troubled, or perhaps he was too tired.

Then he said that he could not dictate any more and asked me to copy out what I had got down in shorthand, and to bring it with me the next day at twelve. I promised to do so without fail. It struck eleven, and I said that I must go home. Dostoevsky asked me where I lived. Learning that I lived in the Peski suburb, he said that he had never in his life been in that neighbourhood, and did not know where it was. But if it was far he would send his servant with me. As it was far away and he insisted that the woman should see me home, I had to say that I was going to spend the night with some relations who lived quite close to him. Dostoevsky saw me to the hall, and called the servant to light me down the stairs. As Fedosya and I were going downstairs I asked her what was her master's patronymic. I knew, from his novels, that his Christian name was Fiodor, but I did not know his father's name.

In the Stoliarny Lane it was quite noisy : drunken people were coming out from the public houses ; and I felt alarmed. Happily I soon came across a cabman and he agreed to take me home for 40 copecks. I urged him to drive quickly, and as he turned out to be a good-natured old fellow, we began talking, just to kill the time, and he told me all about his village. At last I reached home. I had to wait a long time till the *concierge* woke my people. My mother had thought that I was going to spend the night at the Snitkins', and she had told the servant to bolt the door and to go to bed. I gave mother a full account of my day and told her with rapture of how Dostoevsky was frank and nice. But, not to grieve mother, I did not tell her of the painful impression I had taken away with me—an impression more unpleasant than any I had hitherto experienced—and this despite the interesting way in which the day had passed. And the impression was, indeed, painful : for the first time in my life I had seen a man unhappy, deserted and badly treated, and a feeling of deep compassion and sympathy was born in my heart.

Although there was comparatively little to copy out of the work dictated the previous day, I wanted so much to write it in a clear hand that I arrived half an hour late. I found Dostoevsky in great agitation. " I was beginning to think," he said, " that you found work with me difficult, and that you would not wish to come any more. I did not write down your address even, and was afraid that what I had dictated to you yesterday might be lost." I apologised for being late and said that if I were to stop working with him I should certainly let him know beforehand, and return the dictated original. He began telling me that it was incumbent on him to finish the novel by 1st November. " Meanwhile," he said, " I have not yet decided on the plan. I know that the length must be not less than seven folios of Stellovsky's editions ; but what the novel is going to be like I don't know." To my question as to whether the novel was to appear in a monthly magazine, he gave me a detailed account of his business relations with Stellovsky, the publisher. The story was, indeed, a revolting one. It must be said that Dostoevsky owed much money ; debts taken over by him after his brother's death and after his review *Epocha* had stopped publication. The creditors worried him terribly ; they threatened to seize upon his property and to put him in prison. The urgent debts he had to meet amounted to three thousand roubles, and he had been trying to find the money, but with no success. When all attempts to persuade the creditors to wait some time longer had failed and Dostoevsky was driven almost to despair, then the publisher Stellovsky came forward with the offer to buy the copyright of all Dostoevsky's works for publication in three large volumes. For the copyright Stellovsky offered to pay 3,000 roubles, on condition that Dostoevsky gave him a new novel, of seven folios large size, in a two-columned page. Dostoevsky's position was critical, and he agreed to all conditions, just to save himself from the debtors' prison. The agreement was made in April, 1866, and Stellovsky deposited three thousand roubles with a Notary Public to be paid to Dostoevsky's order. The three thousand roubles Dostoevsky handed over the very next day to the creditors. Thus out of the three thousand roubles obtained for his copyrights he received no ready cash at all. But the most revolting thing was this : quite soon it became clear that the three thousand roubles had passed again into Stellovsky's pocket. Having then bought up for a mere trifle Dostoevsky's bills from the creditors, Stellovsky forced him to accept extremely bad terms. The price for the copyright of all the works, three thousand roubles, was in itself scandalously small, in view of the success of Dostoevsky's novels, especially after the publication of *Crime and Punishment*. But the cruellest thing of all was the clause requiring Dostoevsky to deliver the new novel by 1st November, 1866. In case of non-delivery Dostoevsky was to pay a heavy fine ; and should the novel not be delivered by 1st December of the same year, Dostoevsky was to lose his copyright, which would then pass to Stellovsky in perpetuity. That man was a cunning and astute exploiter of our authors and musicians (as for instance of Pisemsky, Krestovsky, Glinka). He was always looking out for people who were in a difficult position and used to catch them in his net. I think that by stipulating for the delivery of the new novel at a fixed date, with a heavy fine for non-delivery, Stellovsky was certainly calculating on appropriating the copyrights of Dostoevsky's books. Dostoevsky at that time had been absorbed by his work on *Crime and Punishment* (running as a serial then), and in view of the great interest it aroused among the public, he wished to complete it to the best of his ability. And then to deliver ten folios of a new novel! Knowing the sickly state in which Dostoevsky nearly always was, Stellovsky counted on the chance that he would not have the time or the energy to execute two works simultaneously, and then, according to the agreement, he would acquire the copyright of Dostoevsky's works for ever. And this would certainly have happened had not God given Dostoevsky the strength to finish his new novel in time. That was the state of Dostoevsky's affairs then. He also told me that, as it seemed almost impossible to write the novel during that one month of October, his friends —Maikov, Milyukov and others—had suggested that he should give them the plan of his novel, and each one of them would write a part of it, so that the three or four of them in combination could manage to have it done in time. But Dostoevsky preferred paying a fine or even losing his copyrights to signing his name to a work which he had not written.

However little I knew the world and its affairs at that time, yet that business of Stellovsky astonished and revolted me.

As usual, tea was brought in, and Dostoevsky began dictating. But he seemed to find it difficult to settle down. He often stopped, thought, asked me to read over what I had written, and after an hour he declared that he was tired and that we had better have a rest. We began talking, but Dostoevsky was perturbed and passed from one subject to another. He again asked me my name, and forgot it instantly ; twice he offered me cigarettes, although I had told him that I did not smoke. Then the conversation turned on the Russian authors who always interested me. Replying to my questions, Dostoevsky, as it were, put aside the thoughts that were besetting him and spoke calmly and even gaily. He spoke of Turgenev as a man of great talent ; he was only sorry that the latter lived abroad for long periods, and so had forgotten Russia and Russian life. He spoke of Nekrasov as a friend of his young days, and placed his poetic gift very high. About Maikov he said that he considered him one of the wisest and best of men.

He began dictating, and became again irritable and perturbed. Evidently he found it hard to settle down to work. I explained it by his not being accustomed to dictating ; hitherto he had written his works without the help of others. Soon after four o'clock I was making ready to go home, and promised to bring a fair copy of that day's work. When I was leaving, Dostoevsky surprised me very much. He said : " What a large chignon you wear ; are not you ashamed to wear false hair ? " I said that I had no chignon, only my own thick, nice hair. Such a remark on his part seemed to me strange and unceremonious. That day Dostoevsky gave me a ream of the thin mail paper with hardly visible lines, on which he usually wrote, and showed me what margins to leave.

Thus began and continued our work : I used to come at twelve and stay till four, and during those four hours he dictated to me for three half-hours, sometimes more, and between the dictations we talked. With joy I began to observe that Dostoevsky was more and more getting used to the new way of writing, and that every day he seemed quieter. Especially was this seen when I counted the number of my written pages and compared them with a printed page of Stellovsky's edition ; after which I could tell precisely the number of pages dictated to me. The growing number of pages greatly cheered and pleased Dostoevsky, and he would ask impatiently: "How many pages did we do yesterday?" Our talks were many, and every day he unfolded before me a sad page of his life. A deep sympathy was stealing into my heart at his accounts of painful circumstances, of which he seems never to have been free, and from which he cannot free himself even now.

It also seemed strange to me that I never met any member of his family. I did not know of whom the family consisted (he did not speak of it, and I could not ask Fedosya, as Dostoevsky himself always saw me to the door). Yet one member[1] of his family, whom I took to be his cousin, I met, I believe, on the fourth day of my visits to his flat. I was just coming out of the gate when a young man stopped me. I recognised in him the dishevelled youth whom I had seen in the house during my first visit. Close to me he seemed more ungainly than at a distance : he had a swarthy, almost yellow complexion, black eyes with yellow pupils, thick curly hair and tobacco-stained teeth. "You don't recognise me," he said familiarly, "I saw you at my father's. ('So that is his son,' I thought.) I do not want to come in during your work; but I am curious to know what shorthand is like, the more so as I myself am going to start learning it. Please," and without any ceremony he took my portfolio, opened it, and there in the street began examining my notes. I was so confused by that familiarity that I let him rummage among my papers. "It is a curious game," he said, as he handed back my portfolio.

During my three visits to Dostoevsky he appeared to me so kind and sympathetic that it seemed strange

---

[1] This was Pasha, Dostoevsky's stepson, by his first marriage.

to me that such a nice man could have a son who was so free and easy and almost impudent. . . .

Between the dictations our conversations were quite lively. I ceased to fear the " famous author " and spoke to him as frankly and freely as I would have talked to an old friend, or to my father. I asked him about various events in his life, and he readily gratified my curiosity. He told me fully of his imprisonment in the Peter and Paul Fortress, how he communicated with the other prisoners by knocking on the walls ; he spoke of his life when he was serving his term of hard labour, and of the convicts he had known there. Sometimes he complained of his difficult position, of his burdens, of his debts. He spoke of foreign countries, of his travels, of his meetings with various people. He told me of his Moscow relations, of whom he was very fond. He also told me that he had been married, that his wife had died two years ago, and he showed me her photograph. To tell the truth, I did not like her very much : she looked so old, forbidding, almost dead. Yet, as he told me, the photograph had been taken a year before her death.

But it so happened that all the stories told by Dostoevsky were sad ones. I was grieved that his life had been so bitter and hard. I once asked him : " Why do you recall only unfortunate events ? Why not tell me of your happiness, of how happy you have been ? "

" Of my happiness ? But I have never experienced happiness, I have always been waiting for it. I recently wrote to my friend, Baron Wrangel, that in spite of all the misfortunes that had befallen me I still dreamed of happiness ; that I dream of beginning a new life."

It was painful to hear that such a good and gifted man had never yet been happy, and now in his almost old days was dreaming of happiness !

He told me of the court he had paid to Anna Korvin-

Krukovsky; how she had given him her word to marry him, and how he had released her, fearing that, with their opposite convictions, they could not be happy. And he spoke of her a great deal as of a sensible, kind-hearted and talented girl.

Once Dostoevsky told me that he was on the point of making one of these three decisions: to go to the East—to Constantinople and Jerusalem—and perhaps remain there for good; to marry someone; or to go abroad to play roulette and become a gambler. The attempt to solve these problems preoccupied him a good deal, and he asked me what I thought would be the best solution. I said that if he had to make a choice between those three decisions, the best thing he could do would be to choose marriage. " And do you think I could marry? " he asked. " Or perhaps you think that nobody would marry me? But whom should I choose: a sensible or a kind woman? " " Certainly, a sensible one," I answered. " No, if I am to choose, I'd choose a kind one so that she should love and cherish me," said Dostoevsky.

As we talked of marriage in general, the conversation turned on my own case, and Dostoevsky asked me why I had not married. I said that two men were paying me attentions, but I did not love either, I only respected them; and I should like to marry one whom I could love. Dostoevsky ardently supported my view that one ought to marry " for love," and that for a happy marriage " respect " alone was not enough.

Once, in the middle of October, when Dostoevsky was dictating to me, A. N. Maikov suddenly appeared in the doorway of the study. I had seen his portraits, and therefore recognised him at once. Entering, he remarked jocularly on the patriarchal way in which Dostoevsky lived: the door into the flat was half open, there was no servant about, and anyone could come in and take away the whole flat. Dostoevsky seemed to be pleased at Maikov's coming, and he introduced me at once as his zealous assistant, saying : " A. N. Maikov ; my zealous collaborator, Anna Gregorevna Snitkin." I must not conceal the pleasure it gave me to hear Dostoevsky admitting and valuing my assistance. Hearing my name, Maikov asked me if the late Snitkin was a relation of mine. Maikov was in a hurry to leave and said he did not want to interrupt our work. I suggested an interval for rest, in which I could copy out the dictation. Dostoevsky accepted the suggestion, and they both went into the next room, and stayed there talking about twenty minutes. Coming in to say good-bye to me, Maikov asked Dostoevsky to dictate something to me. Dostoevsky complied with his wish and dictated to me half a page of his novel. Then I read my notes aloud. Maikov examined the notes and said : " No, I can't make that out."

Maikov produced a very pleasant impression on me. As a poet I had loved him before, and Dostoevsky's praise of him only strengthened my impression.

The longer the time went on the more Dostoevsky got into his stride. He no longer dictated to me monologues thought out at the time, as he did at the beginning. He worked at night, and dictated to me from his notes. At times he managed to write so much during the previous night that I had to sit at home late after midnight to copy out the dictation. But then with what triumph would I announce next day the growing number of pages ; and how pleased I was to see that my assurances that the work was progressing and would be ready in time, made him smile happily. Both Dostoevsky and myself entered into the life of the characters of the new novel (*The Gambler*), and both he and I had favourites and bugbears among them. My sympathies were with the grandmother who had gambled away a fortune, and also with Mr. Astley (the Englishman), and I despised Pauline and the hero of the novel, whom I could not forgive for his faintheartedness and his passion for gambling. Dostoevsky, on the contrary, was on the side of the gambler, and said that he himself had experienced many of his feelings and sensations. He assured me that one might possess a strong character and manifest this all one's life, and yet not have strength enough to conquer in oneself the passion for roulette. The characters of the novel became living people to us, and we argued about them. I often wondered at my courage in expressing my views, as well as at the extraordinary indulgence with which the great writer listened to my childish remarks and opinions. His indulgence to my words I attributed to his extraordinary kindness, and I felt deeply grateful to him.

During the three weeks of my work with Dostoevsky all my former interests had receded into the background. With Olkhin's permission, I no longer went to his lectures; I saw very little of my friends. For the all-important thing to me was the work for Dostoevsky and those most interesting conversations which we had during the intervals between dictations. I compared our conversations with the talks of the young people of my circle; and how empty and insignificant those talks appeared to me compared with the ever new subjects discussed in the conversations of my favourite author. Each time I left him I was under the impression of ideas new to me; at home I felt sad and dull, and I lived in the expectation of my coming next meeting with Dostoevsky. I thought with sadness that our work was nearing completion, and with it our daily meetings would end. I realised what a blank my life would be when those interesting and animated conversations would no longer be open to me. And how surprised and delighted I was when Dostoevsky gave expression to the same idea that was worrying me.

Five days before the end of our work he said to me as I was leaving :

" You see, Anna Gregorevna, we have got to know one another, we have met on friendly terms every day and got quite accustomed to talk together ; and now, when the work is over, all this will come to an end and we shan't meet one another. Indeed, I shall be sorry ! I shall miss you. Where could I see you ? "

" But, Fiodor Mikhailovich," I said, " two mountains never come together, but two human beings may."

" But where ? " he asked.

" Well, in society, at the theatre, at concerts," I replied.

" But you know," he said, " that I go very rarely into society or to the theatre ; and what is the good of meeting in society when one sometimes can't say a word to another. Why don't you invite me to your house, to meet your family ? "

" Please do come, we shall be glad to see you. I only fear that you may find mother and myself uninteresting company."

" When may I come ? " he asked.

" Well, we can fix the time when we have finished our work," I said. " Surely the work is the most important thing now."

One day as I came to work I found Dostoevsky agitated. He was worried by the fear lest Stellovsky, in order to put into operation the clause respecting the fine, might employ some subterfuge and refuse to accept the manuscript. I began to reassure him, and promised to inquire what was to be done in such a contingency. That same evening I asked mother to go to see a friend of hers, a lawyer. The latter advised that the manuscript should be delivered either to a Notary Public or to the police inspector of the district where Stellovsky resided, and that an official receipt should be taken for it.

On 29th October the last dictation took place : the novel, *The Gambler*, was finished. Thus, from 4th to 29th October, in twenty-six days, a novel of seven folios, in a two-columned Stellovsky edition, had been written.

Dostoevsky was very glad, and said that he wished, in celebration of the safe delivery of the manuscript, to give a dinner at a restaurant to his friends (Maikov, Strakhov, Milyukov), and invited me to join them. He asked me if I had dined before at a restaurant. I said I had not. " But you will come to my dinner ? " he asked. " I want to drink the health of my dear collaborator. Indeed, without your help I could not have finished the novel in time. So you will come, won't you ? "

I said I would ask mother ; but in my own mind I decided not to go. I thought that with my shyness and lack of social experience I should cut a dull and silent figure, only spoiling the general merriment.

Next day, 30th October, I went to Dostoevsky's— not to work, but to hand over the copy of the dictation done the day before. Dostoevsky met me with particular warmth. When he saw me, he got up to greet me, and I noticed that he even blushed. As usual, we counted the pages and were glad that there were so many. Dostoevsky wanted to go through the novel that day to get a general impression of it, to make a few corrections, so as to take it to Stellovsky next day. He then gave me the fifty roubles for my work, and shook my hand several times, thanking me for my collaboration. Then we talked a great deal and with animation.

I knew that 30th October was Dostoevsky's birthday, and therefore I had decided to put on my silk lilac dress instead of the ordinary black costume. Dostoevsky, who had always seen me in mourning, was flattered by my attention, and said that lilac suited me very well and that, owing to my train, I looked taller and more graceful. How pleased I was to hear his praise ! But my pleasure was spoilt by the visit of Emily Dostoevsky, the widow of Dostoevsky's brother, who came to congratulate him. Emily Dostoevsky behaved to me in a dry and haughty manner, which surprised and even hurt me. Dostoevsky was displeased with his sister-in-law's tone, and became more cordial and attentive to me. He offered me a book that had just come out and himself led Emily Dostoevsky aside and began going through some papers with her. At that moment A. N. Maikov came in. He bowed to me, but evidently did not recognise me. Maikov asked Dostoevsky how the novel was getting on ; but Dostoevsky, engaged in conversation with Emily, gave no reply. Then I resolved to answer for Dostoevsky, and said that the novel was finished the previous day, and that I had just brought the last pages of the copy. Maikov then came up to me, held out his hand and apologised for not having recognised me at once. He explained it by his being short-sighted, and also by the fact that in my black dress I had seemed to him shorter. He began inquiring about the progress of the novel, and asked my opinion of it. I was fascinated by the new novel, which had become so dear to me, and I said that there were in it three characters (the grandmother, Mr. Astley, and the enamoured General) which were extraordinarily alive and good. I must have talked for quite twenty minutes, easily and freely, to that dear and nice man. Emily Dostoevsky was somewhat surprised and even shocked that Maikov showed me so much attention and cordiality ; yet she did not alter her dry tone, considering it beneath her dignity to regard with decent feeling a mere shorthand writer.

Maikov went away, and I was making ready to go, wishing no longer to contemplate Emily's sour looks or to endure her haughty tone. Dostoevsky tried to persuade me to remain ; and wishing to smooth over the unpleasant impression caused by this meeting with his relation, he saw me to the hall and reminded me of my promise to invite him to our house.

I confirmed my promise. " When can I come to you—to-morrow ? " he asked.

" No, to-morrow I shall not be at home, I have an engagement at my sister's," I replied.

" The day after to-morrow, then ? "

" No, I have a shorthand lesson."

" Then, on the second of November ? "

" On Wednesday I am going to the theatre."

" Christ ! All your evenings seem to be occupied. Do you know, Anna Gregorevna, I think you say all this on purpose, simply because you do not want me to come to see you. Tell me the truth."

" I assure you," I said, " we shall be glad to see you. Come on 3rd November, on Thursday evening, about seven."

" Thursday ? What a long time to wait. I shall miss you ! " he said.

I took his words for a sweet compliment.

So the happy time passed, and dull days came to me. During the last month I had got used to hurrying cheerfully to my work, to meeting Dostoevsky with joy, and to carrying on our animated conversations, so that now it had all become a necessity to me. All my former habitual occupations lost their interest for me and seemed to me empty and futile. Even the promise of Dostoevsky's visit did not give me any joy. On the contrary, it weighed heavily on me; for I realised that neither my good mother nor myself could be interesting company for such a gifted and clever man. If interesting conversations had taken place between Dostoevsky and myself, it was due, I thought, to the fact that they turned on a subject which occupied us both. But now Dostoevsky would come to us as a visitor, who was to be " entertained." I began thinking of subjects for our talks on the evening of his visit. I was afraid that the impression of a wearisome journey to such a remote place as we lived in, and of a dull evening spent in our company, would efface in so impressionable a man as Dostoevsky the memory of our previous meetings, and that he would resent being burdened with such a tedious acquaintance. Despite my longing to see him I was now quite willing that he should forget his promise and not come to us.

But, being a person very much alive, I tried to occupy myself and to distract my gloomy mood. I went off to my sister's for the day, played with her child, and in the evening I told her and her husband of my work and of my visits to Dostoevsky during the whole of October. Working in the afternoons with

Dostoevsky and copying out in the evenings, I had had little time left, and could only see my sister now and then by snatches ; and therefore I had many stories to tell, the more so as she, curious to know all about Dostoevsky, asked a good many questions. When I had answered her questions, my sister remarked : " You are wrong in getting infatuated with Dostoevsky. Indeed, my dear Netochka, your dreams cannot be realised, and the Lord be praised for it ; particularly as he is so ill, so old and so burdened with debts ! "

I replied hotly that I was not " infatuated with Dostoevsky," that I did not dream of anything particular, but that I was glad to talk to a great writer, and that I was grateful to him for his constant kindness and attention to me.

On my way home I turned over in my head what my sister had said to me, and I asked myself : " Am I really infatuated with Dostoevsky ? Is it indeed the beginning of love ? If so, it is a mad idea ! No, evidently my sister has exaggerated ! "

Next day I went to the shorthand lesson. At school I was told that the doctor had forbidden Olkhin, in view of his illness, to go out of doors, and that Olkhin had asked his pupils to come to his house. I went there. Olkhin congratulated me on the successful completion of my work. Dostoevsky had written to him to thank him for recommending me. Without my assistance, he said, he could not have managed to finish the work in time. He added that he had found working with the help of shorthand quite convenient, and he hoped to use it in the future. Olkhin said that he was satisfied with this opinion on the first pupil of his who had undertaken successfully independent work. I gave Olkhin five roubles, the stipulated ten per cent. of my salary, and I gave his children two pounds of sweets.

To my great surprise I noticed a certain feeling of hostility towards me on the part of my colleagues. Evidently most of them considered themselves quite competent in shorthand and were hurt by the preference shown to me. Miss Alexandra I., as the boldest, made it quite clear to me, and declared rather sharply that she would *demand* the next work that came in and would not give it up to anyone. I assured her that I made no claim on future work ; that I rather wished to go on with my studies so as to catch up my colleagues. She had just heard from me about Dostoevsky's coming visit, and she announced that she would come to me on Thursday for the whole evening. Apart from her desire to make the acquaintance of the famous novelist, she was going " to ask Dostoevsky to find work for her either as a shorthand writer or as a translator. He knew all the reviews and with his introduction she could get work anywhere." Her contemplated visit was terribly unpleasant to me. Dostoevsky would have not only to spend a tedious evening with us, but, thanks to Alexandra's insistence, he would also have to take upon himself the business of finding work for her. And besides (I must confess it), I was afraid that Alexandra, with her cleverness and audacity, would produce on Dostoevsky a too favourable impression, as compared with me ; and somehow I did not desire this. Added to which, my desire to see Dostoevsky again and to talk to him was becoming more ardent every day, and it seemed to me that the talkative Alexandra would spoil our conversation. But how to get rid of her, seeing she had invited herself ? I thought for a long while and was greatly worried about it ; and then I decided on a feminine stratagem : to call on her on Thursday morning and to tell her that Dostoevsky had paid us his visit the previous night, on Wednesday, and so was not coming on Thursday. That little lie was disgusting to me ;

but what could I do if I feared her rivalry so much ?

On Thursday I bought excellent pears, of the sort Dostoevsky liked, and various other things with which he used sometimes to treat me. I arranged the tea-table and at seven o'clock I began waiting for him. It struck half-past, then eight o'clock, but Dostoevsky did not come ; and I decided that he had either forgotten or changed his mind. At half-past eight he arrived. I met him with the question : " How did you manage to find us ? "

" That is all right," Dostoevsky replied. " You speak as if you were sorry that I had found you. And I have been trying to find your house ever since seven o'clock ; I have driven round and round. Every one knows that there is a Kostromskaia Street, but how to get there, no one could tell; so that I drove about inquiring in all the little shops. At last I found a kind fellow who stood on the step of the cab and showed the cabman where to drive."

My mother came in, and I introduced Dostoevsky to her. He kissed her hand gallantly and told her that he was greatly obliged to me for my help with his work. While mother was preparing the tea Dostoevsky told me of the troubles he had met with in delivering the novel. Stellovsky was not at home, he had left for the country, and his people could not say when he would return. Then Dostoevsky took the manuscript to Stellovsky's office ; but the manager flatly refused to accept the novel as he had had no instruction or order from his employer to that effect. To the Notary Public Dostoevsky came too late and the office was closed ; at the district police office there were no chiefs present in the afternoon, and he was told to call later on. He spent the day in anxiety, and only at 10 o'clock in the evening he managed to deposit the manuscript with the Inspector of the

Police, and received a formal receipt. And Dostoevsky took it out of his pocket and showed it to me.

We sat down to tea and began talking as pleasantly and unconstrainedly as ever. The topics of conversation I had prepared had to be put aside, so many new and interesting ones came up. Dostoevsky quite fascinated my mother, who was so shy of the " famous author." Justice must be done to Dostoevsky: he knew how to " fascinate " people. He could be enchanting, and many a time afterwards I saw people, who were even prejudiced against him, fall under his influence and charm.

We began talking of how he had passed the last four days. He was having a rest and was going to rest for another week, and then he would start on the third part of *Crime and Punishment*. " I want to ask your assistance, my good Anna Gregorevna," he said to me. " I found it so easy a way of working that I am going to dictate my further writings, and I believe you will not refuse to be my collaborator." I replied that I should be pleased to help him, but I wondered how Olkhin would regard it, if I was to take on fresh work, which he had perhaps intended to give to some other pupil of his. " But I have got used already to your way of working and am perfectly satisfied with it. It would be strange if Olkhin wished to recommend someone else, whom I do not know and who may not suit me. But perhaps you yourself do not want to work with me ; then, of course, I shan't insist." Dostoevsky was obviously annoyed that I had not agreed at once. I began saying that Olkhin would probably make no objections to my continuing to work for Dostoevsky, but as a mere matter of politeness, I must ask him. And then I told Dostoevsky that many of my colleagues were looking askance at me for the preference shown me by Olkhin, and one lady had even made a few biting remarks on the subject.

" Who dared do that ? " Dostoevsky said.

" A young lady, Alexandra I., but I have revenged myself on her by not introducing her to you."

And I told him of my " feminine stratagem."

" Why did you do it ? " he asked.

" I was afraid she would make too favourable an impression on you (I had to confess), and also I wanted to talk to you and to ask you many things, and I should hardly have been able to do it in the presence of a young lady unknown to you."

Dostoevsky was evidently pleased with my confession.

About eleven o'clock he said good-bye, and took my word that at the next lesson, on Monday, I would talk over the matter with Olkhin, and let him know the result. We parted on the most friendly terms, and I returned to the dining-room quite enchanted with an evening marked by such animation and friendliness. But ten minutes later our maid came in and told us of an unpleasant incident. The cabman whom Dostoevsky had engaged for the evening had left his cab for a few minutes to go into a shop. While he was away the cushion of the seat had been stolen. The cabman was in despair, saying that his employer would deduct five roubles from his wages ; but Dostoevsky promised to pay him the money.

I was so grieved and upset. It seemed to me that that annoying incident would affect Dostoevsky's attitude to us, and that he would no longer want to come to see us, at such a remote place where he could be robbed, seeing that his cabman had been robbed. At the thought that the impression of that wonderfully spent evening might be effaced by this annoying incident I almost cried.

The 6th November was a Sunday and I was to go to a birthday party given by my godmother. She lived a long way off and I began to make ready quite early. To pass the time I sat down to play the piano and did not hear the bell ring ; but hearing steps in the next room I guessed that someone must have called. I looked round and suddenly saw Dostoevsky standing in the doorway. I instantly shut the piano and walked towards him. "You know," he said, " I have been missing you all this time, and this morning I was wondering whether I should come to see you or not. Would it be convenient ? Would not your mother and yourself consider my speedy visit too strange : he was here on Thursday and he comes again on Sunday ? Well, I decided after all to come to you to-day and, as you see, I am here ! " I said that mother and I were not society ladies, and that we were glad to see him. But this time there was no animated conversation : I only answered Dostoevsky's questions. I was annoyed that on so cold a day the drawing-room was not warm enough. Dostoevsky observed : " How cold it is to-day here, and how cold you yourself are to-day." I was also somewhat vexed that, owing to Dostoevsky's visit, I should be rather late for my godmother's.

Seeing me in a bright silk dress Dostoevsky asked if I was going out. Learning that my godmother lived near Alarchin Bridge, Dostoevsky suggested that he should take me there in his cab. On our way, at some turning, he put his arm round my waist to support me. But, as a girl of the 'sixties, I had a prejudice against all such marks of attention, as the kissing of a woman's hands or the putting of an arm round her waist in helping her to get out of a cab. So I said to Dostoevsky : " Please do not trouble : I shall not fall out." He was hurt by my refusing such a trifling service, and said : " How delighted I should be if you did fall out ! " I burst out laughing and peace was restored. All the time we talked cheerfully. Saying good-bye to me, Dostoevsky grasped my hand and made me promise that I would come to him on Tuesday to talk over the work on *Crime and Punishment.*

The 8th November, 1866, is one of the greatest days of my life : on that day Dostoevsky told me that he was in love with me, and asked me to be his wife.

It was a sunny, frosty day. I walked to his house, and therefore I was half an hour late. Dostoevsky seemed to have been impatiently waiting for me ; and as soon as he heard my voice, he came out into the hall.

" At last you have come ! " he said happily and began helping me off with my coat and scarf. Together we went into the study. There, on that day, it was bright, and I noticed with surprise that Dostoevsky was agitated about something. He had an excited, almost rapturous expression, which made him look quite young.

" How glad I am that you have come ! " he said. " I was so much afraid that you might forget your promise."

" But what made you think so ? " I replied. " Don't I always keep my word ? "

" Pardon me, I know that you are always true to your word. I am so glad to see you again ! "

" I also am glad to see you, and in such a happy mood, too. Has something pleasant happened to you ? "

" Yes, it has ! Last night I had a wonderful dream ! "

" Only that ? " I asked and burst out laughing.

" Don't laugh, please. I attach great importance to dreams. My dreams are always prophetic. When I see my late brother Misha in my dream, and particularly when I dream of my father, I know that something unfortunate is going to happen to me."

" Tell me your dream then ! " I asked.

" You see that rosewood box there ?   It is a present from a friend of mine, a friend of my Siberian days, and it is precious to me.   In it I keep my manuscripts, letters and things dear to me from their old associations. Well, I dreamt that I was sitting before that box and going through some papers. Suddenly something flashed among them, a bright little star.   I kept on going through them, and the little star now appeared, now disappeared.   I got interested ; I began to sort the papers slowly and among them I found a tiny little diamond, very bright and shining."

" What did you do with it ? " I asked.

" Here is the unfortunate part ; I don't remember ! Other dreams succeeded and I don't know what happened to the diamond.   But it was a good dream ! "

" People, I believe, interpret dreams by their opposites," I said, and instantly regretted my words.

Dostoevsky's face changed quickly, as though overcast.

" So you think," he said sadly, " that nothing happy is going to happen to me ? That it is only a vain hope ? "

" I cannot interpret dreams, and I do not believe in them at all."

I was very sorry that his happy mood had vanished, and I tried to put him into a good humour. To his question, what dreams I usually had, I gave him a laughing answer.

" Most often I dream of the headmistress of our school, a stately lady, with old-fashioned ringlets, who is always lecturing me for something or other.   I also dream of a yellow cat, which once jumped on me from off our fence and frightened me awfully."

" Oh, baby, what a baby you are ! " Dostoevsky repeated several times, laughing and glancing caressingly at me. " And your baby dreams ! Well, did you have a good time at your godmother's party ? "

" A very good time. After dinner the old people sat down to play cards, and we young people spent the evening in the host's study in lively conversation. We had two very nice and jolly students with us."

Dostoevsky's face was again overcast. I was surprised at his quick changes of mood. Not knowing the symptoms of epilepsy, I thought that such a quickly alternating mood must be the sign of an approaching fit, and I felt frightened.

During the time I came to work for him Fiodor Mikhailovich had got into the habit of telling me what he had been doing and where he had been going on the previous day. So I hastened to ask him now what he had been doing lately.

" I have been planning a new love story," he said.

" A new one ?   Is it interesting ? " I asked.

" To me it is very interesting ; only I cannot manage the end. It is the psychology of a young girl that presents the difficulty. If I were in Moscow I should ask the advice of my niece, Sonechka ; but now I must ask your help."

With pride I prepared to " help " the great writer.

" Who is the hero of your novel ? " I asked.

" An artist, not a young one ; well, briefly, a man about my own age.' '

" Do tell me, please ; go on, do," I asked him, intrigued by the new love story.

And in answer to my request he came out with a brilliant improvisation. Never, either before or after, have I heard from Fiodor Mikhailovich such an inspired story. The further he went on, the clearer it seemed to me that he was speaking about his own life, only changing names and circumstances. There was in it nearly everything that he had told me before in snatches and fragments. Now his detailed consecutive account explained to me a good deal in his relations to his late wife and to his people.

In the new love story there was a gloomy childhood, the early loss of a beloved father, and fatal circumstances (a grave illness) which tore away the artist for ten years from his life and art. Then his return to life (the recovery of the artist), his meeting with a woman, with whom he had fallen in love, the torments he endured on account of that love, the death of his wife and of his beloved sister ; then poverty, debts.

The spiritual state of the hero, his loneliness, disappointment in his friends, his thirst for a new life, his need of love, his passionate longing for happiness were presented with such fire that they seemed to be the experiences of the author himself, and not merely the product of his artistic imagination. Fiodor Mikhailovich spared no dark colours in describing his hero. In his words, the hero was a prematurely aged man, suffering from an incurable disease (paralysis of the arm), gloomy, distrustful ; true, he had a tender heart, but he was incapable of showing his feelings. The artist was perhaps gifted, but he was a failure, who had not even once in his life succeeded in embodying his ideas in the forms he had been dreaming of, and therefore he was always tormented.

Recognising Dostoevsky himself in the hero of the love story, I could not restrain myself from interrupting him.

" But why," I asked, " did you wrong the hero of your love story so much ? "

" I gather he is not sympathetic to you ? "

" On the contrary, he's very sympathetic. He has a good heart. Think only what misfortunes he has had to bear, and how well he has borne them ! Surely any other man who had gone through so much sorrow in life would have become embittered ; but your hero still loves people and comes to their help. Indeed, you are not fair to him ! "

" Yes, I agree, he has indeed a kind, loving heart. And how glad I am that you understood him ! "

" At that decisive period of his life," Dostoevsky, went on, " the artist meets a young girl of your age, or perhaps a year or two older. Let us call her Anna so as not to call her the heroine. It is a lovely name—— "

His words strengthened my belief that by his heroine he meant Anna Korvin-Krukovsky, his late fiancée. At that moment I quite forgot that my name, too, was Anna—so little did I think that his story had any reference to me. The subject of the new love story must have originated, I thought, in the receipt of a letter from Anna Krukovsky from abroad, of which Dostoevsky had told me recently. My heart contracted painfully at that idea.

The portrait of the heroine was painted by him in quite different colours. According to the author, Anna was gentle, sensible, kind, full of life, and possessed great tact in dealing with people. Attaching great importance then to feminine beauty, I could not restrain myself from asking :

" Is your heroine good-looking ? "

" She is not a beauty, of course, but she is not at all bad looking. I love her face."

It appeared to me that Dostoevsky had betrayed his secret, and my heart contracted. A hostile feeling towards Anna Krukovsky stole into me, and I remarked :

" I think, Fiodor Mikhailovich, you have idealised your Anna too much. Is she, indeed, at all like that ? "

" Just like that ! I have studied her carefully ! The artist met Anna in artistic circles and the oftener he saw her the more he liked her, and the stronger in him grew the conviction that with her he could find new happiness. And yet that idea presented itself to him as something impossible. Indeed, what could he, an elderly, sick man, burdened with debts, give to that young, healthy, joyous girl? Would not love for the artist become a terrible sacrifice on her part, and would not she bitterly repent afterwards having joined her fate to his? And is it likely that a girl, so different in character and in age, could love my hero? Would not that be psychologically false? That is what I should like to have your opinion about, Anna Gregorevna!"

"Why is it not possible? Surely, if your Anna is not a shallow coquette, but possesses a kind, responsive heart, why should not she fall in love with your artist? What does it matter that he is ill and poor? Does one love anyone for his appearance or for riches? And where is the sacrifice on her part? If she loves him, she will be happy and will never have occasion to regret it!"

I spoke ardently. Dostoevsky looked at me in agitation.

"And do you seriously believe that she could sincerely fall in love with him and for life?" He was silent for a while, as though hesitating.

"Put yourself for one minute in her place," said he in a tremulous voice. "Imagine that that artist is myself, that I have declared my love to you and asked you to be my wife. Tell me, what would you say?"

Dostoevsky's face expressed so much agitation, such anguish of heart that I at last understood that it was not simply a literary discussion, and that I should be dealing a death-blow to his pride and *amour-propre* if I gave an evasive answer. I glanced at his agitated face, so dear to me, and said,

"I should answer that I love you and shall love you all my life."

I shall not record the tender loving words which Fiodor uttered in those unforgettable minutes: they **are** too sacred to me.

I was astonished, almost crushed by the burden of my happiness, and could not believe it for a long time. I remember, when an hour later Fiodor began telling me of his plans for our future, and asking my opinion, I said :

" But I can't think of anything now !   I am so happy ! "

Not knowing when we could be married and what turn circumstances might take, we decided not to tell anyone yet about our engagement except my mother. Fiodor promised to come and spend the following evening with us, and said he would wait impatiently for our next meeting.

He saw me to the hall and carefully tied my scarf. I was on the point of opening the door when he stopped me with these words :

" Anna Gregorevna, I know now what happened to the little diamond ! "

" Do you remember your dream ? "

" No, I don't remember the dream. But I have found the diamond and shall keep it all my life."

" You are mistaken, Fiodor Mikhailovich," I said with a laugh. " You have found not a diamond, but a pebble."

" No, I am convinced that this time I am not mistaken," he said earnestly.

Ecstasy filled my soul on my way back from this meeting with Fiodor Mikhailovich.   I remember that I was talking aloud almost all the way, unconscious of the passers-by.

" God, what happiness ! Can it be true ? Isn't it a dream ? Will he be my husband ? "

The noise of the crowded street somewhat sobered me, and I remembered that I had been invited by my relations to a birthday party. I went into a confectioner's shop to buy a birthday cake. My soul was in raptures, everyone seemed kind and lovely, and I wished to please everybody. I could not help saying to the German girl who waited upon me : " What a wonderful complexion you have and how beautifully your hair is done ! "

At my relations' house I found many guests, but my mother was not there yet, although she had promised to come to dinner. I was upset : I so much wanted to tell her of my happiness.

The dinner was a merry one, but I behaved rather queerly : either I laughed aloud, or fell into silences and did not hear when spoken to. I gave wrong answers and even addressed one guest as " Fiodor Mikhailovich."

At last my mother arrived. I ran into the hall to meet her ; I embraced her and whispered in her ear: " Congratulate me, I am engaged."

I had no time to say more, for our host and hostess were coming to meet her. The whole evening mother looked at me inquiringly, trying to guess whom of my admirers present I was going to marry. It was only on coming home that I told her that I was going to marry Dostoevsky. I wonder if my mother was glad at the news : I rather think not. A woman of the world, with a long experience of life, could not help foreseeing that my coming marriage would be bound to bring many anxieties and sorrows, on account of my future husband's frightful illness, as well as of his lack of means. But she did not try to dissuade me (as others did afterwards), and I am so very grateful to her. Yet none could have persuaded me to give up my marriage which, later on, despite its many painful aspects (his illness, and his debts) turned out to be true and real happiness for us both.

The following day, the 9th November, dragged on oppressively slowly. I could not do anything, recalling all the time the details of yesterday's conversation.

I even wrote them down in shorthand in my note-book.

Fiodor Mikhailovich arrived at half past six, and began with an apology for coming half an hour before time.

" But I could not wait any longer, I so much wanted to see you ! "

" Nous sommes logés à la même enseigne," I said, laughing. " I, too, did nothing all day long, and kept on thinking of you ; and now I am so glad that you have come ! "

Dostoevsky instantly noticed that I was wearing a light-coloured dress.

" On the way I was wondering all the time whether you would take off your mourning, or remain in your black dress. And now you are in pink ! "

" But how could it be otherwise, if I feel so happy ? Certainly, until we announce our engagement, I shall wear mourning out of doors ; but for you, at home, I shall wear bright colours."

" Pink suits you very well," he said. " In it you look younger still and seem a little girl."

My youthful appearance evidently troubled him. Laughingly, I began to assure him that I should age very quickly. And though that promise was made as a joke, owing to various circumstances it soon actually turned out true. That is to say, I did not age quickly, but I tried both in my dress and in my talk to be quite serious, so that the difference of years between me and my husband soon became almost unnoticeable.

My mother came in. Fiodor kissed her hand.

" You are already aware," he said, " that I have asked for your daughter's hand. She has agreed to be my wife, which makes me very happy. But I want your approval. Anna Gregorevna has spoken so warmly of you that I have got to have a high regard for you.   I give you my word that I will do all I can and more than I can to make Anna happy.   And to you I will be a most devoted and loving relation."

(In justice to Fiodor I must say that throughout the fourteen years of our marriage he was very respectful and kind to my mother ; he loved her sincerely and esteemed her.)

Fiodor uttered this little speech solemnly, but in some confusion, as he himself confessed to me later on. My mother was very much moved, she embraced Fiodor Mikhailovich, asked him to love and cherish me, and burst into tears.

(Their marriage took place on Feb. 15th, 1867. The couple went abroad on 14th April, 1867, intending to remain away a few months. Circumstances, however, delayed their return until the spring of 1871. Mme. Dostoevsky's *Diary* for 1867 deals almost exclusively with Dostoevsky's gambling during the first two months of their staying abroad.)

DIARY OF MME. DOSTOEVSKY

Dresden, 1st May, 1867.[1]—In the evening we talked about Fedya's[2] departure for Homburg. It makes me shudder when I think of him going away, and myself being left here alone. What shall I do then? I can't even imagine how lonely and sad I shall be, sitting by myself in these three wearisome rooms without Fedya, without whom I can't live. I persuaded him not to be anxious about me, I said that I should not get ill, that nothing would happen to me, that every-thing would be all right. He asked me to write him every day; I shall do it with the greatest joy; that, at least, will be some comfort. Then he said that, evidently, our not being together would be quite easy for me; that, evidently, I did not love him. But he is wrong. If I am reconciled to his going there, it is not at all for the chance of his winning money at roulette, which, to tell ·the truth, I believe in very little; but I see that he is beginning to fret here, to become irritable. This is quite understandable: he is all the time alone, not a friendly face, nor a man with whom he can exchange a word. I am thankful that we manage to get books here to read; otherwise he would perish from boredom. To go there (to Homburg) is his desire, his idea; why then should not I satisfy it? Otherwise he will keep on turning it over and over in his head and give himself no peace. I shall be comforted by knowing that he will divert himself a little and will return to me loving me as before;

[1] The Dostoevskys arrived in Dresden on 19th April, 1867.
[2] Fedya; affectionate diminutive of Fiodor.

although I can't complain of his not loving me. We read in the evenings and are silent for hours; at moments I glance at him or he at me with a pleasant smile, ever with joy. I am very happy. That evening we talked for a long while. He said that if he succeeded in winning there, he would come to fetch me, and we should make our quarters there. This would be nice. Yet, I wonder; perhaps, it would not be. Perhaps it would be the best if he did not go there at all.

Thursday, 11th May, 1867.[1]—To-day is a rainy day, cloudy; terrible loneliness. I began sewing and finished my lilac dress; am presently going to the post office. I had a presentiment that I should get still more unpleasant news. I walked there very slowly; received a letter, read it and saw that Fedya evidently wished to remain there longer and to go on playing. I wrote him immediately, saying that if he wished he might remain there, that I should not expect him before Monday or Tuesday. I think that he will remain. What can I do? Probably it must be so. If only he could get out of his head that unlucky idea that he is going to win. I was very sad.

Dresden, 12th May, 1867.—I got up early this morning in the belief that Fedya was coming home to-day. I meant to go to the railway station, but I called first, I don't know why, at the post office; and there I found a letter from Fedya. He says that he received my letter, but not the money sent by me through the banker, and therefore he was obliged to wait there. Is not this a pretext for remaining there longer? It's a funny letter. Fedya complains of terrible toothache, and asks me to be patient for a

---

[1] Having left his wife alone in Dresden, Dostoevsky spent the eleven days from 4th May till the 15th at Homburg, playing roulette.

little while longer.   Well, what's to be done ?   I wrote him to say that he might stay on a bit longer.

Dresden, 13th May, 1867.—At 12 p.m. I went to the station, but there was no Fedya.   Then to the post office, and, walking there, I anticipated a letter from Fedya announcing that he had lost everything and asking for more money to be sent him.   And so it turned out indeed.   I instantly wrote him and called on the banker ; but he was just closing and said that he would open again at 3 p.m.   I returned home.   On my way I had a cup of coffee.   I took the money to the banker.   But this time my dress seems not to have inspired him with great respect ; for he kept me standing for a long time, and did not see me to the door, as he did yesterday.

Monday, 15th May, 1867.—I had already lost hope of meeting Fedya to-day, when suddenly he appeared in the distance (at the railway station).   For a minute I gazed fixedly, as if not trusting my eyes.   Then I rushed up to him ; and I was so glad, so glad, so happy !   He has changed a little, probably as the result of travelling.   He was a little flushed, yet our meeting was so joyous.   We took a cab.   On the way home Fedya told me of his ill luck. . .   I was very sorry, yet at the same time terribly happy, seeing that he has at last come back . . . I was all the time looking with admiration at him and I was infinitely happy. When we were having tea he asked me if any letter had come for him, and I gave him *her*[1] letter.   Either he really did not know whom the letter was from, or he pretended not to know ; but he just ripped the envelope open, then glanced at the signature, and began reading.

[1] Mlle. Souslov's.   See Part II, " Dostoevsky and Mlle. Souslov."

All the time he was reading that letter I watched the expression of his face. He read and re-read the first page for a long time, as if he could not make out what was written there. Then, at last, he read it through and blushed scarlet. His hands seemed to tremble. I pretended not to know whom the letter was from and asked him what Sonechka (a relation of Dostoevsky) was writing about. He said that the letter was not from Sonechka, and gave me a bitter smile. I have never yet seen such a smile on his face. It was a smile either of contempt or of pity. Indeed, I do not know, but it was a pitiable, lost smile. Afterwards, he became terribly distrait, and he could hardly make out what I was saying.

Tuesday, 16th May.—To-day we woke up rather late. We have no watch now (Fedya pawned it at Homburg), and therefore we do not know the time. I began trimming my black dress ; while Fedya paced the room all the time, like one lost, looking for something, as though he had lost something, and went through his correspondence. It was obvious that S.'s[1] letter had moved and offended him. But I should so very much, so very much like to know his opinion of conduct of this sort.

Saturday, 3rd June, 1867.—We went to the *Grand Jardin* to hear Wagner's *Field March* from *Rienzi*. It is a charming thing. We sat till the end and then went home. For the first time now abroad, and for the second time in my life, I walked arm-in-arm with Fedya. He proposed it, and I agreed with joy. I was delighted to walk arm-in-arm with him, although I had to make gigantic steps ; for Fedya is taller than I, and his step is longer.

Then we spoke about nobility. He said that I was

______

[1] Mlle. Souslov's.

" ready to sell father and mother for money," not only my husband. When I protested against this, he said that there was not a nobler creature in the whole wide world than I, but that he was not going to praise me for it yet, because I was still young, and because these were the first beginnings. He said that I did not know life at all, that if I had known life I should never have married an old, toothless, licentious old sinner. I replied that all he said was untrue, and I loved him awfully and was frightfully happy. . . .

We spent the whole evening in perfect peace ; I was very happy and laughed like mad. Fedya also did not frown. When I think how his character has changed—it is wonderful ! Formerly he used to be so irritable, and shouted so at people at home, that at times I was terrified for my future with him. I thought if living with me does not change him, then my life will be torture. But now that has all gone, although our circumstances are by no means brilliant. Coming to say good-night to me, Fedya said that I made him both happy and unhappy. Unhappy, because if he were now by himself, it would be easier for him to endure his difficult position ; but now he was afraid on my account. It distressed him that I suffered discomforts and privations. I assured him that his apprehensions were absolutely wrong ; that I did not at all suffer as much as he thought. Actually, in myself, I am much worried over our sad financial position. What is Katkov's[1] answer going to be like ? What if he suddenly refuses ? What shall we do then ? It is intolerable to go on like this.

Wednesday, 7th June, 1867.—To-day we slept very late. As we have no watch, we do not know the time. I think I slept for twelve hours. I got up, and began

---

[1] Katkov, Editor of *Russky Vestnik*, to whom Dostoevsky applied for money *in advance* for his contributions.

reading and translating. Fedya began drinking tea. As he had an epileptic fit last night, he was hard to please, and the tea seemed distasteful to him. He asked me to let him pour out the tea himself, and I replied : " Please do." He did not like my reply, got angry and shouted. It hurt me ; but I said nothing, blushed scarlet and went into the next room. Five minutes had not passed before Fedya came into the room quite gay, and said that he apologised. I, too, very happy, got up and said that I was not at all cross with him, nor could I ever be angry with him. Thus our quarrel ended. I dislike quarrelling : it pains me so much, my thoughts turn all melancholy, and I lose all desire to do anything ! I would rather give in ; anything for the sake of peace. Fedya has been telling me all day that I am " good," that I am a " saint," that I am free from sin, that he regards me more and more as a "saint," as a "model" of a woman, "sinless," " patient." My dearest Fedya ! I am not worthy of his praises, I am not at all so good as he thinks ; but his words are dear to me. (I once said to Fedya that I should be terribly unhappy if he considered me silly. He said that I was very sensible, that I possessed a rare understanding.)

Friday, 9th June, 1867.—We had lunch out and came back home. Fedya lay down for a rest, and I wrote a letter to Vanya [her brother], and took it to the post office. When I returned, Fedya suggested we should walk together to the library to change our books ; but I was so tired that I could not accompany him. When he came home, he asked me if we should go for a walk ; I said "yes." Both Fedya and myself are very much upset by the fact that there is no reply from Katkov. Our money is coming to an end, we see no chance of getting any, and we do not know at all what to do. Poor Fedya is very gloomy. He is upset and now gets cross over trifles, of which he used to take no notice before. His bad humour is also reflected in his behaviour towards myself : he tries to pick quarrels. I, too, am terribly anxious about our position ; I also get irritated and can't restrain myself. For instance, to-day such an absurd scene took place, in which we acted like children. We walked almost as far as the *Grand Jardin.* Fedya wanted to return home, but was undecided. I said : " If you want to go home, let us go home then ! " He became awfully angry, and turned back. A moment later, however, when I said that I should like to rest for a while in the garden, he quickly turned in that direction ; but he said he was not going to sit there more than five minutes. I replied : " If we are going to have a rest, we ought to sit there not five minutes but half an hour, or else we had better go home." As he persisted, I said we had better walk home, or I would do so myself. And as he kept on walking towards the garden, I turned back. Why did I do it ? All our quarrels occur because we are both upset and worried by our uncertain position. Lord, help us to get out of it ! We love each other so much and are so happy, and but for our bad circumstances and money anxieties, we should be the happiest of people. And now we are quarrelling like little children ! In half an hour's time Fedya came home. He was very gloomy. When he began drinking his tea he said that I had moved the table just to spite him. I said it was stupid to say that I wanted to spite him. Then he began teasing me. He said that now he had no money, but he was bound to get money, and that anyhow I ought to respect him. It offended me terribly. What ! To think that I respect people just for their money ! I said that I did not at all value him on account of his money, that if I wanted to be rich, I could have been rich, for I could have

married T., who had made court to me (Fedya said
he had heard that before), that I was not out for
wealth, but loved him, Fedya, for his mind and soul.
I was so wrought up that I could not restrain myself
and burst into tears.   But we soon made it up.   When
we had tea I said that I was going to write an abusive
letter the next day.   Fedya asked : " Why abusive ? "
and I said that abusive letters should be answered by
abuse.   He asked me to whom I was going to write,
and I said : " To a certain lady who has recently
abused me."[1]   I said I was not going to put up with
insults, particularly when I had not deserved them ;
that he himself had said that one ought to put people
in their places.   Fedya said that it was wrong to repay
evil with evil, that it was better to forgive.   I replied
that I thought quite differently.   Then he kissed me
several times and looked at me, and I looked at him
smiling.   Several times he screwed up his eyes and
said : " You are spiteful ! "   I said perhaps I was, but
not towards him.   He glanced at me very attentively
and evidently tried to guess what was in my mind.
Then I went into the next room and began to write.
After some time he came in, called me *" littérateur,"*
" literary wife," and asked me what I was writing.
I said : " A letter."   " May I know to whom you are
writing ? "   " No, you may not," I said.   " Still ? "
" No, I shan't tell you."   Then he advised me to go
to bed.   He was evidently very curious to know ;
moreover, I think he guessed the person to whom I
was going to write. . . .

Friday, 23rd June, 1867.—The day was cloudy,
worse luck.   It was raining, and I thought that we
were not likely to go out.   We had tea and coffee,
and Fedya went to the station casino taking with

------

[1] To Mlle. Souslov.

him fifteen louis d'or and several thalers besides; but he promised not to start playing to-day and, in any case, not to stake all the money. Left at home, I began taking out my dresses, sewing hooks on, mending my skirt and generally overhauling my wardrobe. I felt awfully lonely, sad. I don't know why I felt it so acutely. I did not want to see anyone, to go anywhere; but I just wanted to lie down here, in the dark room, and to stay like that the whole day. Nearly three hours passed and then Fedya came. He told me he had lost all the money he had on him. We have now exactly fifty louis d'or; it is still possible to go on. I dressed and went with Fedya to the casino. It is a rather large building, with a great hall in the centre and two side halls. The casino is called *Conversation.* "At last I am going to see roulette played," I thought as I entered the hall. But I imagined it much more magnificent than it was. At a large table, in the middle of which is placed the roulette, there sit six croupiers (they pay out the money); two at each side of the table and one at each end. But I had better describe the play later on. We looked on a while, and then Fedya suggested that I should stake a five-franc piece. I put the money, as he advised, on *impair*; but it came out *pair*, and I lost. Then Fedya began to play. He played for a long time, and then left off, carrying away, besides our own money, about two hundred five-franc pieces. And then we went to have dinner. On returning home Fedya decided to put away his winnings in a leather bag and not to touch them, unless all our capital went. We packed the two hundred five-franc pieces into the bag. After dinner we went back to the casino, had coffee and Fedya read the newspapers. Then we entered the hall again. Our luck was undecided for a long time; but it ended in our winning fifty francs, and then we went home. It was rather late, about ten o'clock, and I had to go home. The fifty francs were also put into the bag. Having seen me home, Fedya returned to the roulette table ; but after some time he came home and saying that he had lost all the five louis d'or, asked me to get some money out of the bag. He asked me to order tea as he would be back presently. I was sure of what was going to happen ; and, indeed, before half an hour had passed he returned and said that he had lost all. (I forgot to write down that before dinner we went looking for rooms. We found two rooms at eight florins a week and are going to move in there to-morrow.) Poor Fedya is very upset. But what's to be done ? We have still forty-five louis d'or left.

Saturday, 24th June, 1867.—We got up rather early ; but I felt so ill that I could not bring myself to go out to pay the deposit for the rooms. I think that the cause of it is my present state (of pregnancy). We went out to have another look at the rooms, and bought tea on our way. We took the rooms, promised to move in in an hour, and returning home asked for our bill. When it was brought I was astonished. For two days we had to pay twenty-three florins—simple robbery ! But what can we do, we must submit. (They charged for tea, 1 florin 36 kreutzer, that is, 96 copecks, for one tea.) We left one franc for the waiter, and half a franc for the chambermaid. From the hotel we engaged a porter who carried our things to the rooms. All that day I was awfully unwell : sick, with a green face and dull eyes. When I came to our new rooms, I immediately lay down on the couch and did not get up the whole day. We have spent five louis, and Fedya has taken another ten to try his luck again. There remain thirty louis. . . . Fedya went off to play, and I fell asleep. I slept for a long time ; suddenly, opening my eyes, I saw Fedya standing at the head of my bed. He was terribly upset. I understood that he must have lost all the ten louis ; and so it turned out. I began persuading him not to be grieved, and asked him if he wanted me to get him some more money. He asked for another five louis. I gave them to him immediately ; and he thanked me awfully, as if I had, indeed, conferred a favour on him. I asked him to go to the restaurant to have a meal ; for I did not feel well enough to accompany him. He went away at four, promising to return soon. I began waiting for him—five o'clock, seven o'clock—still he had not come back. I waited for him and I thought if he were here I would ask him to fetch me some bread ; for I began to feel hungry. I was lying in bed all the time, I kept waking all the time. I could not sleep, and cried, and felt awfully miserable. At last I asked the landlady to bring in candles and to send for a loaf. And the time was passing—nine, ten o'clock, and Fedya was not back. I pictured him having an epileptic fit at the casino, and being unable to explain where he lived. I imagined that he was dying, and that I should not be in time to speak to him. These thoughts tormented me so that I decided that if he did not come by eleven o'clock, then, however poorly I felt, I would go to the casino to find out what had happened to him. But at eleven o'clock Fedya came ; he was terribly upset. He said he had been trying to get away for the last three hours ; but he did not know what to do. He had won as much as four hundred francs and wished to win more ; but, though he was anxious and tormented on my account, he could not tear himself away from the game. I consoled him, and assured him that it did not matter, that all was right, that nothing had happened to me during his absence, that the only thing was to get calm and not to worry. But he begged me to give him the chance of reproaching himself for his stupid weakness ; and he asked to be forgiven, I don't know for what. He said that he was unworthy of me, that he was a scoundrel, and that I was an angel, and many such like impossible things. With difficulty I managed to set his mind at peace. To divert him, I asked him to go and buy candles, sugar and coffee. On coming back, he asked me to send him out again to fetch something for me. I begged him to stay. Poor Fedya, how sorry I am for him ! (I forget : to-day he decided to throw away his old purse which had brought him ill luck. I gave him my thaler to buy a new one. I also gave him a florin for luck, and he put it in the purse. He bought gloves for me, made at Grenoble, not in Paris.) I managed to calm him. I am terribly sorry for his sake that all this upsets him so much : I am even afraid that he may get an epileptic fit.

Baden, Sunday, 25th June, 1867.—To-day we had twenty-five louis. Of these Fedya took five ; and when he left, he asked me to be dressed by the time he returned, so that we might go together to the post office. After he left I felt very sad ; I was sure that he would lose that money, too, and would torment himself again. Several times I began crying, and felt as though I were going mad ; but Fedya came back, and I asked him quite indifferently : " Have you lost ? " " Yes, I have," he replied, in despair, and began again to accuse himself. He said pathetically that he reproached himself for his weakness for gambling, that he loved me, that I was his beautiful wife, and that he was not worthy of me. Then he asked me to give him some more money. I said : " I won't give you any money to-day, but I may give you some to-morrow." On no account would I give him any to-day, as he was bound to lose it and torment himself again. But Fedya implored me to give him at least two louis ; so that he could go to the tables and get relief. There was nothing to be done, I gave him two louis. Fedya was in a state of agitation. He asked me not to consider him a scoundrel who took away from me the last penny in order to gamble it away. I implored him to be calm. I assured him that I did not at all consider him in that light, that he was free to lose as much as he liked. He went away, and I cried very much. The way in which he tormented and worried himself distressed me ; and I was anxious about our future in a foreign country with so little money. Fedya came back quite soon and said that he had lost. (There remain eighteen louis.) We went to the post office, and Fedya asked me to take with me three louis. He said that if he lost those three, it was settled that we should leave Baden next day ; for there was no sense in staying on any longer here. There were no letters for us at the post office, and they suggested we should call later. Meantime we went to the casino. Fedya began playing and lost his money. On our way home, after deciding to leave the next day for Geneva, we met Goncharov[1] to whom Fedya introduced me. Goncharov told me that Turgenev had seen Fedya the day before, but had not come up to him as he knew that players do not like people to come up to them. As Fedya owes Turgenev fifty roubles, he really must call on him ; otherwise Turgenev might think that Fedya does not want to call on him for fear lest Turgenev may ask for his money back. Therefore Fedya wants to call on Turgenev to-morrow. When we returned from the casino Fedya said that he would probably play more cautiously if I were not with him. He said that he had decided to try the last resource—to play as cautiously as possible ; but as

---

[1] **Well-known Russian novelist.**

I was with him, he was in a flutter. I was afraid lest he should reproach me for being in his way, and I offered to let him take another three louis and to try his luck for the last time. He was wonderfully glad ; he began calling me all sorts of endearing names. He said he would rather have a bad-tempered wife who would scold him, than such a gentle wife as I am who forgives him and, instead of scolding, only comforts him. It pained him that I treated him so meekly. He was wonderfully glad. Fedya went out to change the money, and I sent to the restaurant for dinner. They charged one florin and brought us four courses, very good, but German soup, with eggs, beaf-steak, veal cutlets, and cherry cakes. All the dishes, Fedya said, were quite good ; and all this for a florin—it is rather cheap. After dinner we had very good coffee with cream. Fedya then went to the casino, and I stayed at home and was wonderfully calm. I thought: " Well, let him lose that money, but then we are going to Geneva to-morrow, and there we shall again be peaceful and happy." Before Fedya left we talked about money and decided that twelve louis was too little to take us to Geneva and to support us there till we received money from Moscow ; and that it would be so nice to wait and not to ask the Moscow people for money. Fedya suggested that we should pawn our belongings ; but I told him that I had left my bracelet behind in Petersburg. I said that I had asked mother to send it on to me to Dresden, and probably she had sent it ; but it must have arrived there after we had left. Fedya returned quite soon from the casino having won forty thalers, and we put the money in the bag. Fedya says that he had won fifty thalers, that he then put ten thalers on the *middle* and lost. And then he thought of me and decided to leave the casino at once. I was pleased, not so much with the money, as with the resolution he showed in leaving the game when he had decided to leave. Fedya suggested we should go for a walk to the station, to hear the band. We went there. To-day there were lots of people there, mostly local inhabitants, but not so many foreigners. We walked for a while, listening to the band ; then we entered the hall of the casino and took a place near the croupier. I now saw for the second time a Russian lady who always stakes gold and always wins ; she generally puts on *numbers*, but also on *zéro*. But what surprises me is this : I noticed that she put three times on *zéro*, and won every time. I wonder if she plays fair. One of the croupiers here who hands over the money, a young blackhaired man, is always turning to her. He smiles and glances at her and talks to her freely. Can there be some under-standing between her and him ? Perhaps, as croupier, he knows by certain signs when *zéro* is going to come out, and he signals to her in some way, for she wins on *zéro* unerringly. Only once has she staked without winning. That Russian lady is remarkably well dressed (diamond earrings), in a bright lilac dress, with a white silk waistband and lilac sleeves, trimmed with white lace— wonderfully nice. I should like to know who she is ; for her face, and the faces of her friends, seem familiar to me. Fedya had bad luck to-night—he lost all the fifteen thalers. Behind me stood a German woman with her husband, who wrote down on a piece of paper the winning numbers. She held a thaler in her hand for a very long time ; she meant to stake it, but hesitated for a long while. Then she staked it at the same time as Fedya, and lost. Then she rummaged in her purse for a long while, got another thaler, staked it, and lost. How unlucky ! Perhaps that was her last thaler, and to lose it—how hard on her ! There was also a young girl here who staked a thaler and lost it. Perhaps hers, too, was the last one she had. They say that the local inhabitants try their luck on Sundays and lose all they have saved in the week. What a pity ! An old woman with a yellow hat several times staked five-franc pieces and won each time ; so that even I was surprised. On whatever she staked she unfailingly won ; I believe she got away with twenty-five five-franc pieces. Near me stood a young man who staked gold pieces. He generally put on *rouge* or *noir*, and, as it piled up, he staked *à la masse* five louis, all *à la masse* ; so that at one moment he had fifteen louis *à la masse.* He put ten of them on *noir*, and lost. He blushed terribly : I think he was very much annoyed to lose so much. Fedya having lost all his thalers, we left the hall. On our way home I said to him : " I am sorry that I came with you ; if I had not been there, perhaps you would have won." But Fedya thanked me and said : " Bless you, my dear Anya ; if I die, remember what I now say to you, that I bless you for the happiness you have given me." He said that that was above everything to him, that he was unworthy of me, ; that God had given me to him as a compensation, that he prayed for me every day, and was afraid only lest all this might change. He said that now I loved and cared for him, but that love would pass, and then all would be changed. But I believe that nothing of the kind will happen, and that we shall always love one another as ardently as now.

Baden, Monday, 26th June, 1867.—To-day was a sad day. I have never been so terribly sad ; I simply do not know what to do. To-day we had twelve louis and twenty-five thalers. Fedya took fifteen thalers and went to the tables. He first called on Turgenev, but did not find him at home ; for Turgenev is at home only up to mid-day. Fedya lost his fifteen thalers and came home. A little later he went to the casino again, taking another fifteen thalers. But he soon came back, saying that he had lost again, and begged me to give him another fifteen thalers. I gave them to him. There

remained only four thalers ; for we paid one for dinner.
I persuaded Fedya to have his dinner here. He went
to the tables, and I to the post-office. There were no
letters. I bought envelopes, and then went for a walk
to *Lichtenthalerstrasse* and further out of town. I felt
very uneasy. When I returned, Fedya, too, came in a
few minutes, and, with a pale face, said that he had lost,
and asked me to give him the last four thalers. I gave
them to him ; but I was sure that he was bound to lose,
that it could not be otherwise. Over half an hour
passed ; he returned home, having of course lost, and
said that he wished to have a talk with me. He put
me on his knees, and began imploring me to give him
five louis. He said he knew that that would leave us
only seven louis, and that we should not have enough to
live on. He said he knew all that perfectly ; but what
could he do if he could not set himself at peace ? He
said that if I refused him the money, he would go mad.
He was in a terrible state of agitation. I argued with
Fedya that it would be very difficult for us to go on with
so little money. But I did not say much, I only asked
him to calm down and to postpone playing till
to-morrow. But Fedya said that if he put off till to-
morrow he would only be tormenting himself all the
time ; that it was better to end it all to-day than to be
tormenting himself all day and all night. I certainly
could not withstand his argument, and gave him the
five louis. " You are behaving very nicely so far," said
Fedya, " but when you are older, when you have
become ' Mme. Anna Dostoevsky,' you won't allow me
to behave in the way I am doing now. You will say
that previously you were foolish. You will say : ' If
my husband wanted to make a fool of himself I should
not have allowed him to do so. A wife ought to stop
her husband behaving like that.' " He said that the
way I acted was much the best ; for I was winning him
by my kindness and meekness. He loved me more and

more. Fedya went to the casino and asked me also to go somewhere ; otherwise I might feel too lonely sitting by myself at home. I was quite calm, although I felt distressed. Well, had I not calculated that we should have to do with seven louis ; why trouble then ? I went out for a walk in the direction of the old castle. To reach the garden you have to climb steep flights of steps. In the garden there are several terraces, from which a beautiful view opens on to the casino and the neighbourhood. I walked there for a long while, and then went home. As I came down the steps near the open door of a house, I noticed a boy of about eight, who sat peacefully with his books, studying. I asked him where he lived. He said he lived in that house, and always came out on the steps to do his lessons, and went to a Catholic school. I took a great liking to the boy— he is not at all dull, as the Germans are, and at once understands what he is asked. I talked for a long time to the boy, and then went down the rest of the steps. When I got home Fedya was not yet back ; but he soon returned and said that his heart had ached for me all that time, and that he had not stopped thinking of me all the while. Out of the five louis which he had had from me, he had lost very little ; and he asked me to come out with him to hear the band at the casino. I changed my dress, and we went out ; we walked for a short while, and then went into the hall. Fedya began playing, now winning a little, now losing a little. At last he had only one louis left. We crossed to another hall, and Fedya started playing again—winning and losing alternately. When we had again only one louis left the croupier announced the last three throws. Fedya put his louis on the red, and won. The second time he put on *passe,* and won. So he had now three louis. The third and last time he put on the twelve middles —and won again two louis. Thus we had our five louis back, exactly as when Fedya began. That surprised us very much and, I must say, also delighted us. If we had not won anything, at least we had lost nothing. We were so glad that all the way home we laughed happily, and Fedya kissed my hands and said no man in the world was happier than he.

Baden, Tuesday, 27th June, 1867.—This morning Fedya wanted to pay a visit to Turgenev ; but he was so late in getting up that he put it off. Again we had twelve louis ; Fedya took five and went to the tables. After he left, I became terribly sad ; I was quite sure that he would lose again and torment himself again. I cried bitterly. My apprehensions came true : Fedya returned home in the greatest despair. He said he had lost all, and began begging me to give him two more louis, saying that he must play on, that he must without fail. He fell on his knees before me, imploring me to give him two more louis. Seeing him in such despair I certainly could not help agreeing. I gave them to him, and now we are left with only five louis. I asked him not to go there to-day. I said that in such a state of agitation he was bound to lose. But it was of no avail. He could not help himself, and off he went. A rather long time passed, and I was sure that he could not remain there so long with so little money. At last he returned, and said that he had pawned his wedding ring and that he had lost all he had. He asked me to give him three more louis to redeem the ring ; for it might be lost. He had pawned the ring for seventeen francs, and it had to be paid immediately. There was nothing to be done but to give him the money ; thus we were left with two louis and one gulden. But Fedya was in such despair that I dared not talk to him ; so I gave him the money. He went away and returned after some time. He had managed to redeem the ring and to win at roulette five louis, which, together with the money we had, made eight louis. He gave me three louis, and five he took for himself to stake again. The pawnbroker refused to accept interest for the ring ; so Fedya gave him a franc for his trouble. We sat down to dinner, for I was very hungry. Whilst I was waiting for Fedya, I worried awfully : I cried, cursed myself, the roulette, Baden, and all. I am simply ashamed of myself, for I have never been like that. But after the crying I felt easier. After dinner Fedya went again to the tables. This time I was singularly calm ; I decided that he was going to lose the five louis and therefore it was no use fretting. I dressed and went for a walk as far as the hill St. Michel, where the Russian church stands. . . I came home a little before Fedya. He returned and told me that he had won some money. When he counted it, it turned out that he had won sixteen louis. So, with the five louis in our bag we have twenty-one louis—a fortune undreamed of lately. I was delighted because it improved our position. Fedya suggested we should go to hear the band in the casino garden. We went there, but to my annoyance we had not left the money at home. We walked for a long time, and listened to Rossini's *Stabat Mater*, a wonderful work, a great hymn that penetrates the soul. I wonder if there are many such wonderful musical pieces. Fedya highly appreciates the *Stabat Mater* and always listens to it with reverence.

Baden, Wednesday, 28th June, 1867.—This morning we got up at ten. Fedya went to pay his visit to Turgenev, with whom he remained for an hour and a half. Afterwards Fedya went to the tables, taking with him five louis. There remained at home ten louis. I went to the post-office, but there were no letters for us. I wanted to prolong my walk ; but as it was very hot, stifling, I put it off till the evening, when it would be cooler. I came home and started reading Soloviov's History, when our maid Marie began tidying up the place, and kept on sending me from one room to another. Marie looks about eighteen ; but when we asked her how old she was she said she was fourteen. She is such a baby ! always happy, gay and laughing. She has become quite friendly with us, and regards us as her own people, and so she is always happy with us. But she is wonderfully stupid. She never understands at once what she is told ; and although I say the same thing to her every day, she takes no heed. Thus, for instance, she brings no spoon for the soup when we dine at home ; I tell her each time, but she keeps on forgetting. To all questions she answers gaily and readily with a thundering *Ja*. I was cross with her this morning ; for she kept us waiting a long time for our tea and coffee. But I did not show her that I was cross. The making of tea takes them a long time here. They say that the tea must be in the teapot for at least three-quarters of an hour to taste really well ! When I came back from the post-office I felt ill, and decided to lie down. Recently all sorts of funny longings come into my mind. Now I want pastries, now mushrooms, now cabbage pies, which I had never liked before ; now I want new cucumber, or something sour or salty. All at once I longed for a fresh cucumber, and I asked Marie to go and to buy me a small one. I gave her six kreutzer and she brought me such an enormous one, over a yard long, I suppose, and so thick that it might last four days. . . . Fedya came home and said with vexation that he had lost ; that people had been pushing him and preventing him from playing quietly. He asked me to give him five louis. He told me that he had won seventeen, but he went on increasing the stakes, and lost everything. Of course, I gave him the money. There are five louis left ; but I have now got a bit used to these happenings, and they do not upset me so terribly. When Fedya went away, I felt wonderfully quiet, as though it were not our very last money. I think he must have been there over an hour, during which time I lay on the couch looking at the wall, and thinking. This has now become my favourite occupation. Fedya came back. He appeared to me very pale, and, thinking he had lost, I began consoling him, saying that the loss did not matter, and so on. But then Fedya told me that he had not lost, but had won a little ; and he showed me his purse. " A little ! " Forty-six pieces ! A whole purse of gold ! I was so glad, for now our life is secure (with my five we have now fifty-one louis). I was so pleased ; for these winnings will help us to carry on, and there will be no need to ask Turgenev to lend us money till we get some from Katkov. Fedya said that he was awfully lucky to-day. He staked gold and each time made good ; so that everyone was surprised at his luck. I immediately sent for dinner. Then we remembered that we had no coffee. Fedya at once proposed to go out and to fetch coffee, candles and wine. I am always surprised at Fedya doing the shopping. Well, who would have supposed—I mean, could I have believed—that that grave man, whom I had met for the first time on 4th October of last year—such a stern looking man—could busy himself with such trifles and talk with German shopkeepers about candles and such things. Fedya went off, and when they brought in the dinner I arranged it all on the table. Unexpectedly I went up to the window, and I saw Fedya, not through the window, but reflected in the window pane, carrying a bouquet in his hands. I began expecting him. But instead of him a tiny little boy about eight came in. He brought in a whole basket of fruit. I took it from him, and saw it contained raspberries, apricots, peaches and gooseberries. Fedya himself had called at the wine shop and in a few moments he appeared. Marie asked the boy to sit down ; but the funny little thing dared not do so at first. Then he sat down on the very edge of the chair and kept on looking at me awfully funnily.

Fedya came in and gave me the bouquet; I was so delighted that I kissed Fedya several times. I am so grateful to my dear darling Fedya for his attentions to me. He knew it would give me great pleasure, and he went out of his way to get the bouquet for me. I generally value Fedya's least attention to me. For instance, when I go to bed I say to him: " Bye-bye, Fedya," and he comes to me to say good-night, and each time I am unspeakably glad and happy. So in this case, too, I was very, very happy. Fedya told me that when the proprietress of the wine shop *Stadt Paris* (whose acquaintance he had already made) saw the bouquet, she exclaimed: " What a magnificent bouquet!" Fedya replied: " I am taking it to my wife." All the German women in the wineshop were extremely pleased by this, that is, by his attention to his wife. The bouquet is indeed superb: pink and yellow roses in the middle, violets and carnations as a border, and all beautifully arranged. We sat down to dinner. The dinner, as if to correspond, was also very good, and passed off merrily. We had now fifty louis and could go on quite securely. I asked Fedya to do me the favour of not going to the tables to-day; for I had observed that if one won, one ought not to go back the same day, otherwise one would lose. And why, indeed, not be satisfied? But Fedya asked me for five louis just to try his luck; perhaps to-day was his lucky day and he would win more. Not to give him the money was impossible; so I gave it him and was sure that he would lose it. After dinner we went out together, first to the post-office, but there were no letters for us. Fedya went on to the tables, and I went, as he directed me, to the left of the casino, to walk by the pond. I walked a rather long distance, I should say about a mile and a half or even more, and then turned back home. There is one thing which worries me in my walks, and that is the fear that I may have a fainting fit. Suddenly I feel bad, and I am afraid of falling into a swoon. And I am terrified, too, by the thought that I may stumble on one of the steps—there are many such steps on my walks —and fall down. The consequence might be very bad ; it might mean a miscarriage. I don't want that to happen ; I should then consider myself very unfortunate. Besides, I know that that would distress Fedya, who often talks and dreams with me of our coming child. Well, I had been walking back for over an hour when I came into an avenue called the Promenade. I was just turning into it when I suddenly noticed Fedya, who was sitting on a bench, and, so he told me, had been waiting for me a long time. He said that he had been pushed about, and therefore had lost. He asked me to give him five louis so that he might win back what he had lost. We went home, and I gave him the money : although I was quite sure that he would lose again. One can't reckon on continuous good luck. After a short while, indeed, Fedya returned and said that he had lost. He asked me to come for a walk to the casino. It was still daylight, and so I did not like going to a place where all the ladies are so smartly dressed. I must confess, I am not particularly pleased at having always to wear my ordinary black costume, which does not look at all nice among their brilliant dresses. Yet, I don't much care about the opinion of the ladies. In spite of my objections Fedya asked me to come with him and to take two louis ; again I knew beforehand that they would be lost. But Fedya remarked that I was probably grudging him the money ; then, of course, I gave it him. I was not at all grudging him the money ; but I knew for a certainty that he would not win to-day. When we got there it was still clear daylight ; but the lamps were lit, and it was an unpleasant sight. As a rule I do not like the time when it is not dark yet and the light of the day is struggling with the light of the lamps—it is not a pleasant sight.

To wait until it got dark we entered the hall and went to the tables. Fedya at first began to win ; but then, through staking unwisely, he lost everything, including his two louis. This made him terribly angry ; so not knowing on what to vent his anger he began cursing because it did not get dark sooner. We came out into the avenue and took a seat on a bench where some Germans were sitting. Fedya comforted me all the while, saying that his losses did not matter ; as though I needed that consolation ; I was calmer than he. I implored him not to worry. I said that, taking into account what we still had, his losses were a mere trifle. When it grew quite dark we went to hear the band. To-day an orchestral and not the usual military band was playing, and it played pieces meant for solo cornet-à-piston or for the flute. They were all such sad melodies, quite out of place. Gay polkas and valses should be played here, but not sonatas. If they want to play more serious pieces, they ought at least to make a better selection ; for who can be interested to hear a solo on a cornet-à-piston ? Fedya and I could not stand it any longer, and we went home. While we were having tea Fedya told me of his visit to Turgenev. According to him, Turgenev[1] was terribly vexed, and awfully bitter, and turned the conversation all the while on his new novel, *Smoke*.[2] Fedya, however, made no attempt to talk of the novel. Turgenev was furious over the reviews in the papers ; he said he had been reviled in the *Golos* and the *Otechestvennya Zapiski*, and in other journals. He also said that the nobility, led by its Marshal, Philip (?) Tolstoy, wanted to strike his name off the register of Russian noblemen, but for some reason this had not materialised. And he added : " if only they knew what pleasure it would have

---

[1] See Part II, " Dostoevsky and Turgenev."

[2] Turgenev's novel, *Smoke*, appeared in the *Russky Vestnik* in the first three numbers of 1867.

given me if they had done so." Fedya, as usual, spoke to him somewhat sharply. For instance, he advised him, since he lived so far from Russia, to buy a telescope in Paris, and to point the telescope on Russia, so as to see what was going on there ; otherwise he would never be able to make things out. Turgenev declared that he, Turgenev, was a realist ; but Fedya replied that he only thought he was one. When Fedya said that he had observed in the Germans nothing but stupidity, and constant cheating, Turgenev was terribly offended, and declared that Fedya had mortally offended him ; for he had become a German [in sympathy], was, indeed, a German, and not at all a Russian. Fedya replied that he had not known it at all, but that he was very sorry to hear it. Fedya, so he told me, went on talking to him rather humorously, which made Turgenev still more angry ; and then he told him definitely that his [T's] novel, was not a success. They parted, however, on friendly terms, and Turgenev promised to send us his book. He's a strange man—fancy being proud of having become a German ! It seems to me that, as a Russian writer, he had no need to renounce his nationality, still less to consider himself a German. And what good have the Germans done him ? He grew up in Russia, she brought him up and was enthusiastic over his talent. And he has renounced her. He says that, if Russia went under, the world would be none the worse for it. How wrong it is for a Russian to speak like that ! Well, let it pass ; though I know that Fedya was terribly angry and agitated at the baseness of renouncing one's country.

I went to bed at ten o'clock, as I was rather tired and dull : I have no books to read. While I prayed and made preparations for the night, Fedya sat and waited, so he told me, to see whether I would or would not say the usual " Bye-bye, dear Fedya." He thought that I was cross with him. We had a talk and parted great

friends.   He began pacing his room, and I fell asleep to
the sound of his steps.   My nerves are so unstrung that
I dream of all sorts of strange things.   So I dreamed of
my father, then of a young man who lends Fedya four
thousand francs.   They go together to the tables ; and
I know that robbers are waiting on the road and will
attack and murder them.   I feel such distress and
anguish about what is going to happen to Fedya that
I awake !   Then it occurs to me that the workmen in
the smithy, above which are our rooms, may rob us.
I get up from my bed and ask Fedya to bolt the door,
which frightens him.

Thursday, 29th June, 1867.—Such a fine day to-day.
I believe I woke up about eight.   But I did not get up ;
for Fedya did not go to bed till four.   I was afraid of
making a noise and waking him.   At ten o'clock Fedya
woke up, and no longer wanted to sleep.   I ordered
tea.   Marie came in, bringing a card from Turgenev.
He had driven up in a cab, and, after inquiring if we
lived there, had asked her to take up his card.   Probably, he did not want to come in, so as to avoid speaking to Fedya : yet he had to pay a visit out of politeness.
Queer: fancy making a call at ten in the morning !
Perhaps it is the German way ; still it is strange.   Marie
amuses us very much with her little ways ; when she
speaks she always employs her fingers to point to the
object she is speaking of.   Fedya paced the room for a
long time, and at one o'clock he went to the tables,
taking eight louis.   Of the fifty we had yesterday only
thirty remain, and they would be quite enough, provided they do not go with the same speed as those we
had before.   I was quite certain that Fedya would lose
them, and that he would come asking for more.   And so
it happened : Fedya lost the money, and explained the
circumstance by the fact that close to him stood an
Englishman who smelt of so very strong a scent, that

it was impossible to bear it, and so he lost. Fedya asked me to give him five more louis ; I gave them to him, and there remain twenty-five. Well, I thought, if our money goes with such rapidity, it won't be long before we are left with ten louis. When Fedya went off, I, too, went out for a walk, but in the opposite direction. When I came home, I had to wait a long time for Fedya, who said that he had won a little. He showed me forty louis ; so that now we have again sixty-five pieces, sixty in the bag and five which Fedya took. But he was much annoyed : he was in luck, and won, but then put fifteen louis on the twelve last numbers and lost. It was those fifteen louis he was annoyed about. He suggested that he should go out and fetch some wine and peaches. While he was out, Marie brought the dinner from the restaurant—a very good dinner ; they simply surprise us by their attention. Fedya came back and again brought me a bouquet, a small one, but still a charming one. Indeed, Fedya is spoiling me. He also bought gooseberries, cherries, peaches and apricots. . . . After dinner he said he was going to the tables to play, not for excitement, but just for a bit of fun, and that if he lost the four louis (he had spent a louis on the purchases), he should not mind it at all. . . . Soon he came back ; he had lost, and was vexed, and suggested I should come with him to the tables and take with me five louis. He said that perhaps he would not call there at all ; but he spoke of his desire to try a new system—to stake on *zéro* ; then perhaps he might win. There was nothing to be done, save to take five louis and to go back. . . . We entered the hall. I suggested to Fedya that, as I had not a lucky hand, I should not stand near him, but sit down at some distance. I sat down in a corner. But Fedya's luck did not improve. He put on *zéro*, it came out twice, and yet he lost. This annoyed him awfully, and he left the hall in gloom. As we were walking in the garden, he began saying that it would be nice now to go home. I had better remain at home, and he would take another five louis and return to the tables, perhaps to win. At first I objected and said that he had already won, and it ought to be enough for to-day ; but it was no use, and I had to agree. He asked me not to be angry, as though I ever felt angry with him ; he kissed my hands, saying God forbid that my love for him should ever disappear. I replied, that my love for him would never change. We came home. I gave him the money. He went to the tables, and I stayed at home and began making tea, which, I must say, the people here don't know how to make. Fedya came soon and said that he had lost everything. In the evening he told me that he was as attached to me as a child is to its mother, that he loved me very much, and was afraid of vexing me. I comforted him, saying that we had still a lot of money left : fifty louis in our circumstances is a great deal of money. All through the evening Fedya was very dull and irritable ; he had evidently lost all hope of winning, and such gloom came over him that I was extremely sorry for him. As for me, I was quite calm ; for surely with to-day's gains we have back all the money we had at our arrival. And my ideal is : to have sixty louis, and to live quietly until we go back [to Russia]. That's all I want, and then I should be very satisfied and contented. . . . Late at night Fedya came to say good-night to me and told me marvellous stories of his love for me.

Friday, 1st July, 1867.—I got up to-day at ten, and, as Fedya says, I must have made a noise with my boots, so that I woke him ; and he, poor thing, went to bed only at four, just at the time when the workmen in the smithy downstairs began moving out a cart. . . I usually don't take any notice of the noise downstairs, having got used to it ; but Fedya, who is less at home, is annoyed by it. I was grieved because I knew that,

if Fedya has not his sleep out, he becomes capricious
and irritable. We had coffee, but he did not like it.
Then he went to the tables, taking five louis, and asked
me to get envelopes and sealing wax while he was out.
I went to buy them, and no sooner had I come home
than Fedya returned and said that he had lost, and asked
for another five louis. I gave them to him at once
(there are forty left). Soon he came again ; he had lost,
and asked me for another ten pieces. I was sorry for
him, gave him the money, and said that I was going out
for a walk, as I did not want to remain alone in the
rooms. . . . I came home about four, and thought
that Fedya would have been waiting till I came to send
out for dinner. But he was not there ; and when he
came he said that he had lost all ; and took another
ten louis (there remain twenty). We had dinner ; but
it was a very bad one, as though they knew that it was
not our lucky day. We had to send out for a portion
of veal cutlets. At dinner Fedya was wonderfully
good and tender with me. Then he went to the tables
and won thirty louis, so that we have again fifty ; but
he took five with him and lost them while I was out at
the post office. . . . In the evening we went to the
tables and lost five louis. At first Fedya took four louis
to play, and five he gave to me, saying that I must in
no case give them back to him. But when he had lost
his four louis, he asked me to give him the five louis, or
else he would go home to fetch more money. Of course,
I gave them to him, and he lost them. When we came
home, Fedya began saying that we ought to have some
sweets, and proposed to go out and buy some, and to
get change for paying the landlady. He went out and
brought candles, lemons (as he knew I felt sick to-day,
he wanted to make lemonade for me), oranges, cheese,
and, what surprised me, fine granulated sugar. Such
solicitude on his part greatly moved me—indeed with
him I am as safe as ' in Christ's bosom.' I even feel

inclined to laugh when I see him going out shopping and returning loaded with candles and cheese. He is very fond of fussing about, of preparing tea, and he seems even to take a pleasure in doing it. He is such a fine, such a dear man, my husband, such a dear and simple man, and I am so happy. We had a jolly time over our tea, ate cheese, oranges, and made some fine lemonade. Before going to bed we had a very good affectionate talk. I fell asleep quite happy ; for it is very pleasant to have those forty-four louis in our pockets, if even only for a short time. It's so much better than to have only two louis and to be uncertain as to what is going to happen next.

Baden, Saturday, 2nd July, 1867.—To-day we got up rather early, and I paid our landlady five florins ; I had given her three during the week, and so it makes eight florins (our weekly rent). She seemed to be pleased. While I was getting ready to take to the post-office Fedya's letter to Katkov, which he has at last written, he went out to the tables, but came back very soon, having lost five louis. I gave him another eight (there remain now thirty). I had been reading all the while. . . . I had meant to do some sewing, but I was very sad. I could not even make out why. I am indifferent to everything, as if it does not matter what happens. Nothing makes me happy, my gaiety is gone God knows where. I do not want to go anywhere ; if even we were to win a considerable amount, I should not feel particularly pleased—so indifferent have I become. I have no wish to do anything, either to sew or write or read (it is true, there is positively nothing to read). Fedya advises me to go and read at the library which is attached to the casino ; he says that women go there. Of course I think of going there ; but somehow nothing interests me. It even seems to me that if my mother—whom after Fedya I love above all in the world

—were to come here, even her arrival would not make me feel happy. I should just like to lie in bed with the curtains closed and to think of nothing. I do not know how to rid myself of this apathy. I have even no desire now to leave this place ; it is painful to think of packing and travelling, and being sick—it is best not to think of going away. At last Fedya came. At first he said "no luck," and then showed me a full purse. It contained sixty-one louis, and with our thirty it makes ninety-one. Among the coins there was a piece of forty francs, a coin which he had never been given before. He was going to put that coin into the bag, and then gave it to me as a present ; so that now I am the owner of a gold piece of forty francs. Still I do not know what to do with it, for I want to keep it in case of emergency, or else I would buy a brooch or some other trinket. Fedya told me that he had had a run of luck and everybody wondered at it : he won on whatever he staked. Behind him stood an Englishman, and staked on the same *numbers* as Fedya did ; and Fedya observed that each time he made a stake and looked at the Englishman, he won without fail : such a lucky face that man has. Fedya says that the Englishman's face is so good and kind that it is bound to bring luck. They do not understand each other ; for Fedya does not speak English, and the Englishman evidently speaks no French. They converse by gesture, which I imagine must be very funny. Fedya is such a familiar figure in the place that the waiters usually bring him a chair. He ought to give them a tip for being so obliging ; but I think he has not yet given them anything. And a lady there, Fedya noticed, has twice already given him her seat. While I was putting the money in the bag, Fedya went out to buy sweets. A little afterwards a woman appeared carrying a whole basket of apricots, cherries, gooseberries, prunes and reine-claudes—(it is a kind of fruit named in honour of some Queen, Reine

Claude). . . . They know Fedya in the market place ; three women stand there, and Fedya invariably buys things from each of them. From one he buys fruit, from another cherries, from the third bouquets. Fedya came back soon and brought me a magnificent bouquet. Calling at the wineshop, he showed the bouquet to the proprietress, who knows him as a customer. She asked him how long he had been married, and he said, five months. I think she must have been surprised that after five months of married life the husband was taking bouquets to his wife. . . . We went out together. I went for a very long walk, and coming back I met Fedya, who said that he had lost all and was waiting for me. He said he had lost because behind him stood a rich Pole and a young little Pole, who made very small stakes, but gave themselves airs. This made Fedya so angry that he played carelessly and lost. We came home, and Fedya blamed me for being out so late; but when I told him of my pain, he got frightened and blamed me for walking too fast, saying that he could have waited longer, and that I need not have hurried. Then he asked me to come with him to hear the band, and to take with me five louis. Well, there was nothing to be done ; we took the money, although I was certain that it would be lost. . . . I ought to have mentioned that to-day, when Fedya won so much money, he met Goncharov, who from a desire to show off and to give the impression of not playing at all, but of just having a bit of fun, asked Fedya what *passe* meant. Well, could one believe that a man, who has been seen at the tables for two or three hours at a time, does not know how to play ; but he must have wished to show that " we do not care for that sort of thing ; let others make money in that way." Goncharov asked Fedya how he had been getting on, and Fedya said that at first he had been losing, but that he had got his money back with a certain gain ; he showed him his full purse.

I am certain Goncharov will tell Turgenev about it, and Fedya owes Turgenev fifty or a hundred thalers. I should, therefore, be glad if we could manage to pay Turgenev back while we are here ; for how will Fedya manage to pay him when we return to Russia ? We went to hear the band, but it was very bad ; we called at the tables and lost as usual, after which Fedya became very gloomy. I am terribly annoyed that the whole evening is spoilt. We came out of the casino and went for a walk. Here Fedya showed me his lucky Englishman ; he appears to me . . . like a man who drinks, with his hat tilted on one side, and with a funny face. We walked for a long time. There were many artisans and shop assistants sitting about in grand style on the benches and probably imagining themselves the most superior people in Baden. (In my present state of mind I would prefer not to go to hear the band, but to stay at home. Indeed it would be better ; for the Promenade is filled with smartly-dressed women. It simply makes me ill ! I, too, have ambition, and I don't want to be dressed worse than the others. But I have to wear my black costume, in which I feel very hot, and which, besides, is ugly. But what can I do, if it must be so ?) We came home and sat down to tea ; but I suddenly felt terribly ill. I went to bed, and Fedya came to me several times comforting me, calling me "poor sufferer." He was sorry that I was not well, said he loved me and many other nice things. He spoke with rapture of our coming baby. His sympathy is very, very comforting.

Sunday, 2nd July, 1867. We got up rather early ; I woke at seven, but fell asleep again at ten. But my sleep did not last—the landlady's children scream terrifically. I have never come across such noisy children as hers. Fedya got up cross and quarrelled with me. He got terribly angry with the children and several times mimicked the way they screamed, which was awfully funny. Then he looked at me and saw me laugh ; he too burst into laughter and said : " What a funny thing you are ! I can't be cross with you, you laugh so nicely ! " This morning we had seventy-five gold pieces. Fedya went off to the tables, although I had a feeling that it was going to be an unlucky day ; for I had dreamed that we had gambled away all we had. He first took seven pieces. Then, having lost them, he came back and took another eight ; but the latter went too. Then he came back again and took ten pieces. After a short while he returned and asked me to give him yet another ten pieces. There remained forty. I gave him the ten pieces and went out for a walk. I returned home at four, as I promised, but Fedya was not yet back. At five he came, at last, and was awfully upset. He was very much annoyed that, having just now won forty-four pieces, he had gambled them all away, because he could not stop in time. I, too, was a bit annoyed. We had a very cheerless dinner, although I tried my best to comfort him. Then he took another five pieces, and I went to the post office. There were no letters for us. Fedya returned home and said that he had lost those five as well, and asked me for another five, saying that if he lost them, he would not play any more to-day. I gave him the five pieces ; there remain thirty-two. We could manage on this money quite well, especially as we have a supply of food in now. Fedya went off and has not yet returned. I am writing now and wonder what is going to happen. . . I was greatly mistaken : Fedya did not lose, but won forty-three pieces ; so that we have now seventy-five pieces. . . . As we were coming back from our walk we called at a book-shop. We asked the assistant (on whose bright-coloured waistcoat a bug was crawling) to show us some books. We took two volumes of Gustave Flaubert's *Madame Bovary*, of which novel Turgenev had said that it was the best work in the whole literary world for the last ten years. . . . We met Goncharov, and stopped for a few minutes' talk. I think that Goncharov must have been gambling hard. He says he is going to stay here another fortnight, as he is waiting for a friend.

Monday, 3rd July, 1867. At twelve o'clock Fedya went off to the tables, having on him some six pieces ; but very soon he came back saying that he had lost, and asked for more. I gave him more. He went away and did not come home for a long time. At last he arrived looking very sad and told me that he had lost. I began to comfort him, saying that it did not matter, that it was a mere trifle ; then he suddenly said to me : " Would you like a present ? " and he handed me his purse.[1] There were fifty gold pieces in it and a great deal of silver; so we now had one hundred pieces. He took ten pieces and the silver ; and after staying with me for a while, he went out to buy some fruit, and he gave me his word that he would not go to the tables. I think that if he were to go there he would lose, for he is still agitated. I wonder if he will keep his word or not. . . . As it was a long time before he came back I began feeling uneasy. At last he arrived, but very cross, followed by a boy carrying a basket of fruit. That boy made me very angry. They have got used

---

[1] Note by Mme. Dostoevsky inserted at a later date : " Fiodor had the habit all his lifetime first of distressing a person and then of making him very happy. Thus, for instance, when we were living abroad, in straitened circumstances, and were waiting impatiently for money, he would, after receiving some from the post office, return home looking sad and crushed. I would start comforting him ; then he would go out into the hall or to the landlady's rooms and come back with cakes, fruit and various dainties for which we had been longing for a long time, and with which he would hasten to bring happiness to myself and our family, as soon as he got any money."

to Fedya tipping them, and therefore he stood waiting.
Although I gave him the empty basket, he did not move,
waiting for a tip.   I gave him something and sent him
away ; for I cannot bear a stranger in our rooms.
Fedya bought to-day a lot of peaches, cherries, gooseberries, plums, and pears. He was somewhat irritated
at not going off to play. . . .   After dinner, at six, he
went off to the tables, and I stayed behind, intending to
go out for a walk, as I had not yet been out to-day ;
but very soon Fedya came back, saying that he had lost
the ten gold pieces.   I gave him another ten.   After
the storm Fedya came running home.   At first he told
me that he had lost everything, but when I began comforting him he showed me some seven or eight gold
pieces ; then he suggested that I should have a good
look at his purse.   There were in it seventy pieces.   I
put them with our eighty pieces, so that we have now
one hundred and fifty pieces or three thousand francs.
He had, besides, two forty-franc notes, some gold, and
thirty-five francs.   Fedya said if I wanted anything,
he would fetch it.   I said we needed cheese, oranges and
a lemon.   He went out promising not to go to the
tables.   Some time passed ; the tea got cold, and I
began to wonder if Fedya had not, after all, called at the
tables.   At last he came back with his pockets bulging
with various things.   At first he handed me the cheese,
oranges and lemon ; then he took out of his overcoat
pocket a jar the contents of which I could not make out.
And it turned out to be my favourite, my dream—
preserved mushrooms ! Oh, what a good husband !
What a dear husband to get for his wife Russian
mushrooms in Baden ! It is something that must not
be forgotten. Then Fedya got out of his pocket a
bottle of huckleberry jelly, which he also managed to
find there, then caviare, French mustard—in a word,
everything I am fond of. Is not it sweet ? Have
not I a splendid husband ? He, who remembers

nothing, suddenly remembered the way to the shop, and got the things I so much like.

Tuesday, 4th July, 1867. I woke at seven—the naughty children keep on screaming. To-day we had one-hundred and sixty-six gold pieces, and we could feel secure. Fedya went off to the tables, taking twenty pieces. He did not come back for a long time, and I thought he had lost. At last he arrived very agitated and said he had had a quarrel with a gentleman whose coin he by mistake had raked in. When that man mentioned the fact to Fedya, he immediately gave the coin back to him, apologised, and said that it was due to his absent-mindedness. But the gentleman said : "It was not at all absent-mindedness." Then Fedya went up to him and wanted to take him aside to clear up the matter. But the man replied : " The matter is at an end now." Then Fedya publicly called him "scoundrel," and the man took no offence. That incident irritated Fedya so much that he started playing without any calculation, and lost about forty pieces. He came home to get another twenty pieces, which he wanted to lose in order to show that he did not go there with the object of winning, but in order to stake big amounts and to lose. He wanted to take thirty, but I gave him only twenty (we have left one hundred and twenty-six), but that was quite a big enough sum. Fedya returned soon and said that he had lost. We had dinner, in great agitation, and he went off again. taking another twenty pieces ; but this time he came back awfully soon, saying that whatever he staked he had lost. Then he took another twenty pieces, and lost them. Then he took another ten, and lost ; another ten, and lost. So that we did not even go for a walk. By the evening we had sixty-six pieces left. Fedya had wished to change the rooms ; for the workmen at the smithy prevented him from sleeping, and the landlady's children shouted so much that we did not know what to do. In the evening I implored Fedya to leave Baden ; but he did not want to go, and even got cross with me. Ah, why did we not go away yesterday !

Wednesday, 5th July, 1867. Fedya went off in the morning and took five pieces, which he lost immediately. Then he came back and took another ten, and also the six double-louis-d'or which he had given me as a present, saying that as he always won when staking on *trente et quarante*, he might win now. I gave them to him, but he lost them. (We have forty left). Then he came home once again, taking another five louis. I went out for a walk to the New Castle. There I sat over an hour, reading *Madame Bovary*. I wanted to prolong my walk, but seeing that it was four o'clock I went home. Fedya was not there, but he arrived soon. He told me he had lost everything some time before, that he had already been here, and not having found me at home, he had gone to the reading room to read the Russian papers. After dinner he went to the tables, taking with him five louis, lost them immediately, and returned home to get another five. When he had gone I, too, went out for a walk, to the post office and to get a few things. But Fedya, having already managed to lose his money, noticed me when I was passing the square, and hurried up to me. Although I, too, saw him in the distance, I purposely wanted to postpone as long as possible the handing over to him of the next five louis. There were no letters for us. We went home for the five louis. These too were lost ; and so we are left with twenty louis. Fedya came home rather late, and told me that he had been involved in another incident. A very tall and stout man began jostling him. Fedya protested and the man said that the tables were open to every-body. Fedya told him not to take a place which was not his. Then the man said " this time it won't end like last time." He evidently hinted at the cowardice of the other man, meaning that this time Fedya would not get off so lightly. Fedya heard someone saying " it has started again " ; so they may possibly consider Fedya as a man who picks quarrels. This is too bad, for on the next occasion the croupiers may tell Fedya that he is picking quarrels, and then he will have to stop going to the tables. Fedya said that if we had forty louis, we would immediately leave the place. I should be very happy, the more so that these incidents begin frightening me very much. And Fedya, too, is queer ; why does he take offence at being jostled ? Surely everyone tries to come close to the table, and therefore jostling is inevitable. He says, indeed, that all sorts of incidents take place there, and people are often terribly rude to one another, and that all this does not matter.

Thursday, 6th July, 1867. This morning we had twenty gold pieces—too small an amount ; but what is to be done ? Perhaps we shall manage to improve our position. Fedya went off to the tables, and I remained at home. But soon he came back saying that he had lost, and asked for another five. I gave them to him, and there are ten left. He went out and lost the five. Taking five more, he soon came back and said that he had lost these too, and asked for one more louis. There were now four left. I gave him one louis. He went off, but returned in a quarter of an hour. Well, how long could one louis last ? Very sad we sat down to our meal. After which we went to the post office, and Fedya went off to the tables, taking three louis. All we now have left is one louis. I walked for a long time on the Promenade, expecting him to come out ; but he did not appear. At last he came and said that he had lost these too, and asked me to allow him to pawn certain things. I got out my ear-rings and brooch, and looked

at them for a long, long time.   It seemed to me I was
seeing them for the last time.   I was so terribly grieved,
I loved these things so much, they were Fedya's presents
to me.   I think that those were the only things that
were really dear to me.   Fedya kept saying that he
was pained and ashamed to look me in the face, that
he was robbing me of things dear to me, but what could
he do, we had surely known that it would come to that.
Unobserved by him I bade farewell to the lovely things,
I kissed them.   Then I asked Fedya to go and pawn
them for one month, saying that I would write to my
mother asking her for money with which to redeem
them, for I do not want to lose them.   Fedya dropped
down on his knees before me, kissed my breast, kissed
my hands, saying that I was good and kind, and so
unwell, and that there was no one better than I in the
whole world.   Fedya went off, but when he closed the
door I felt so distressed that I could not restrain myself
and burst into tears.   It was not ordinary crying, it
was a kind of sobbing, with such pain in my chest, and
the pain was not relieved even by my tears.   The tears
did not make it easier a bit.   I was so sad, so distressed,
intolerably distressed.   I envied everyone, I considered
that everyone was happy, only we alone seemed to be
so unhappy.   Everything seemed to me terrible, sad,
painful.   I did not fear so much the loss of the last of
our money, as I feared that everything would become
so empty, so distressing, all these dramas and worries.
We should not be able to think of anything else.   Every
minute we should be thinking about having had one
hundred and sixty gold pieces the day before.   We
were mad not to have gone away, and now we had not
a single penny.   I kept on now lying down on the bed,
choking with sobs, now getting up and pacing the room,
crying aloud.   Only once, I remember, had I cried so
bitterly: it was before my wedding.   But then my
mother was with me and I felt easier ; but here I was

quite alone, I had no dear mother to comfort me.   I was
in such despair that I thought I was going off my head.
I was terribly afraid lest Fedya should come in.   I
wished him to keep away as long as possible ; for on
coming home he would say that he had lost all, and that
we were lost.   Only this morning we were joking and
he had said to me in German : " Wir sind verloren,"
and we had laughed so much.   And now I was in such
despair that I positively did not know what to do.   I
shuddered awfully and almost fainted each time Marie
came into the room.   I thought it was Fedya coming.
At times it seemed to me that it would be best if Fedya
kept away for three days and even longer ;   I would
lie in a dark room all that time and sleep all the time.
I was afraid of meeting Fedya—I was extremely sorry
for him.   Christ, how grieved I was ;   I wonder if I
shall often have to live through such terrible moments.
Three hours, perhaps more, passed and at last Fedya
arrived.   Hearing the bell, I quite jumped from my
seat.   He told me he had lost everything, all the money
he had received for the articles pawned.   He sat down
and wanted to place me on his knees, but I knelt before
him and began consoling him.   Then Fedya said to me
that he had played for the last time in his life, that it
would never happen again.   He leant his elbows on
the table and began to cry.   Yes, Fedya cried.   He said
" I have robbed you of your very last thing, carried it
off and gambled it away."   I began to comfort him, but
he kept on crying.   How distressed I was for him ;   it
is terrible the way he torments himself.   Fedya told
me he had received one hundred and twenty francs for
the ear-rings, the interest was five francs, so that in a
month we shall have to pay back one hundred and
twenty-five francs.   Then we sat for some·time on the
couch, embracing one another.   I was distressed, almost
crushed.   Then Fedya suggested that we should go out
for a walk and get cigarettes.   I agreed and we took a

few turns on the Promenade. Fedya spoke of various plans for improving our position. He said that he had called twice on Goncharov, wishing to tell him everything and to ask for a loan of a hundred thalers, which he hoped to pay him back in a month. But each time Goncharov was out. Then Fedya spoke of Katkov. But how to write to him, especially from Baden—it would be clear that he was gambling. It is a bad look out. Oh, we were fools not to have left Baden even this morning, when we had still twenty louis; we could still have managed to carry on in Geneva. When we came home we lay down on the bed side by side, and Fedya began speaking of various projects by which we could improve our position. He thought of writing to Aksakov, to offer him his collaboration. First he meant to write to Kraievsky[1] to ask him for money (in advance), promising to send him the manuscript of a novel of ten folios by January. But to me the idea seemed impossible. It would mean too much work; the more so as Fedya can hardly manage to write his novel for Katkov. We talked for a long time sorrowfully. I could not bear to look at Fedya. And to be with him was painful, too; for if he had not been there, I could have cried, but in his presence I had no tears. I could not cry: it was too painful. We sat up till eleven, and decided that next day he should go to the tables and try his luck with the last louis: perhaps things would get better again. I went to my room to bed and happily, fell asleep. Fedya woke me at two o'clock to say good-night, and I was so glad that I fell asleep again. I was afraid of lying awake; for sad thoughts kept on obsessing my mind and I could not drive them away. It always seems to me that I am extremely happy in having married Fedya, and that the bad moments are what I have to pay for my happi-

---

[1] Editor of the review *Otechestvennya Zapiski*.

ness. Bidding me good-night Fedya said that he loved me boundlessly ; that if he were told that he had got to have his head cut off for me he would submit to it readily, so much did he love me, and that he would never forget my kindness during those moments. (In the evening Fedya said to me : " How can I help loving you, you are two now ; I love you very much, and our child I adore beforehand.")

Friday, 7th July, 1867. I suddenly saw Fedya sitting on my bed looking at me. I asked him what was the matter, and he said he had come in to see why I was so late in getting up. We talked for a while and I got up. I was ill again. Fedya looked so miserable. Then about one o'clock he took the one louis we had, and I gave him a five-franc note I had saved up, and he went off to the tables. We have now altogether five florins ; but we owe for three days' meals, and to-morrow we have to pay rent for the rooms ; but how ? Fedya came back saying he had lost everything. On his way to the tables he pawned his wedding ring for twenty francs, but it had all gone. And now our desires were quite modest, just to get two or five louis and then we should be happy. But fate is punishing us for not having been satisfied when we had the one hundred and sixty louis, and for having wanted more. God is my witness, I did not want more, it was Fedya who wanted more, and for whom ? Not for himself, but for those bad people at home who torment him so much. Surely, we should not have kept any of the money he had won, it would all have gone to them.

We sat in still greater grief. What should we do now, what could we pawn ? I had a Chantilly lace cloak. I gave it to Fedya. He took it to the jeweller, but the latter said he took only articles of gold and things which were not in his line he could not accept ; but he advised Fedya to go to a certain man called Weismann, who specialised in these things. Fedya called there, but the door was shut. Then he came home, soaking wet from the rain which, as though to spite us had been pouring down all day. Before dinner Fedya called there again, but again the man was out. After dinner Fedya went again, but soon came back saying that the pawnbroker did not take such articles ; but he advised Fedya to go to Mme. Etienne, who kept a shop in the square. Fedya called there, but the proprietress was out, and her sister told him to call next morning at ten ; but she doubted if her sister would take the article. At home Fedya lay down for some time, he was very sad, and then went off to the tables, taking with him my wedding ring which he was to pawn. Of course, nothing could come of it. Fedya was so very sad all day. It pains me to see him like this and to know that I cannot help him. I asked Fedya to go to the reading room and to sit there, for he is bored sitting at home . . . I wanted to go out for a walk. I was already shutting the door, when I heard Fedya coming up the stairs, and, as it seemed to me in the darkness, carrying a bouquet. I immediately thought that in order to make me happy, he had bought a bouquet for me with the half gulden which I had given him. That would be fine—there is no money to buy food for to-morrow and he is buying bouquets ! But Fedya said that, besides the bouquets, he had also fruit. I opened the door and he handed me a beautifully arranged bouquet, crown-shaped, of white and pink roses. Fedya asked me not to suppose that he had brought me gold, as he had only silver. But I was so happy at his winning, however small the sum, that I did not wish for bigger gains. Fedya then handed me the two rings (my second ring had also been pawned for twenty francs) and told me that for that ring he had received from the pawnbroker four thalers and one five-franc note, and with that money he had gone off to the tables. He staked the thalers and lost them. There remained the five francs ; he staked them, and won. He won as much as one hundred and eighty francs, then came down to seven, got up again, then came down to three francs, and so on. At last when he had won again one hundred and eighty francs, he left the tables. From the Casino rooms, he went to our good German and redeemed the two rings for two louis. The German was surprised and asked him, " Have you made all this money on the loan you recently received ? " Fedya said " Yes." The German said : " Do not play, for you will lose everything." He was greatly surprised that Fedya had won such a big sum in such a short time, and suggested that Fedya should redeem now all the articles pawned ; but Fedya said he would do it next time. Probably that old fellow must have lost at roulette, and made a vow, in spite of the temptation so close at hand, never again to gamble ; and now he is firmly faithful to his vow, and warns everyone against that vice. Fedya is very friendly with that German, and he will probably help us again. Fedya said that he had bought me the bouquet with the greatest joy ; for the day before he had cried, saying that he would now no longer be able to bring me any more bouquets or fruit—and now he could do so again. We put the bouquet in water and went out for a stroll, and also to buy food. First we called at the tobacconist to buy cigars, then at the shop where we usually buy our coffee, and got half a pound of such wonderful cheese as I never ate before. While they ground the coffee for us, we went for a walk, and congratulated ourselves on our position. Now at any rate, we can pay the rent, eight gulden, to-morrow. We need not be ashamed before the landlady of having no money. We bought provisions to last us for several days, and we need not beg of Goncharov for some money to live on ; we shall pay for the three dinners, and also for the handkerchiefs. Although the amount we have now is not big, yet it is a relief. We spent supper time merrily and ate the cheese and fruit. We gave some to Marie, who is a very nice girl ; she is an awful baby, giggles all the time, but, to give her her due, she does everything very slowly. Also, we are rid of the necessity of going to-morrow to Mme. Etienne to pawn my cloak, which is indeed fortunate, for she might give very little for it, or even refuse it altogether.

Saturday, 8th July. Fedya went off to the tables, taking with him eighty francs, but he came back and said that he had lost all, and asked me for the last louis we had left. I gave it to him, but of course he lost it—there was no chance of winning, for surely such mad luck does not happen to man. . . . Fedya told me about a Russian who stood yesterday at the tables asking his friend to lend him some money ; but the latter said he would not give him any, as he was sure to lose it. . . . We began examining our belongings to see what could be sold or pawned. We fixed on my fur jacket. Fedya went to a furrier, whom he brought here, but the furrier refused to buy it, as it was worn. There was nothing left for us to do but to take the jacket with us when we go to Switzerland, where it might come in useful. When the German left, Fedya went off and pawned again our rings, but this time my ring which had brought luck yesterday, did not help, and Fedya lost. And so we are now without any money, with the dinners unpaid, but, praise the Lord, our rent is paid and a few provisions bought, such as tea, coffee and sugar. Then Fedya went to all sorts of shops trying to sell my lace cloak ; but everywhere he got the answer that they did not want it, and recommended him to go to other places. They did not even want to look at the cloak, so that Fedya ran about the town for three hours, without any result. They all kept sending him to Weismann, who they said kept a bank and would take anything. Fedya at last went to him. Weismann met him on the stairs, where he was having a quarrel with a woman ; but he asked Fedya in and told him that he did not take such things ; that he took only good articles ; that he used to take other things, but that it was not profitable. Still, he examined the cloak and showed it to his sister. Then they said that they could do nothing for him to-day, but if he called to-morrow at eleven, at Mme. Etienne's, who would value the cloak, then he would be able to say if he could advance anything on it or not.

Sunday, 9th July, 1867. To-day I woke Fedya rather early, so that he should be not late for Weismann. He went off, and I prayed that he might pawn the article so that it should not be lost. At last Fedya came back and brought sixty francs. He told me that when he arrived at Mme. Etienne's shop, it was closed ; then he went to Weismann's, but that, too, was closed. Then he thought all was lost. But then he suddenly saw Weismann in the street, and the latter proposed that they should go together to Etienne. There they waited outside for some time, until Madame came from the sermon and opened the shop. Then Weismann himself went into the shop to have a private consultation with Mme. Etienne. When he came back he said that the cloak was out of fashion and no longer worn, but that he was willing to advance sixty francs on it for a month, and if it was not redeemed in a month it would be forfeited. He told Fedya that on gold articles he allowed a fourth of the value. They must, therefore, have valued the cloak at three hundred francs, and would be glad if it were not redeemed. Then I went to the post office to post a letter to my people, in which I blamed them very much for their long silence, and also asked them for some money. But there I received a letter, read it, and almost burst out crying. Mother wrote that K. could no longer keep the furniture for us, and would appropriate it if we did not redeem it, and a good deal of other unpleasant news. I was so distressed that I nearly cried at the post office. But when I came home I gave way to my tears, and wept dreadfully. At last Fedya arrived ; he came in very pale and fell on his knees before me. He said that all was at an end, that he had lost everything, that he had won forty-five francs but was not satisfied with this and had lost everything. This affected me terribly. I was afraid of his getting an epileptic fit. I told him of the letter I had from home, and of my sorrow. He listened and then decided that he would write to Katkov and ask him to send some money to mother, so that she could redeem the furniture. Then she should pawn the furniture, and send on the money to us. But as we have no money at all to live on now, we should ask mother to send us meanwhile fifty roubles. And so we decided. I sat down to write to mother. I described to her the state in which we were and asked for help. After dinner Fedya lay for some time thinking what to do—whether to call on Goncharov at once, when he would be likely to find him at the table d'hôte, or to wait and go to him to-morrow about ten o'clock, when he would be just out of bed ; for all the times Fedya has called on him at any other hour Goncharov has always been out. Fedya wants to ask him for some money. I advised him to go now so as not to worry himself by getting up early in the morning. Fedya went to the Hotel Europe, but was told that Goncharov was still at dinner, and they advised him to call in a quarter of an hour. He went for a stroll and returned to the hotel just in time to find Goncharov coming out of the hotel. Goncharov's first question was : " Well, how are things with you ? Mine are bad, too bad ! Yesterday I gave a man five hundred roubles and he gambled them away. Then I began playing for him, and won for him a pile of gold, but he lost it all." Then Fedya said to him, " I have come to you to ask a favour. I have gambled away everything—to the very last penny. The day before yesterday I had one hundred and sixty louis, and to-day I have not a single gulden. I have therefore come to you to ask you for three louis." " How much ! " Goncharov exclaimed. Fedya repeated the sum. " Well, that amount I can, of course, let you have, but no more ; for I am going to Paris in a week, and shall therefore need money." Fedya said that he wanted the money only for living expenses, until he got money from Russia, and that he would pay him back in a week's time. Goncharov immediately took his purse from his pocket, and gave Fedya three louis. Fedya said that this would be quite enough for him for small expenses until he got money from Petersburg, and promised to pay it back without fail in a week's time. They parted rather shy of one another. Fedya told him that he had called on him the day before yesterday, but on quite a different matter—he had wanted to give Goncharov some money and to ask him to hand it over to Turgenev—(Oh, why didn't he do what he had wished to do)—and now he had none himself. Goncharov replied that he would have performed that commission with pleasure. Then Fedya asked him not to tell anyone about the loan, and he said that, of course, he would not. So Fedya brought home three louis ; but he dressed immediately and went off to the tables, saying that if he won even fifteen francs he would leave off. I waited for him for a long time. The day was very fine, but I did not go out, as I have had no desire to go out anywhere these last few days. I cried a great deal and prayed God to save us. I was almost sure that Fedya would lose that money, too. He came home about eight, and said that he had won three five-franc pieces ; he said that as soon as he entered the rooms he met Goncharov there, so he felt very awkward. While Fedya was out at Goncharov's I wrote a letter to my mother asking her for money. How unutterably distressed I was at having to write that letter! I know that poor mother will certainly think that we are in extreme want, and she will suffer on our account. My dear, my sweet mother, how dearly she loves us, and how much she wishes for our happiness; and now our constant privations, our continuous requests for money show her our unenviable material position, although she knows that I am very happy for Fedya loves me.

Monday, 10th July, 1867. To-day we got up with a presentiment that we should lose our money. Fedya went off to the tables, but returned soon, saying he had lost. I was now left with one five-franc piece, two guldens and a few coppers. Fedya took the five-franc piece and went away, but came home soon; he had lost. . . . He was in complete despair, he said he had ruined me and that all was lost now. His despair was so great that I did not know how to comfort him. At last he decided that it was no use going to the tables . . . fate was against us.

Tuesday, 11th July, 1867. To-day Fedya got up rather early to go to the furrier; but he did not find him at home. A girl came back with him to fetch my fur cloak, and in the afternoon Fedya called there again. The furrier said he could not give any more than eight gulden for it. Fedya agreed to take them. He took four thalers, three for himself and one he gave to me. He was convinced that he was going to win now. Therefore, his resolution has lasted less than a day, and now he has got again the desire to win, to become rich. He went to the tables and lost. Then he came home and asked me to give him the last thaler, although I had nothing more left. I implored him not to play, for it was obvious that fate was against us. Although he agreed that he might not win, still he took the thaler. Then he came home and said he had lost it. We are without money, possessing one gulden only, and we owe for meals for two days. Fedya wrote to-day to Katkov asking him to send some money to my mother ; I, too, wrote to mother, urging her to send us some temporary assistance, which she could repay herself out of the money she would be getting from Katkov. I wonder what the result is going to be. I paid for the letter twenty-eight kreutzers.

Wednesday, 12th July, 1867. At twelve o'clock Fedya and I went to the man who keeps a bureau. We found him at home, and I talked to him, for Fedya finds it difficult to express himself in German. He gave us Weismann's address ; but we told him that Weismann didn't take wearing apparel. Then he asked for our address, in order that he might send someone to have a look at our things. We went home ; he promised to send someone at two. The man looked at the things, but said that he would send us another little man. . . . Some time later the little man came. For Fedya's winter overcoat he offered eight gulden, for mine six, for Fedya's old frock coat and coat he offered two florins. We showed him our boots, he tried them on and even put a hat on his head, and said he would give us three francs. We wanted four and he agreed.

Thursday, 13th July, 1867. We went again to Mr. Castorph, but he was not at home. We saw his wife and daughter. We talked to her about our clothes, and she seemed to want to buy them for herself ; but we said we would rather pawn them than let them go for good. I talked to her a great deal in German. She promised to send some one to us about three o'clock to have a look at our things. I went home, and Fedya went to see if Weismann was at home. He came back from the reading room and we waited for the woman from Mr. Castorph's, but she did not come. We had a very sad dinner. After dinner I wrote a letter to my mother, in which I asked her again for money, and also enclosed a letter for my sister asking her to lend me twenty-five or twenty roubles for a few days. I wonder if the letter will be successful. God grant it may be. Fedya took the letter to the post office and from there he went to Castorph's. His wife was surprised that the woman she had sent to us had not called, and said that she would call, together with the woman, next morning at eleven.

Friday, 14*th July*, 1867. I got up early and woke Fedya, so that we should be ready by the time the two women were supposed to come. We waited for them till twelve, but they did not call. Then Fedya went there. He did not find the woman in, but saw her daughter, who said she would tell her mother when she came in. The affair seems not to be coming off. Then Fedya went to Weismann and told him he wanted to pawn his things. Weismann told Fedya to bring the things to his place by three o'clock. Fedya said he could not bring them. Then he advised Fedya to take a porter, but Fedya frankly told him that he had no money, not enough even to pay a porter. Then Weismann promised to pay the man himself. I forgot to mention that this morning Fedya called on Goncharov to ask his address in case we should not be able to pay him before his departure. Goncharov did not give his address, but said that the little loan was such a trifle it was not worth bothering about, that we could pay him in Petersburg any time; that it was not worth troubling about. Then Fedya told him he was now trying to get forty francs. Goncharov said he could not let him have them now, for he himself had gambled away a good deal of money, although he had enough for his journey.   Of course, he said, as he was travelling with friends he could always borrow from them, but at any rate he could not lend Fedya anything now. Fedya told me that it seemed to him that Goncharov had gambled away his money and that perhaps he had nothing to pay his hotel bill with.   How annoying that we cannot pay him back !   They parted on friendly terms.   At three o'clock Fedya went alone to see Weismann, but the latter was not at home.   Fedya went there several times to have a look, but each time the door was shut.   At last Weismann himself came to us, and said that he had been waiting at home all the time, and that he could only spare another ten minutes. Then Fedya took a porter and told him to take my two dresses, the green and lilac, to Weismann's.   The latter, seeing the dresses, said that they were out of fashion and so on, and offered Fedya twenty francs for them. Fedya asked for forty, but Weismann said he would not give more than twenty-five.   At last Fedya simply begged him to let him have thirty francs for one month. But Weismann warned him, saying that, if the money were not paid in time, the things would be forfeit.   I hope to God they won't be lost, they cost us so much, and now they may go for seven roubles.   It is simply terrible.   We went out for a walk when in the streets suddenly Fedya noticed that he had his old house-jacket on.   We had to go back to allow him to change into his good jacket.   It seemed to me so funny that I laughed for nearly five minutes.   When he had changed and we came out again, he suddenly frowned and did not want to speak.   I told him that if he were going to go on like that, I should go home.   When I asked him to make it up, he kept silent.   I turned back and went by myself in the opposite direction.   I walked for about an hour, but got very tired and returned home.

I had pains in my stomach and I lay down, but I felt terribly lonely. I wanted to make peace with Fedya and to go out somewhere. I called to him, but, instead of making his peace with me at once, he suddenly declared that, with my caprices, I was spoiling our life. I got cross ; could it be possible, I thought, that such trifles should spoil our life. What sort of fragile creatures we must be, if our love can evaporate so quickly, if on account of an empty word he can say that all our life is spoilt. I did not want to argue with him, and lay down on my bed, shutting the door of my room. But Fedya did not like this, and he opened the door, saying the room was stuffy. I shut it again, but again he opened it and said that it must remain open, that it must be open because of the heat. Then I said to him that if he prevented me from doing what I liked, then I had better leave him, for I did not want to submit. I dressed and went out for a walk. I went to the cemetery and sat there for a long time by a grave. . . . About half past eight I returned home. Fedya was not there. I was afraid all the time that he had gone to the tables. What if he lost our last few francs now, when we have nothing even to pawn ! At last he came back. When I went to bed, he came to me and gave me a friendly good night, and we made it up. I am cross with myself. Why do I pick such empty quarrels? I have such a wonderful husband and I always irritate him.

Saturday, 15*th July*, 1867. Fedya went to the reading room, taking with him a five-franc piece saying that perhaps he would stake it, perhaps not. I sat, ill, at home, reading the New Testament. In two hours time he came back looking very sad. He told me that he had won two five-franc pieces, so that he had fifteen francs ; then he lost one piece and went to the reading-room, and stayed there for a long time. But then wanting to try his luck again, he went to the tables and lost all the money. He was so worried, because with that money we could have paid the landlady, whom we owe a week's rent. It is unpleasant to ask her to wait a while ; for these people understand nothing and positively become very rude immediately they notice that our position has changed for the worse. I was annoyed at his loss, but what is to be done ? To-day it is exactly five months since we were married ; so, although we had very little money, just to celebrate the event, we sent out for some wine.

Tuesday, 18th July, 1867. To-day the weather is dull and I feel so weary. During the last few days, I have been thinking of my coming child, Misha. I am dreaming all the time about the child. Fedya said yesterday that he would go to the tables and win thirty thousand francs, so as to be able to go back to Russia, for he longs to see several persons. I, too, should like to see several persons, but the idea of going back so soon frightens me. It seems to me that Fedya will cease loving me when we go back. It is as though I were not sure of his love. I am afraid that another woman will occupy the place in his heart which I occupy now. It seems to me that he has never loved, that he has only imagined that he has loved, that there has been no real love on his part. I even think that he is incapable of love ; he is too much occupied with other thoughts and ideas to become strongly attached to anyone earthly.

Wednesday, 19th July, 1867. Fedya saw in the papers an advertisement to the effect that a man in Sophienstrasse was buying and selling things. Perhaps that man would also take things in pawn. Fedya went off there, but it turned out that it was the same old fellow who had bought our boots. He promised to take

Fedya's overcoat, and Fedya took it to him. For the overcoat he got six gulden and signed the papers saying that he had sold his coat for eight gulden (two gulden as interest) and, if it was not redeemed in fourteen days, it was to become the property of the old fellow. Thus we had now eight gulden. Fedya began saying that if he went now to the tables, taking only two gulden, he was bound to win. What did it matter, if out of the eight gulden, he were even to lose two, that is a quarter of our fortune ? As Fedya adopted that idea very ardently, it was no use my opposing it : it would only have meant exciting him still more. But I advised him, if he won something on his two gulden, to leave off at once ; but he said that that was impossible. In a word, he conceived the idea of winning a lot of money. Well, if a person gets such an idea into his head, then it is certain that he will not win. And so it happened ; he staked, and lost. He said that no one had even noticed that he had lost . . . On our walk we talked and came to the conclusion that, although we had no money, yet we had love ; we love one another so much. Perhaps others have money but long for love, and have not got it. I agreed absolutely with what he said.

Thursday, 20th July, 1867. After dinner Fedya went to the post office and I remained at home, but I asked him not to open my letter, if he got any for me. He brought me a letter from mother. I suddenly thought that mother could not send us any money. But in the first words of the letter mother said that she was sending us money by the next post. I was very glad that Fedya had not opened the letter, because Vanya[1] sent me again S.'s address,[2] although I knew it already. Fedya would probably have begun asking questions, why and where-

---

[1] Mme. Dostoevsky's brother.   [2] Mlle. Souslov's.

fore I needed that address, etc. It is so much better
that he did not open it. My dear mummie, how much
I love her, my darling, and also Vanya, my brother!
How much I should like to help them now! If I won
two hundred roubles, I would send my darling a hundred
roubles so that she could pay her debt to Yerineevich.
Christ, how delighted she would be! She would pay
her debts and pick up again. But, Christ, I cannot
help her; how it pains me and how ashamed I am!
When Fedya went out for a walk, I felt very sad,
remembering my mother's kindness to me and my own
inability to help her; I cried bitterly, I cried so much.
Then Fedya came back, and we had tea. My head
ached from the walk and from the crying, and I went
to bed early. Fedya was so tender, so good to me, and I
see that he loves me, but I love him madly. I also love
my dear mummie, and how happy I should be if these
two dear creatures were always with me.

Friday, 21st July, 1867. How cross the landlady
made me this morning! I met her in the hall and she
said I had promised to pay her in two days' time, and
why then did I not pay? I told her I had a letter to
say that money was coming to-day. Then she told
me that in August the rent was always higher, for they
had no lodgers in the winter and therefore they must
make up for it in the summer months. As last summer
she was getting twelve gulden per week, she would let
us have the rooms at eleven gulden. How wicked of
her! She knows that we have no money now, and she
wants to take advantage of this to rob us. . . . Then
she let drop a hint about Fedya's gambling; I wonder
how she knows that; I could not quite make out what
she said. . . . They are all wicked people! The
naughty Marie, for instance. I told her to have boiling
water ready and to come up for the coffee, but an hour
passed and she did not come. So before she comes up

with the coffee she has made, another hour will pass, and I have an awful headache and am very hungry. Each minute I am afraid of being sick, and a cup of coffee brought up in time would do me good. I was so annoyed that I cried. Fedya got cross with Marie, but he also got cross with me for crying over trifles. How impatient he is ! Surely, I do not blame him when he happens to have epileptic fits, or when he coughs ; I do not say to him that it bores me, although it does make me suffer. And he can't even bear my having a little cry, and says that it bores him ; it is indeed wrong ; why be so egotistical ? I was very distressed, and even now I am sometimes vexed that Fedya of all people should have just the character which I had so much feared in my future husband—that lack of family feeling. Yes, he simply does not want to trouble about his own family. He is much more worried about Emily, his brother's widow (that silly German woman), that she should be in need of nothing, that her son should not overwork, that Pasha [Dostoevsky's stepson] should not deny himself anything. And yet what *we* feel does not matter to him ; it does not matter to him if we are in want—he does not even notice it. And as I am his wife, and belong to him, it seems to follow that he considers me obliged to bear all these little unpleasant-nesses and privations. Certainly I should not say a word if I knew that he had nothing ; but when I know that we are in want just so that Emily and the rest of the company should not be, when my cloak is being pawned in order to redeem Emily's cloak—then somehow or other an ugly feeling is born in me, and I am terribly pained that the man, whom I value so highly and love so dearly, should display such carelessness and lack of understanding and consideration. He says he is obliged to help his brother's family, for his brother had helped him. But is not Fedya as much obliged in regard to myself ? Have I not given him my life, have I not given him my soul, with the complete desire and perfect readiness to suffer, piovided he is happy ? He does not value it at all, and there it is. He does not consider himself obliged to take care that his wife should be happy, that she should not have to worry every minute about whether there will be anything to eat to-morrow. How wrong, how unjust ! I am cross with myself for my wicked thoughts against my dear, lovable, good husband. Probably I am spiteful.

I went to the post office at twelve ; there was a letter for me. Mother has sent me a draft for one hundred and seventy-two francs on Paris. I called to see the banker and he agreed to change it for me, at a discount of two francs. . . . He gave me seventeen gold ten-franc pieces. On my way to the post office I called at a bootmaker's to show him my boots, which have become impossibly worn down. He shook his head and said that it was no good bringing them on my feet, for he could not do anything with them in that state ; and indeed it seemed to him that they were hopeless, and that it was no use mending them. At last he said that anyway he could not do anything with them during that week. How am I to go about if my boots cannot be mended ? Then I called at a confectioner's shop, which I always pass with envy, and bought there a sweet pastry— with cream and nuts inside—a wonderful pastry. I liked it so much that I bought another for Fedya. . . . He has been cross with me to-day. When he got up he took three ten-franc notes and said that he was taking *my* money—a thing which has never happened before ; for we had decided never to say *my money*, or *your* money, but our money. He went out, as I learnt later, to pay the bill at the grocer's for sugar, etc., that he has recently run up there. He came back in an hour's time, but said nothing to me. I only noticed that he was worried about something ; then he told me that he had lost five thalers. He had first won seven thalers, but was not satisfied and lost all he had. I began comforting him, asking him not to worry. Then we had dinner, and Fedya told me he would take the money, which was intended for the redemption of the overcoat, and instead of redeeming it now he would take the money and go off to the tables. I could do nothing, I gave him the money. . . . We went for a walk and decided how nice it would be if we could win two thalers a day. Then we could gradually redeem all the things we had pawned, and wait quietly till we got money from Katkov. But I thought it impossible. Fedya decidedly has not got will power enough to leave off when he has won two thalers. Immediately he gets the idea that he ought to win not two, but at least fifty thalers. Instantly he begins dreaming of thousands—and because of this everything goes wrong. . . . We discussed for a long time the question of buying new boots for me. I did not tell him that I had sent my boots to be mended, for Fedya does not like old boots. I am afraid that the money will be gambled away, so that it would be as well to secure a pair of boots and not to have to walk, as I have had to do, most carefully hiding my feet. When we came near the house, Fedya got the idea of buying cheese. Then I asked him to buy some ham, for I had long been dreaming of how we should one day buy ham, and I should eat it with vinegar. Fedya went to do the shopping ; and when he came back he had not only cheese and ham, but excellent sausages—and it seemed to me as though I had never eaten such good food.

Saturday, 22nd July, 1867. Fedya went off to the tables, taking with him ten thalers, but returned very soon saying he had lost. . . . He asked me to give him two gold coins and also my three thalers. I gave them to him, but was convinced that he would lose them. So we have now eight gold pieces left. He went off to the tables, but came home quite soon. He said that a Russian lady stood behind him, chattering away all the time ; so he could not concentrate his mind, and in his annoyance he lost all the money. He asked me to give him three more gold pieces. (So we are now left with fifty francs). Christ, how distressed I was,—all my nice things and clothes won't be redeemed now, all is lost. When he came back, I met him with the exclamation—" Don't be agitated, my poor Fedya," for without even seeing his face I was sure that he had lost. Then he began asking me to give him another ten francs—" the last," as he said. He went back and lost. . . . Christ, whenever shall we get out of this cursed mire in which we have got stuck ! I think we shall never get out of it, for we shall keep on sitting here, go on gambling, expecting all the time to win a large fortune. . . . After dinner Fedya had a cup of coffee, lay down at five, and asked me to wake him at half past. I also fell into a doze. But at twenty-five minutes past five Fedya got up, came up to my bed and kissed me. I said " What is the matter, Fedya ? " He turned back, but suddenly fell into an epileptic fit. I got very frightened. I wanted to take him to his bed, but I could not manage it in time. So I propped him up against my bed, for I had not the strength to put him on the bed. He half stood all the time the convulsions lasted. (And that is why his right leg is now aching, because he had leant against the wall.) When the convulsions were over, Fedya began tossing about, and although I tried my best to keep him quiet, I had not the strength to manage it. Then I put two cushions on the floor and quietly placed him on them, on the carpet, so that he should lie more comfortably. I unbuttoned his clothes so that he could breathe more freely. To-day I noticed for the first time that his lips turned quite blue, and his face unusually red. How unhappy I was ! This time he did not come round for a rather long time, and when he began to do so—however bitterly and painfully I felt, I had a desire to laugh, for any words he uttered were spoken in German. He said : " *Was ? Was doch ? Lassen Sie mich,*" and went on with a long string of German phrases. Then he called me by my pet name, and asked for my forgiveness ; but he could not make out what I was saying to him. He also asked me for money to go off to the tables. A fine player, I thought, to play in this state ! Yet it seems to me that in such a state he might win, if he were not swindled out of his money. When Fedya recovered, he got up from the floor, buttoned himself up and asked me to give him his hat. I thought : does he want to go somewhere now ? And I asked him, "Where are you going ? " " Comme ça," was his reply. I could not make out and asked him to repeat what he said, for I thought he said he was going out for sausages. Then I persuaded him to lie down, which he did not want to do, and even began grumbling. " Why was I trying to put him to bed, why was I tormenting him ?" . . . At last he lay down, but slept by snatches, waking every ten minutes. At seven o'clock we went out for a walk, but Fedya suddenly wanted to kiss my hand in the street, and said that if I did not let him do it, he would not consider me his wife. Of course I tried my best to dissuade him : in the middle of the street with people looking on—it would be terribly ridiculous. Then Fedya said he would very much like to have some chocolate. Although a glass of chocolate costs eighteen kreutzer, I agreed and we went into a café. . . .

Sunday, 23rd *July,* 1867. Soon after twelve o'clock, when I came home from the post office (there were no letters for us) Fedya was going off to the tables. He took a ten-franc note, and very soon returned, and asked me for another ten francs. But I said that we had altogether twenty francs left, that there was no one

from whom we could expect any help now, and that until
the money from Katkov came—if it did come—we should
just have to starve. I felt so bitter that I burst out
crying. I told him I was crying because it seemed
to me that we were never going to get out of Baden, that
we should go on playing in expectation of winning a
fortune, that we should have to remain here for months,
and that even with Katkov's money, when it came, we
should keep on playing and losing. Perhaps it was
harsh of me to speak like that, but what could I do?
The first month I suffered and did not say a word, even
when the last penny had gone. But then I had the hope
that mother might help us; there was also the chance
of pawning our clothes and jewellery. But now everything had been pawned and will probably never be
redeemed ; and to go on asking mother for money is
impossible, also it is such a shame. Still I gave the
money to Fedya, but he said that one ten-franc note
would not make three thalers, and he wanted to start
with three. Then I proposed that he should change our
last ten-franc note, but on condition that he should
bring the remaining two thalers home, so that we could
go on for two or three days. Fedya asked me if I could
not trust him to bring the change back? I frankly
replied that I could not. There was nothing offensive
in that, the point being that everyone in the hope of
winning would do likewise. I myself would do that, and
therefore I thought that he, too, would do so. Fedya
took the two ten-franc notes and went off. I felt so sad
that I lay down on my bed and wept bitterly. More
than an hour passed and Fedya came back. I got up
to meet him, when he said he had brought me only one
thaler. I thought that he had won one thaler, and I
was very glad and said that, if he brought a thaler every
day, it would be quite good. My conscience pricked
me for having recently spoken harshly to Fedya, and
I began to apologise. Then he showed me his purse,

and there were in it thirty thalers. Fedya gave me twenty-five, and five he took for himself. As he produced the money, his tone towards me was somewhat caustic ; he said he thought that, if he had lost the money, I should have assaulted him. He went out to buy some fruit, asking me to tell Marie to lay the table for dinner. . . . He was away a long time, and came back terribly angry, saying that he had gambled away the five thalers. . . . Yes, indeed, I must guard Fedya not only against others, but against himself, too, for he has not the least self-control. He will promise, he will even give his word, but he will act quite differently. I am fully convinced that our winnings, amounting at one time to one hundred and sixty-eight louis, were due to the fact that I kept the money, and that I gave him five louis at a time, and no more. Otherwise he would have gambled away everything on the first day of his arrival at Baden. He is a strange man, but how fine ! . . .

Tuesday, 25*th July*, 1867. We ought to send our washing to the washerwoman, but we must wait now, for there is no money to pay for it. I am glad that I had not sent it before, for how vexed I should be if I could not pay the woman. Our last two thalers went the same way as all our other money ; our one and last thaler I must keep for the bootmaker. Poor Fedya came home terribly grieved. He said he would either go off his head, or shoot himself ; for how was he going to pay his debts, his numerous debts, when he had nothing to pay them with. I began telling him that it did not matter very much and that it was not worth while getting into such despair. Then we lay in bed and talked of our situation. Indeed, we are a sort of gipsies—one day we have plenty, the next we are empty. Just recently we were independent people, now we have to run about, pawning things. . . .

DOSTOEVSKY IN A NEW LIGHT

[Here follows a detailed account of how Dostoevsky sold his own clothes to a second-hand dealer.]

When Fedya came to bid me good-night he was in an agitated state. He said that he loved me passionately, loved me so very, very much ; that he was not worthy of me, that I was his guardian angel, sent him from heaven ; that he must correct his ways ; that, although he was forty-five, he was still unfit for family life ; that he must prepare himself for it ; that at moments he still had his fancies. I do not know what he meant by the last phrase ; can it be that he wants to be unfaithful to me ? Well, I do not believe that, but how sad I should be, if it happened. Then he said, " You dreamed that I had sent you away to a boarding school. How could I let you go, if I cannot live without you." He said that if I told him to throw himself down from a tower, he would do it for my sake. I could see that he loved me. He said that at times he was irresistibly drawn to me, that he must speak to me and have a word with me. He also told me that some time ago he had opened a book and tried to obtain from it the answer to the question : " How will Anya take my gambling ? " and the answer had been, " The situation will render your friendship still happier." And, indeed, it is so : we were never so friendly as now, we suffer together, grieve and try to find a way out. Lord help us, and permit us to get out of this cursed town, where we have had so much sorrow. At night I asked Fedya if he thought of Sonichka [the coming baby girl], and he said he thought of her frequently and a good deal, and he added that perhaps after all the child would be a boy. I said that whatever it was I should be happy.

Thursday, 27th July, 1867. To-day he declared more than once that he had not expected to have such a wife as I was, that he had never hoped that I should be so nice, not reproaching him for anything, but on the contrary, trying only to comfort him. Then he said that if I was always going to be like that, he would be re-born, for I had given him many new emotions, new thoughts, many fine feelings, so that he had begun to grow a better man. I was delighted. But towards the end of the evening we quarrelled because I had laid down on my bed dressed. I felt tired, lay down and fell asleep, and I could not get up to undress. He got angry about it, but when he came to bid me good-night we made it up and he prepared everything for my sleep, that is, matches and tea, as he always does.

Saturday, 29*th July,* 1867. To-day we must pay our rent to the landlady, but we have no money ; I shall have to apologise. We have only twelve kreutzer left, which are to be given to the porter (for taking the things to the pawnshop). We have no sugar, and I had no tea in the morning, because of it. Then Fedya went to Weismann, and the latter told him to take down the things at two o'clock. We don't know how much he will give for them, perhaps only twenty francs ; and according to Fedya's calculations, we shall have to wait another eleven days at least until we hear from Moscow. Fedya called at the post office, but there were no letters for us. We lay down and talked of our unenviable position. We said how in the future we should remember it all : the terrible heat, the landlady's screaming children, the smithy with its hammers mercilessly knocking all day, and not a sou, all our belongings pawned and likely to be lost, stuffy rooms, the bells ringing, no books to read, and the prospect of having no food. May God not allow our position to become still worse, for I do not know what we should do then. Then Fedya went to Weismann's. But when he came home with the porter, our landlady stood at the gate and saw him. She was talking to a neighbour, and pointed to our floor and to the porter. When Fedya came out of the house, she went to her husband in the smithy, probably to tell him that we were taking our things away to the pawnshop, and therefore our rent would not be paid. Fedya got from Weismann thirty francs ; but he immediately went off to the tables and lost eighteen. He came in pale and worried. I was simply astounded, I could not restrain myself and said : " It is sheer stupidity." I was not so much annoyed by his loss, as by the fact that he simply couldn't rid his mind of the idea that he was going to become rich through playing roulette. It is this idea that makes me wild, for it has done us so much harm. . . .

Sunday, 30th July, 1867.—In the evening I had a cup of tea, and as I had pains in my side, I went to bed at once, and fell asleep. I slept, I believe, till one o'clock in the morning, and when I woke I had no foreboding of any storm. But it appeared that Fedya had felt hurt by my going to bed so early. He paced the room all the time, muttering to himself. In a word, he was in a violent agitation. I asked him what was the matter. He said it was no business of mine. Then he said that he had been suffering the last seven hours ; that I deliberately refrained from talking to him, that I kept away from him—which I decidedly had not done. I asked him to calm himself and not to make a noise with his boots ; for the landlady slept quite close by and would be cross if he woke her children. I spoke loudly, but I did not shout. Suddenly Fedya announced that if I was going to shout, he would jump out of the window. He was in terrible despair, he kept shouting that he himself was to blame and that he realised our difficult position. Suddenly without any connection he said that he hated me. I got dreadfully offended by this and nearly burst into tears. I went into the other room and told him that it was " ignoble " of him to be saying : first, " You have made me so happy," and then, " I hate you." When I lay down, Fedya came up to me and said that he had not wanted to hurt me, that he was completely upset, that his conscience tormented him for worrying me and for our impecuniosity, and that before I used to be so happy. Of course, it is true, I was twenty times happier and quieter than I am now, for we had no squabbles then. But I was very much hurt. We bade one another good-night, and as I could not go to sleep for a long time, Fedya asked me several times if I had any pain, and implored me to wake him if I felt unwell. I promised him to do so. But I am certain not to wake him, for he could be of no help to me, he would only get alarmed. Poor, poor things that we are, and all because of that cursed roulette ! But for that constant impecuniosity, we should be quiet and happy. But God will help us, it must end some time.

Monday, 31st July, 1867.—Before saying good-night Fedya told me that he valued me and knew my character, that he respected my character, but that at times I had flashes of anger. I asked him to forgive me. I was so sorry and annoyed with myself for picking quarrels and being unable to restrain myself. But it seems to me that my pregnancy is to blame for this : it spoils my disposition and drives me at moments to obstinate caprices. I forgot to mention that Fedya had called in the evening at Messmer's, the grocer's, where we buy our provisions, and he wanted to run up an account for tea, sugar, and candles, all of which we need, but can't pay cash for. When he came home he said that the proprietor was out, there was only his assistant there, and as there were customers in the shop, he had felt it awkward to ask for things on credit. Poor, poor Fedya, how he must suffer !

Tuesday, 1st August, 1867.—To-day we got up, preoccupied by the idea of how to get some money. We now owe for dinners for four days, and if we don't pay they won't send us any more. We must pawn my lilac dress, the only article now left unpawned. We have nothing else left, all our resources are exhausted. I did not want Fedya to go to Weismann's ; I preferred going there myself. But, of course, I should not give Weismann my name, so that he should not know that I was Fedya's wife. We argued for a long while about it, but Fedya decided, however painful and vexing it might be, to take the dress there himself. It had to be done in such a way that our landlady should not see that a parcel was being carried out from our rooms. For that purpose, I made the dress into a very small bundle, and Fedya carried it under his overcoat, which he threw over his arm, although he felt terribly awkward. He went off at twelve o'clock, and while he was out I began washing his shirt and handkerchiefs. Then I went out to get some starch. They could not make out in the little shop what I wanted, and advised me to go to another shop, to the shoemaker's. It cost me a lot of trouble to explain to them that I wanted starch for ironing, and not for any other purpose. I came home and began ironing ; it was about two o'clock, but Fedya was not back. . . At last he came and told me that Weismann had not been at home, and his sister had asked Fedya to sit a while and wait for him while they were having their meal—she and another woman with an enormous Adam's apple, who fell asleep there and then at the table. Fedya waited for over an hour. (Poor, poor Fedya ! He such a fine, talented, noble man, and has to wait at a Jew's house, for Weismann is probably a Jew.) Fedya wanted to go, but Weismann's sister said that she had sent someone to find her brother in the town. A nice thing—Fedya thought—Weismann, interrupted in some business, would come home to find Fedya wanting to pawn a dress ; he might get cross and refuse to accept it altogether. Then Fedya could not bear it any longer, and went away, saying he would call again. On his way he called on Mr. Jorgel [the pawnbroker]. To Fedya's surprise, Jorgel, who, as his wife said, was seventy, has a wife of thirty, who looks not more than twenty-five. The most surprising thing is that Jorgel has a boy of four, the very likeness of his father, and also a baby of eighteen months, also his, and at the age of seventy ! That is vitality ! Jorgel seemed to have been struck by the beauty of the dress and allowed twenty francs on it, a sum which Weismann would not have given. Fedya asked Jorgel's wife to take care of the dress, and she put it with the shawl, in which it was wrapped, into a sheet, and placed it in the wardrobe, so that it should be kept clean. The interest is enormous : for three weeks, on a sum of seven florins, he charges four florins. Weismann has a tenderer conscience. He charged us only two francs for thirty francs, which is a small interest. Fedya took a great fancy to Jorgel's baby girl, speaking with a particular fondness of her lovely little eyes. Fedya put the pawn ticket on my ironing board, and himself went out to change the money and to buy cigarettes. . . . We went to the post office. There was a letter from my mother saying she had sent us a hundred roubles. From the post office we went to the banker's and received there one hundred and fifty-six gulden notes. But, afraid of losing the money, Fedya divided it ; he took a hundred gulden, and gave me fifty. . . . When we came home I asked him to go and redeem some of our things, but implored him not to call at the tables ; and I said that if he did not give me his word not to call there, I should have to accompany him. Fedya seemed offended and asked what I meant by accompanying him. I said, that being with him, I should beseech him, implore him not to call at the tables. . . . In a quarter of an hour Fedya came back and brought my ear-rings and rings. Then we went for a walk. Fedya took me to the reading room, and himself went off to the tables, saying that he would be back presently. . . . I sat for over an hour, and then decided to call at the tables. There I found him. He stood close to the table and I saw a pile of silver near him. I had thought he had lost, but he won, therefore I decided to call him away, otherwise he would lose again. . . . I touched his arm, but as he had a stake on, he did not stir, but kept on looking to see if he were winning. Then he noticed me ; but as he had won, he had to wait for the money to be passed over to him. We came out. It was terrible to look at him : he was all flushed, with red eyes as though drunk. . . . When we counted the money it turned out that Fedya had lost only something over a gulden. . . .

At three o'clock Fedya came to me to say good-night. He was very kind and nice, said that he loved me, that in spite of our having a squabble now and then it did not matter, that he had never been so happy as he was then. Then he went to his room, to bed. A quarter of an hour later he asked me something, and he seemed falling asleep ; when suddenly, ten minutes later, his epilepsy came on again. I jumped off my bed, but had no candle. I rushed into the other room and lit the candle. Fedya lay with his head on the edge of the bed, and if I had come a minute later he would have fallen down. The fit did not last very long, and was not very violent, yet his convulsions were intense. Then he came round, kissed my hands, embraced me, and when he completely came round, he could not understand why I was sitting there, and asked me : " Had I a fit last night ? " I said that it was only just over. He kissed me, said he was passionately in love with me, that he adored me. After a fit, he is afraid of death. He began saying that he was afraid he would die before long, and asked me to look at him. To reassure him I said I would lie down on the couch near his bed ; then, if anything happened to him, I should hear it instantly and get up. He was very pleased. But he continued to be afraid. He prayed and said that it would be hard on him to die now, to part with me and not to see Sonichka or Misha. He asked me to take care of our future child, and also to come and see if he was alive when I got up in the morning. But I told him to go to sleep, and said that I should not sleep till he fell asleep. Five o'clock struck. The smiths began getting up. First they made a noise over our heads (they sleep in the garret), and then they came down into the smithy and started hammering. I could not sleep. Fedya got up at eight, smoked, then he had a look in the glass and saw two red marks on his face. His head ached terribly.

Friday, 4th August, 1867.—To-day was an unlucky day. Early in the morning I recognised the omen, when I looked up at the belfry, the weathercock on which represents a figure of the Apostle Peter. I noticed that the Apostle had turned his back on us ; and I had observed, whenever he stood facing us, holding his keys in his right hand, that it was a good omen, that is, that our affairs would prosper. I also had noticed that on our very worst days, when we lived from hand to mouth and had to pawn everything, the figure of Peter stood in such a position that his face could hardly be seen. So it was also to-day. Fedya went off to the tables, taking forty gulden, and asked me to stay at home, although I wanted to go out for a walk. We decided to pay four louis to redeem some of the things we had pawned. Then we should feel a bit more comfortable. But Fedya decided to postpone redeeming the things till two o'clock ; for he thought he might not find the pawnbroker in before that hour. Meanwhile he went off to the tables, and lost. Then he came home, took another four louis, and lost them, too.

He came home again, took another three, and lost them. Finally he came again to take the last gold piece and the remaining thirty francs. He went off, but did not return for a long time ; so that I decided to go out for a walk to the New Castle. . . . I came home at four, but Fedya was not back yet. At last he came. He said he had not touched the golden piece, only played with the thirty francs and had won nearly four louis, thirty francs and ten or twenty two-gulden pieces. I asked him not to go to the tables after dinner, but to wait till to-morrow, and I asked him to take me for a walk. But he refused, and after dinner went off to the tables again. But this time fortune turned her back on us : Fedya lost all the silver money. I went to the post office, and on my way home I met Fedya at the corner of the street, and he said that he had lost all the money. He asked me to give him another four louis. I gave them to him. He went off and lost them. He came back very soon, and said that he could not leave off, that he must go on playing. Well, I could do nothing. I saw that it was no good asking him to stay at home, and I gave him the last gold piece, so that now we are left with only forty gulden in notes. After some time, he came home and said he had lost, and asked me to come out for a walk with him. We went out, but I was in no mood for walking : so sad and bitter did I feel. Above all I was grieved that Fedya had not listened to me and had not redeemed our things in the morning.

Saturday, 5th August, 1867.—At twelve o'clock Fedya went off to the tables, taking twenty gulden of our last forty. But of course, pursued by ill luck, he lost them. He came home and took another ten. He did not return for a long time. At last he came back and brought me a letter which he had received at the post office and which he had opened, saying he did not know whether it was for him or for me. The letter was from my mother, and she wrote that she had paid only three months' interest on our pawned furniture. I was so sad and distressed by the fact that only yesterday we had money to redeem the things we had pawned here, and yet acted in the same way as we did with our furniture in Russia. Then, when Fedya said : "Curse the furniture," I became so distressed at the idea that perhaps our furniture would be lost that I began to cry and could not stop. Fedya calmed me, asking me not to cry. But what could I do? All the money we had here was gone, and all our things were pawned, and I was distressed at not knowing whether we should get money from Russia. We began counting how much we needed to redeem our things, and found it would take about a hundred gulden, if we included the ring which Fedya had pawned this morning for twenty francs. It was distressing. I cried, and when he got suddenly cross with me (because I cried), I too lost patience and said that he had lost because he did not take my advice. . . . Fedya replied that gambling was a passion, that is why he did not take my advice ; but in other matters he always did as I wished. I was so vexed and pained that I said that his idea of winning millions at roulette was ridiculous and, in irritation, I called him "benefactor of mankind." Fedya got hurt and asked me what I meant by it. He was very much hurt. I certainly repented of having called him that name. But indeed, whenever he wins, I am always annoyed at hearing him say that he must help this person, make a present to that person, do something or other for a third. I am sure, that if we were to win, only the wicked people [the people at home] would benefit by it, and we ourselves would get nothing. Then Fedya decided to go to the public baths before dinner. I was very glad at this, for he had intended to go there some time ago, but kept on postponing it. Before he went out we made it up and had a final reconciliation ; and he even forgave me for calling him " benefactor."

Sunday, 6th August, 1867.—A very fine, bright day, but it will probably be very hot. I got up rather early. I was so sick, worse than ever ; but after that I felt perfectly well.

After he had drunk his tea, while he was dressing, Fedya suddenly said to me that yesterday I had been insensitive. I was indeed pained to hear it, particularly because I always thought that Fedya was a man who understood my sensitiveness. Christ ! What a number of times I could have made things unpleasant for him, if I had wished it. Could not traits be found in him on which one could seize and have a good laugh ? I always tried to avoid that in talking to him, I was always afraid of hurting him. I remember when I used to come to him to work, I never asked him questions. It seemed to me indelicate to ask him anything. Let him tell me himself. If he wants to, he will tell me himself ; but I must not ask him questions. I go about wearing a ragged dress, an ugly black thing ; but I say nothing to him, and I should perhaps like to have a decent dress. I think perhaps he himself will remember it, perhaps he will say that I need a summer dress, which is so cheap here. Surely, he thought of himself, when he bought a suit in Berlin, and ordered clothes for himself in Dresden ; yet he did not think then that I too had to have something, that I was so badly dressed. If I say nothing to him about this it is simply because I feel shy of speaking about it. Perhaps he will guess it himself, why speak to him ? Moreover, he does not seem to have the slightest idea that he hurts me by giving money to Pasha,[1] and to his relations, while my clothes and furniture are pawned.

When he gambled madly, was not I the first to com-

---

[1] Dostoevsky's stepson.

fort him, was not I the first to suggest to him without hesitation that he should pawn my things ; yet I knew they would be lost. Did I ever reproach him for losing so much money in gambling ? On the contrary, I comforted him by saying that it did not matter, that no attention should be paid to such a trifle. No, he does not value it all, and now he says that I am not sensitive ! Really, after this it is decidedly not worth while being sensitive. If I were now to start shouting and having constant quarrels, then perhaps he would remember that I had been very sensitive towards him, and that he ought not to hurt me by unjust reproaches. Fedya went to Jorgel's to redeem his coat ; while I stayed at home and felt so terribly sad at the great injustice he had done me, that I simply did not know what to do. That is his gratitude for my not blaming him ! Really, it is not worth while restraining oneself. Indeed, Marie Dmitrievna [Dostoevsky's first wife] called him galley-slave, scoundrel, jail-bird ; and yet she scored easily over him. When Fedya returned from Jorgel's he came up to me and asked me why I was so gloomy. He recited a poem . . . and said that he had not meant to hurt me when he said I was insensitive. He must say that I was delicate morally, that there was no one like me in that respect, but that I was not outwardly delicate. It turns out that all this was due to the fact that I sometimes call him " a little silly, little stupid !" How absurd to accuse me because of that foolish habit. I did not at all want to quarrel, therefore I assumed the air of not being cross. Then Fedya went off to the tables and asked me to pray for him, that he should not lose. At two o'clock he came back saying that he had won thirty gulden. I was very glad, for this somewhat increased our capital.

In order that he should not go off to the tables again I asked him to come for a walk with me. First he refused, then he went.

[The entries in the Diary for 7th, 8th, and 9th
August contain the usual tale of gambling and
losing and of visits to the pawnbroker. They also
record the receipt of one hundred and fifty roubles
from Mme. Dostoevsky's mother.]

Thursday, 10th August, 1867.—When Fedya came
home about eight in the evening, before I actually saw
him, I asked him something. But the question was
inopportune. Fedya, in terrible agitation, ran up to me,
and with tears said that he had lost, lost everything,
even the money I had given him to redeem the ear-rings.
To reproach him was impossible. I was distressed to
see poor Fedya crying and despairing. I embraced
him, imploring him for the love of Christ, for his love
to me, not to cry and not to torment himself. Fedya
called himself a scoundrel, said that he was not worthy
of me, that I must not forgive him, and cried so bitterly.
I calmed him at last, and we decided to leave Baden
to-morrow. Fedya gradually became quiet and asked
me to give him the one hundred and seventy francs
which we still possess, to go to Weismann's to redeem
an article or two. But as I have the right now not to
trust him, I said I would accompany him. I waited
outside Weismann's shop, and when Fedya came out
we counted our money : we had one hundred and sixty
francs in gold and thirty francs in various coins. Fedya
suggested that we should go to the railway station to
find out at what time the train goes to Geneva, and also
the cost of the fares. Although it was a good distance,
we walked there, and all the time Fedya kept kissing my
hands, and asking me to forgive him. . . . We found
out that there were two trains, one in the early morning,
the other at five minutes past two in the afternoon.
We decided to take the afternoon train. . . . We
returned home about nine o'clock. Fedya evidently
wished to go to the tables again and to take with him

all the gold he had on him ; but, as it was so late and as I was with him, he put off his intention till to-morrow. Arrived home, we intended packing our things, but instead began talking. Fedya began arguing how nice it would be if, out of the one hundred and sixty francs we had, I gave him a hundred. Then perhaps he might win and our fate would change for the better. Now— he argued—we were in such a bad position, it was simply terrible. Who could help us now? Where was the benefactor who could get us out of our embarrassed position ? Fedya had said to-day that he would write to Maikov, explaining the whole situation and asking him to get a hundred roubles for us ; that although Maikov himself had no money, yet he would probably manage to find this sum. This proposition seemed to me very wrong. How can we worry Maikov with such a request? How can we make him raise money for us, which he may not even be able to do? Then Fedya limited his demand to fifty francs and finally to forty. I saw that he had a desperate desire to try his luck again. I was afraid that he would reproach me later for robbing him of the opportunity of winning. He embraced me and asked me to give him forty francs for the last flutter ; he said that now he was bound to win. There was nothing I could do ; anyway we are lost. So perhaps it is better to satisfy his desire and to give him the forty francs ; for if I agree he will feel calm and not distress himself so much. We decided to put off the packing till to-morrow, to get up early in the morning and to do it at once.

Friday, 11th August, 1867.—At eleven o'clock Fedya went off to the tables. After having packed his and my trunk in the early morning, I sat down to write a letter to mother. When I had finished the letter Fedya returned and said that he had not only lost the forty francs which I had given him, but that he had also pawned his ring at Moppert's and had lost that money as well . . . I wanted to reproach him ; but he fell on his knees before me, asking me to forgive him, saying that he was a scoundrel, that there was no punishment too severe for him, but that all the same I must forgive him. However much I was grieved by the loss of the money, yet I had to give him twenty francs to redeem the ring. But when he began counting our money, we found that we should have to pawn my ear-rings to have enough to take us to Geneva. . . . The twenty francs I gave him seemed to cheer him up immensely. He said he would never forget the fact, that when we had no money at all, I gave him twenty francs and told him he might go to the tables and lose them ; that he would never forget my goodness. Fedya went to Moppert's and got an advance of one hundred and twenty francs on the ear-rings, to be redeemed in two months' time. From there he went off to the tables. I asked him for the love of God not to stay there long ; for our train was due to start in a very short time. In about twenty minutes he returned home saying he had lost. I asked him not to trouble, but to help me to fasten the trunks. . . . He went out to get a cab. We had still forty minutes in which to catch the train. He returned bringing with him a loaf and half a pound of ham, and we began eating very quickly. I never ate so quickly before, and Fedya kept on hurrying me. We were both terribly exhausted. The sweat poured down our faces. We drove up to the station, bought our tickets for Geneva, and got into the train. . . .

DIARY OF MME. DOSTOEVSKY

On April 14th, 1867, the Dostoevskys leave Petersburg for Germany.

„   „ 19th,   they arrive in Dresden.

„ May 4th,   F. M. Dostoevsky goes to Homburg to play roulette, Mme. Dostoevsky remaining in Dresden.

„   „ 15th,   F. M. Dostoevsky returns from Homburg to Dresden.

„ June 21st, „   The Dostoevskys go to Baden, staying there from June 22nd to August 11th, F. M. Dostoevsky playing at the tables.

„ Aug. 11th,   The Dostoevskys leave for Geneva.

Mme. Dostoevsky's Diary begins with the date April 18th, 1867 and ends with the entry for August 12th, 1867.

CHAPTERS FROM
MME. DOSTOEVSKY'S
REMINISCENCES

FIODOR so often spoke of the certain " ruin " of his talent, if we remained any longer abroad, and was so tormented by the thought that he would not be able to keep his family, that, as I listened to him, I too was driven to despair. To relieve his anxiety and disperse his gloomy thoughts, which prevented him from concentrating on his work, I had recourse to the device which always helped to distract and amuse him. As we possessed then about three hundred thalers, I said that it would be worth while to try once more our luck at roulette. I pointed out that as he had occasionally happened to win, there was no reason why we should not hope that our luck would turn this time. I certainly did not entertain any hope of his winning at roulette, and I also was very sorry to part with the hundred thalers, which it was necessary to sacrifice ; but I knew by experience of his former visits to the tables that, after those exciting emotions, after satisfying his craving for risk, his passion for gambling, Fiodor would return home calmed, and that then, realizing the futility of his hopes of winning at the tables, he would sit down with renewed strength to his novel, and in a couple of weeks would make good his losses. My idea of his going to play roulette pleased my husband very much, and he did not oppose it. Taking with him one hundred and twenty thalers and stipulating, if he lost them, that I should send him money for his return fare, he left for Wiesbaden, where he stayed for a week. As I had expected, his playing ended in disaster. Including his travelling expenses Fiodor spent one hundred and eighty thalers—quite a considerable sum in our circumstances. But the cruel torments which he experienced during that week had such an effect upon him that he decided *never* again in his life to play roulette. And this is what my husband wrote me on 28th April, 1871 : " A great thing has happened to me ; the filthy fancy, which has *tormented* me for ten years (or more accurately, since the death of my brother, when I found myself suddenly crushed by debts) has vanished. I used perpetually to dream of winning ; I dreamt seriously, passionately. Now that is all over and finished. This was actually the *last* time. Do you believe me, Anya, that now my hands are unbound ? Gambling was a chain about me ; but now I shall think of work and I shall not dream for nights on end of gambling as I used to do."

I, of course, could not all at once believe in such great happiness as Fiodor's indifference to roulette. He had promised me not to play so many times before, and never found the strength to keep his word. But this time the happiness was realized. That was indeed the *last* time he played roulette. Later on, during his travels abroad (in 1874, 1875, 1876, 1879) Fiodor never once went to a casino. It is true that roulette was soon forbidden in Baden ; but roulette tables were to be found in Saxony and in Monte Carlo. The distance would not have prevented my husband from going if he had wished to play. But he was no longer drawn to it. It was as though Fiodor's " fancy " of winning at roulette was a sort of diabolical suggestion or disease, of which he suddenly and for ever cured himself. He returned from Wiesbaden cheerful and calm, and immediately sat down to the continuation of his novel, *The Devils*. He foresaw that our going back to Russia, settling in a new place and the expected increase of our family would not allow him to do much work there. All my husband's thoughts were turned to the new period opening before us, and he speculated on how he would find his old friends and relations, who, he thought, might have changed considerably in the last four years. In himself he was conscious of certain definite changes in his views and convictions.

By the end of June, 1871, we received from *The Russky Vestnik* the money due for Fiodor's novel ; and without losing a day, we began to settle our Dresden affairs (in other words, to get our things out of pawn and to pay our debts), and to pack. Two days before our departure Fiodor called me into his room and handed me several thick bundles of manuscripts written on large size paper, and asked me to burn them. Although we had discussed the matter before, I felt so sorry that I began to implore my husband to allow me to take them with me. But Fiodor reminded me that at the Russian frontier he would without a doubt be searched and his papers taken away from him, and that then they would be lost, just as his papers taken by the authorities at the time of his arrest in 1849 had been lost. We also had to bear in mind that we might be detained at Verzhbolovo [the frontier] until Fiodor's papers had been examined by the authorities, and this, in view of my state of health, would involve a risk. However sad I was to part with the manuscripts, I had to yield to Fiodor's insistent arguments. We lit a fire and burnt the papers. Thus were destroyed the manuscripts of *The Idiot* and of *The Eternal Husband*. I was especially sorry to lose part of *The Devils,* which represented a particularly original variant of the novel ' with a tendency.' I only managed to save the notebooks for the above named novels : these I handed over to my mother, who intended to return to Russia in the autumn a few months later. . . .

As I close the account of the foreign period of our life I must say that I remember it with the most profound gratitude.   True, in the course of the four years spent by us in voluntary exile, we passed through hard trials : the death of our first-born daughter, Fiodor's illness, our constant lack of money and insecurity of work, Fiodor's unfortunate passion for roulette and the impossibility of returning to Russia.   But those trials were for our good : they brought us closer together, made us understand and appreciate one another and created that firm mutual attachment, thanks to which we were so happy in our married life. . . .

Abroad we had no society at all, except casual meetings with passers-by.   But during the first two years Fiodor was even glad of this complete isolation from society.   The death of his brother Michael, his struggles with hardships and failures, and the unpleasantness caused him by the literary confraternity—all combined to tire him out.   Besides, he considered that for a thinking man it was, at times, extraordinarily good to live in retirement, away from current, ever agitating events, and to devote himself entirely to his thoughts and dreams.   Later on, after he had returned to the round of life in Petersburg, Fiodor more than once recalled with regret the advantages he had enjoyed abroad, the perfect leisure he had had for thinking out the plan of a work or for reading a book, without hurry, and with complete surrender to the mood of the moment.

---

[1] The Dostoevskys left Dresden in June, 1871, and arrived at Petersburg on 8th June, 1871, after staying abroad for over four years.

And what a number of profound joys our life abroad had given us, besides the external beautiful impressions ! The birth of our children, of which Fiodor had always dreamt, filled and brightened our life ; and with gratitude I say : " Blessed be the years spent abroad in the sole company of this wonderful man ! "

In spite of many troubles, continual lack of money and moments of depressing boredom, that long isolated life had a good influence on the growth and manifestation in my husband of his Christian ideas and feelings. All our friends and acquaintances, on our return from abroad, said to me that they did not recognize Fiodor, so much had his character changed for the better, so much gentler, kindlier and more charitable to people had he become. His habitual intolerance and impatience had almost entirely disappeared. I must quote from N. Strakhov's *Reminiscences:* " I am perfectly convinced that those four years spent by Dostoevsky abroad were the best period of his life, that is, a period which above all brought him profound and pure ideas and feelings. He had worked very intensely, and often experienced want ; but he had the peace and joy of a happy married life, and nearly all the time he lived in complete retirement, I mean, away from all those big events which might have tempted him to desert the direct way of developing his ideas and his profound inner work. The birth of children, the care of them, the mutual sympathy between husband and wife, even the death of the first child—all these are pure, sometimes lofty experiences. There is no doubt that during his retirement from Russia, in his new situation, and as a result of long and quiet reflection, there occurred that particular unfolding of the Christian spirit that had always lived in him. That essential change was evident to all his friends, when Dostoevsky returned from abroad. He continuously turned the conversation on to religious themes. Moreover, his manner changed, taking on a greater gentleness, which at times even assumed a character of perfect meekness. Even his features bore a trace of that frame of mind, and a gentle smile appeared on his lips. . . . "

Fiodor himself in later years remembered our life abroad with gratitude.

Friends and relations noticed a great change in me, too : from a timid, shy girl I had become a woman of resolute character, who could not longer be frightened by the struggle with troubles or, to speak exactly, with debts, which at the time of our arrival at Petersburg had reached the sum of twenty-five thousand roubles. My cheerfulness and vitality remained with me, but showed only in our family, among relations or friends. In the presence of strangers, especially in the company of men, I behaved with the greatest reserve, confining myself to cold politeness. I more often kept silent and listened than expressed my opinions. My women friends assured me that I had aged terribly during those four years, and reproached me for paying no attention to my appearance, and for not dressing fashionably. Though I agreed with them, I did not want to change. I was firmly convinced that Fiodor loved me not only for my appearance, but for the good qualities of my mind and character, and that we had reached during that period " a fusion of souls," as Fiodor put it. My dowdy appearance and my obvious avoidance of men's company could only act favourably on my husband ; for it provided him with no occasions of displaying that bad trait in his character—groundless jealousy.

Having finished his novel, *The Devils*, Fiodor was very undecided as to what he should do next. He was so worn out by his work on it and so dissatisfied with it, that it seemed to him wearisome to start at once on a new novel. To realise the idea which he had formed while we were living abroad, that is, to publish *The Journal of an Author*, as a monthly review, was out of the question. To meet the cost of the publication of the *Journal* and of the maintenance of our family (not to speak of the payment of debts) quite considerable sums would be needed, and there was also the question as to whether the *Journal* would be a success, and if so how great that success would be, for it was intended to stand for something quite new, for something which up to that time had not been undertaken in literature either in form or contents. And in case of failure we should be placed in a desperate position.

Fiodor hesitated very much, and I cannot say what decision he would have made, had not Prince P. Meschersky at that very time proposed to him to become editor of the weekly *Grazhdanin*. That journal had been founded a year ago under the editorship of G. Gradovsky. Concerned with *The Grazhdanin* were a few people of like views and convictions. Some of them : K. P. Pobedonoszev, T. I. Fillipov, N. N. Strakhov, A. N. Maikov and E. Belov were sympathetic

---

[1] See Mme. Dostoevsky's *Reminiscences*, relating to the years 1871–2, in the volume *Dostoevsky : Letters and Reminiscences*, translated by S. S. Koteliansky and J. M. Murry, published by Chatto & Windus.

to Fiodor, and the idea of working with them appealed to him. No less pleased was he at the possibility of sharing with the readers the hopes and doubts that had been maturing in his mind and heart. In the pages of *The Grazhdanin* he could realise his idea of *The Journal of an Author* although in a form different from the one it subsequently assumed. From the financial point of view the proposition was satisfactory. The editor's salary was fixed at three thousand roubles ; for his articles entitled *The Journal of an Author,* as well as his political writings, he was to be paid separately. Altogether he would be getting about five thousand roubles a year. The monthly receipt of a definite sum of money had also the advantage of allowing Fiodor to devote himself to his work without having to tear himself away in order to find the means of subsistence—. worries which acted most prejudicially on his mood. Yet in consenting to become editor of *The Grazhdanin,* at the request of persons sympathetic to him, Fiodor did not conceal from them the fact that he was assuming the editorship only temporarily, as a respite from his literary work, and in order to get more intimately acquainted with current actualities. When the urge of creative work arose in him, he would give up an activity so uncongenial to his character.

The autumn and winter of 1872 passed without any troubles, and we were all well. Thanks to that circumstance and to our improved material position Fiodor's mood changed for the better ; he felt free from worry and frequently went out to the dinners given by Prince Meschersky, to N. P. Semionov's evening parties, and to the Saturday gatherings of the much-esteemed I. P. Kornilov. At Kornilov's one was sure of meeting the most representative people of the literary, scientific and bureaucratic world. Fiodor went to the theatre very little, as he did not like to go there by himself ; and I could not accompany him for fear of leaving the children in the sole charge of our old nurse. But I remember I once went with him to a party given by the Kashpirovs, on which occasion Pissemsky read his new novel, *The Burghers*. His reading made no particular impression.

The beginning of 1873 was marked by an undertaking which was of great importance in our life, namely, the publishing by ourselves of F. M. Dostoevsky's novel, *The Devils*. With that book was laid the foundation of our publishing activity, which, directed for the first eight years by myself and my husband, was after his death continued by me alone for a subsequent thirty years.

One of the hopes we had for improving our financial affairs was the chance of selling the book rights first of *The Idiot* and then of *The Devils*. While we were abroad it was difficult to arrange the matter ; and it did not greatly improve on our return to Russia (in 1871) when we had the opportunity of carrying on personal negotiations with the publishers. By every publisher to whom we turned we were offered a very unprofitable price : thus, for instance, for the book rights of two thousand copies of *The Eternal Husband* we had been paid one hundred and fifty roubles, and for the book rights of *The Devils* we were offered 500 roubles to be paid in instalments spread over three years.

Even when he was young Fiodor dreamt of being his own publisher ; he also talked of it while we were living abroad. I, too, became interested in the idea, and gradually tried to learn the conditions of book publishing and distribution. Once as I was ordering some visiting cards for Fiodor, I got into a conversation with the manager of the printing house, and asked him the conditions of book publishing. He explained that most books were printed on a cash basis, but if the author had a considerable literary reputation, and his books sold, then any printer would readily print on a six months' credit, on condition that, if the money were not paid during that time, a certain interest was to be charged on the remaining debt. On the same credit terms one could also get the paper. He also told me the approximate price of the publication I had in mind, that is, the cost of paper, printing, stitching and binding. According to his estimate, the publication of three thousand copies of *The Devils* would come to about four thousand roubles. The price was to be fixed at R3·50 copecks, for the three volumes, printed in large fine type, on a good-quality paper. Out of the gross receipts of 12,250 roubles if all the copies were sold, a discount of forty to fifty per cent. would have to be made to the booksellers ; but even then, if the novel were a success, there would still remain a profit of about four thousand roubles.

At that time no author published his works himself, and if there appeared such a bold fellow, he paid for his boldness with a loss. There existed several book-sellers : Basunov, Wolf, Isacov, Kozhanchikov, who bought the copyrights of books, published them and distributed them all over Russia. Books published by learned societies or by private persons, used to be taken by the booksellers on a commission of fifty per cent. and at times of sixty per cent. on the pretext that the storing and advertising of books (which was done very sparingly) cost a great deal of money. The result would be that many books published on a commission and storing basis were returned to the owner unsold ; sometimes even in a damaged condition. I was indignant that the lion's share of the profit (fifty to sixty per cent.) had to go to the booksellers, from whom, according to the unfortunate publishers, one could not get accounts for years. And I was thinking how to find a way of selling the books myself and for cash, and so of getting rid of the system of commission and storage. I made enquiries in bookshops as to what discount they got, but I received the vaguest replies ; as, for instance, that the discount depended on the book, that the discount was as high as forty or fifty per cent. and even higher. Once as I was buying a pamphlet I asked the price of a book ; I was told that it cost four roubles. I purposely asked them to let me have it for R2·50 copecs, on the pretext that they surely got fifty or sixty per cent. discount. The assistant was indignant and declared that they got only twenty or twenty-five per cent., and only got thirty per cent. on a very few books. From these inquiries I gathered clearly what a discount had to be given to the book-sellers and how it varied with the number of copies taken.

When we told our friends and acquaintances of our intention to publish our book ourselves, we had to listen to many objections. They advised us not to undertake a thing which we did not understand, which, through our inexperience, would only ruin us, and would add to our old debts some thousands of roubles. But these dissuasions had no influence on us, and we made up our minds to realise our idea. We bought paper from the firm of A. I. Vargunin, the best paper manufacturer of that time ; and on the advice of N. N. Strakhov we gave the printing order to Panteleyev Brothers. November and December of 1872 and part of January, 1873, were spent on getting out the book. I read one set of proofs, Fiodor read his own set, and I went through his corrections, transferred them to my copy, and read the proofs again so as to avoid misprints.

About the 20th of January, 1873, the book was ready and a certain number of copies was delivered at our house. Fiodor was satisfied with the appearance of the book and, as for myself, I was quite charmed. Before the publication of the book Fiodor took it to one of the big booksellers with whom he had been having dealings for many years, in the hope that the latter would wish to order a certain number of copies. " Well, send us two hundred copies on commission," the bookseller said. " What discount ? " Fiodor asked. " Not less than fifty per cent " was the answer. Fiodor made no reply. He returned home worried, and told me of his failure. I, too, was upset, for the bookseller's proposition to take two hundred copies on commission did not at all please me. I knew that, even if he sold the copies, it would be two or three years before we got the money from him.

Then there arrived the momentous day of our life. On 22nd January, 1873, there appeared announcements in the papers of our publication of *The Devils*, and early in the morning there arrived a messenger from M. V. Popov, the bookseller, who, contrary to the custom of the trade, used to buy all new publications. I came out into the hall and asked the man who had sent him and what he wanted. " We saw your announcement," he said, " so I should like to take ten *Devils*." I got out the copies, and with some agitation I said : " The price is thirty-five roubles, the discount is twenty per cent., so you have to pay me twenty-eight roubles." " Why such a small discount ? Can't you make it thirty per cent. ? " the man asked. " No, I cannot." " Well, twenty-five per cent. ? " " Really, no," I said, but in my own mind I was very uneasy : suppose he were to go away, and I missed my first customer ? " Well, if you cannot, then here is the money," and he handed me the twenty-eight roubles. I was so glad that I gave him thirty copecks for a cab. A little later a boy came from a bookshop, which supplied the provinces, and bought ten copies ; he also, after some bargaining, agreed to the twenty per cent. discount. A man from Glasunov's came and said he would take twenty-five copies if I gave him a discount of twenty-five per cent. In view of the big order I had to give it him. Some one else called for copies. About midday there appeared a dashing assistant from the bookseller whom Fiodor had previously gone to see, and said that he had come to take away two hundred copies on a commission basis. Encouraged by the success of the first sales, I said that I did not sell copies on commission, only for cash. " But Mr. Dostoevsky," he said, " promised to let us have them." I said that Mr. Dostoevsky had published the book, but I, his wife, looked after the sales, and that many booksellers had already bought copies for cash. " May I see Mr. Dostoevsky himself," the assistant persisted, evidently reckoning on my husband's yielding the point. " Mr. Dostoevsky worked all night and I am not going to wake him before two o'clock." The assistant suggested that I should let him have the two hundred copies and " we will pay Mr. Dostoevsky later." I remained firm, and telling him what discount we were allowing, and on what number of copies, I said that only five hundred copies had been delivered to us, and that I expected to sell them that day. The assistant went away, but an hour later another assistant, less assured, arrived and bought fifty copies for cash at a thirty per cent. discount.

That day I was impatient for Fiodor to wake up, so much did I want to boast of the success of our sales. I may add by the way that when he woke, Fiodor was always ill-tempered and disagreeable and did not like to be talked to or to be asked anything at that hour. It was only after he had completed his toilet, had drunk a glass of very hot coffee, and gone into his study, that I was allowed to go to him to tell him all the news, pleasant and unpleasant, which had occurred since the previous night. During those hours Fiodor was always in the pleasantest mood : everything interested him, he inquired about all sorts of things, called in the children, played and sported with them. So it was this time too. After he had talked to the children, I sent them off on some errand to the nursery, and myself sat down in my habitual place by the desk. Seeing that I kept silent, Fiodor glanced at me mockingly and asked : " Well, Aneckha, how is our trade ? " " It is getting on fine," I replied in the same tone. " And you have surely succeeded already in selling one copy ? " " Not one, but one hundred and fifteen," I said. " Indeed ? . . . Well, I congratulate you ! " Fiodor continued in a bantering tone, thinking that I was joking. " But, am I not telling you," I said with annoyance, " why don't you believe me ? " and I got out of my pocket the list of copies sold together with a pile of notes, about three hundred roubles. As Fiodor knew that we had only very little money in the house, the amount I showed him convinced him that I was not joking. After four o'clock the bell started ringing again : new customers appeared. *The Devils* had had a great success when it was running as a serial in the *Russky Vestnik*, and now there appeared to be a number of people who wanted to have the novel in book form ; and the booksellers who bought copies in the morning sent again for fresh supplies. I was more triumphant than ever, especially seeing that Fiodor was greatly interested in the success of the book and that he was very glad. But how great was my triumph when that day, about seven o'clock in the evening, Kozhanchikov, the bookseller, came to us and wanted us to sell him three hundred copies for bills, at a discount of only thirty per cent., saying that any bank would take his bills. Fiodor came to discuss the matter with me. Having no idea what bills were, I advised Fiodor to invite Kozhanchikov to tea and to have a talk with him. Meanwhile I took a cab and went to the printers, who lived close to us, to ask their advice. Fortunately I found one of the Panteleyevs and he told me not to lose such a big order ; he assured me that Kozhanchikov's bills could readily be discounted, and he even agreed to take the bills in payment of our debt at the printing office. With that information I came home, and Kozhanchikov, an experienced tradesman who always carried with him stamped blanks for bills, immediately issued three bills for seven hundred and thirty-five roubles, and Fiodor gave him a note to the printers for the corresponding number of copies.

In a word, our publishing activity started brilliantly, and the first three thousand copies were sold before the year was out. The sale of the remaining five hundred copies dragged on for a while, for we ceased to advertise the book. I won't say that we had no losses in our first experiment, for a couple of swindlers took advantage of our inexperience ; but these losses only taught us to be more cautious and not to fall in with propositions which sounded excellent, but turned out to be detrimental. In the end, after deducting commissions and paying all expenses, we made . . . roubles net.[1] We mutually agreed not to take a single rouble out of the money realised from sales, and we counted our profit only after the whole edition had been paid for. To that system—of not mixing my personal money with the publishing money—I adhered throughout the whole course of my publishing activity. Apart from the advantage of being our own publishers, we were able to apply the profits thus made to freeing ourselves from our old debts. The assurance that we had no longer got to look out for publishers, but that we could publish ourselves and at a much bigger profit than if we sold the copyright, was of enormous importance to us. I must say that the title of the novel [*The Devils*] served to those who came to buy it as an excuse for calling the book all sorts of names. Not to distract myself from my secretarial work, I only counted the copies and reckoned up the amounts ; and the customers were attended to by my cheerful maid. They would come in

---

[1] In the original the amount is not stated.

and say to her : " Let us have a dozen devils," or " I've come to fetch half a dozen demons," or " give me five fiends," etc. They called it either 'demons,' or ' fiends,' or ' Satans.' Our old nurse who frequently heard these appellations complained to me and assured me that since ' Satan ' got into our house, her charge (my boy) had become restless and did not sleep so well at night.

Fiodor always worked at night when perfect stillness reigned in the house and nothing could disturb the flow of his thoughts. He dictated to me in the afternoons, from two to three, and I remember those hours as the happiest of my life. . . . As he finished his dictation, my husband always addressed me like this :

" Well, what do you say, Anechka ? "

" I say it is grand ! " I would answer. But that " grand " Fiodor would interprete to mean that the scene, just dictated by him, was done well, but that it did not particularly strike me. And on my immediate impressions my husband set great value. It always so happened somehow that the passages in his novels which moved or depressed me, acted in the same way on the majority of the readers, of which fact my husband would learn from his talks with his readers or from the opinions of the critics.

I wanted to be sincere, and did not express praise or admiration when I did not feel them. My husband valued my sincerity very much. Nor did I conceal my impressions. I remember how much I laughed at the talks of Mme. Khokhlakov and of the General in *The Idiot,* and how I teased my husband about the speech of The Crown Prosecutor in *The Brothers Karamasov.*

" What a pity you are not a Crown Prosecutor ! You could send the most innocent man to Siberia, with your speech."

" So you think I've managed the speech well ? " Fiodor asked.

" Remarkably well ! " I answered. " Yet I am

sorry that you did not choose the law ! You would have risen to the rank of General, and I should now be Mme. General, and not the wife of a retired sub-lieutenant ! "

After Fiodor had dictated to me the defending counsel's speech (in *The Brothers Karamasov*) and had asked me the usual question, I replied :

" Now I can only say this, why did not you, my dear, become a counsel?   You would make the most thorough criminal whiter than snow.   Surely you have missed your vocation !   You've managed the counsel splendidly ! "

But at times I also shed tears.   I remember my husband dictating to me the scene in which Aliosha and the boys return from Ilyushechka's funeral (*The Brothers Karamasov*).   I was so moved that with one hand I copied from his dictation, and with the other I wiped away my tears.   Fiodor noticed my agitation, came up to me, and without saying a word, kissed my head.

Fiodor thought highly of me, and attributed to me a much deeper understanding of his works than, I think, was actually the case.   He was convinced, for instance, that I understood the philosophical side of his novels. I remember how, after he had dictated to me the chapter on ' The Grand Inquisitor ' (*The Brothers Karamasov*), I replied to his usual question :

" You know, I really understood very little of it. I think that, in order to understand it, I ought to have had a philosophical training."

" Wait," my husband said, " I'll put it more clearly to you."

And he told me of the idea in terms which I could more easily understand.

" Well, is it clear now ? " he asked.

" No, it is not clear even now.   If you were to make me repeat it, I should not be able to do it."

" Why, you understood it !   I conclude this from the questions you have been putting me.   And if you can't express it, it is because of your lack of a sense of form, of style."

I may say here, by the way, that the longer my life with its accompanying sad complications went on, the more widely opened to me were the works of my husband and the more deeply I began to understand them.

From our life at Staraia Roussa I recall the occasion on which Fiodor read to me the chapter of his novel (*The Raw Youth*, Part I, Chap. X), in which the girl hangs herself.   On finishing reading, Fiodor glanced at me and exclaimed :

" Anya, what's the matter with you, darling ?   You are pale.   Are you tired, are you ill ? "

" You have frightened me ! " I said.

" My God, does it indeed produce such a painful impression? How very sorry I am ! How very sorry ! "

On receiving my card, the Captain immediately invited me into his room, asked me to sit down, and enquired what was my business.   He brought out from his desk a rather thick portfolio, in a blue wrapper, and handed it to me.   I opened it, and to my great surprise, I saw that it was " The Case of the Retired Sub-Lieutenant Fiodor Mikhailovich Dostoevsky, kept under secret police surveillance and temporarily residing at Staraia Roussa."   I perused several pages, and said to him laughingly :

" Well ? So we are under your enlightened surveillance, and you probably know everything concerning us ?   I must say I did not expect it ! "

" Yes, I know of everything that is taking place in your family," the Captain said pompously. " I can say that I have been quite satisfied with your husband up till now."

" May I repeat your compliment to my husband ? " I asked.

" I beg you to tell him that he is behaving excellently, and that I hope that he won't give me any trouble in the future."

On coming home, I told Fiodor what the Captain had said, and laughed at the idea that a man, like my husband, should be under the surveillance of a silly policeman.   But Fiodor received my news with pain.

" What a number of evil-minded persons they keep

---

[1] The Dostoevskys spent the whole of 1874 in Staraia Roussa. As the novelist was advised by his doctor to go again to Ems for a cure, Mme. Dostoevsky went to the local Captain of the Police to ask for a passport for her husband to travel to Germany.

no eye on," Fiodor said, " yet they suspect and watch me, a man, devoted with all his heart and thoughts to the Tsar and the country. It does hurt ! "

Thanks to the loquacious Captain, a very annoying circumstance, the cause of which we could not understand, has now been cleared up. We could not understand why letters sent by me from Staraia Roussa to my husband at Ems, were not sent off the same day, but were kept back by the post office for a day or two. The same thing happened with Fiodor's letters to me from Ems. And the fact that my husband did not receive my letters in time not only caused him anxiety, but even drove him at times to fits of epilepsy (as is seen from his letter to me of July 16th, 28th, 1874). Now, it became clear that our letters were subject to secret examination, and that their despatch depended on the discretion of a police Captain who was often away for two or three days in the country.

The secret examination to which the authorities subjected my correspondence with my husband (and possibly all our correspondence) went on in later years, too, and caused my husband and myself not a few anxieties ; but we could not rid ourselves of that inconvenience. Fiodor himself did not raise the question of obtaining relief from this ; moreover, informed persons assured him that, seeing that he had been permitted to be editor and publisher of *The Journal of an Author*, the secret surveillance of his activities must have ceased. However, it continued till 1880, when, during the Pushkin festival, Fiodor happened to mention the matter to a highly-placed personage, who gave an order for terminating it.

On 18th May, 1876, an incident took place which I
recall almost with terror.   This is how it happened.   A
new novel by Mme. Sophie Smirnov entitled *The Strong
Character* was running as a serial then in *The Otechestvennya Zapiski*.   Fiodor was on friendly terms with
Sophia Smirnov and valued her talent very highly.
He was interested in her latest work, and asked me to get
him the numbers of the monthly as they appeared.   I
chose those few days, when my husband had a rest
from his work on *The Journal of an Author*, and brought
him the numbers of *The Otechestvennya Zapiski*.   But as
journals are lent by the libraries only for two or three
days, I urged my husband to read the journal quickly
so as to avoid paying a fine at the library.   So it was
also with the April number.   Fiodor read the novel and
spoke to me of how our dear Sophie (whom I, too,
valued very highly) had succeeded in creating a certain
male character in the novel.   That evening my husband
went out to some gathering, and after seeing the
children to bed, I began reading the novel.   In it, by
the way, was published an anonymous letter, sent by the
villain to the hero, which ran as follows :

" Dear Sir, Noblest Peter Ivanovich,

As I am a perfect stranger to you, but take an
interest in your feelings, I venture to address these
lines to you.   Your nobility is sufficiently well-
known to me, and my heart is pained at the idea,
that despite all your nobility, a certain person, who

is very close to you, is so basely deceiving you. Having gone away with your blessing to a place four hundred miles off, she, like a delighted dove spreading its wings and soaring upwards, has no mind to return to the marital home. You have let her go to your own as well as to her ruin, into the claws of a man who terrifies her, but who fascinates her by his flattering addresses. He has stolen her heart, and there are no eyes more beautiful to her than his. Even her little children are loathsome to her, if she gets no loving word from him. If you want to know who this fellow the villain is, I must not reveal his name, but look for yourself among those who frequent your house, and beware of dark men. When you see the dark man, who loves haunting your doors, have a good look at him. It is now a long time since that fellow has crossed your path, and you are the only one who does not notice it.

Nothing but your nobility compels me to reveal this secret to you. And if you don't trust me, then have a look at the locket which your wife wears round her neck, and see whose portrait she wears in that locket near her heart.

Your ever unknown well-wisher."

I must say here that lately I had been in the best of moods ; my husband had had no epileptic fits for a long time, our children were perfectly well, our debts were gradually being paid, and the success of *The Journal of an Author* was marked. All this strengthened my characteristic cheerfulness, and under the influence of the anonymous letter, just read, a playful idea flashed across my mind—to copy that letter (changing the name and striking out certain lines) and to send it by post to Fiodor. It seemed to me that, as he had only yesterday read that letter in Mme. Smirnov's novel, he would guess at once that it was a joke, and we should have some fun. There also occurred another idea to me, that my husband might take the letter seriously. In that case I was interested to see how he would regard it : whether he would show it to me, or throw it away into the waste-paper basket. As usual with me, I had no sooner thought of the idea than I put it into execution. At first I wanted to write the letter in my own hand-writing ; but as I had been copying for Fiodor every day, and my handwriting was too familiar to him, I resolved to cover up my joke and began copying out the letter in a rounder handwriting than mine. But it turned out to be a hard job, and I spoilt several sheets before I managed to write the whole letter in a uniform hand. Next morning I posted it, and in the afternoon it was delivered to us together with other letters.

That day Fiodor was out later than usual, and returned only at five o'clock and, not wanting to keep the children waiting for their dinner, he just changed and came straight into the dining room, without looking at his letters. The dinner passed off merrily and noisily. Fiodor was in a good mood ; he talked a good deal and laughed, as he answered the children's questions. After dinner, with the usual cup of tea in his hand, he went into his study. I went into the nursery, and in about ten minutes' time I entered the study to see the effect which my anonymous letter had produced.

I sat down in my usual seat by the writing table, and purposely asked Fiodor something to which he had to give an answer. But he kept a gloomy silence, and paced the room with heavy steps. I saw he was upset, and instantly I felt sorry. To break the silence I asked him : " Why are you so gloomy, Fedya ? "

Fiodor gave me an angry look, walked across the room a couple of times and came to a stop just facing me.

" You wear a locket ? " he asked in a choking voice.

" I do."

" Show it to me."

" What for ? You have seen it many times."

" Show—me—the locket ! " Fiodor shouted at the top of his voice.

I realised that my joke had gone too far, and in order to reassure him I began undoing the collar of my dress. But I had no time to take the locket out. Fiodor could not restrain the anger which had seized him. He quickly rushed to me and caught my chain with all his strength. It was a thin chain which he himself had bought for me in Venice. It broke instantly, and the locket remained in my husband's hand. He quickly swept round the table and, with his head bent down, he began opening the locket. Not knowing where to press the spring, he fussed over it for a long time. I saw how his hands trembled, and the locket nearly slipped from them on to the table. I was very sorry for him and terribly angry with myself. I began to speak in a friendly tone, and proposed to open the locket for him ; but Fiodor with an angry nod of his head refused my help. At last my husband opened the locket and found there —on one side the portrait of our little daughter, on the other—his own portrait. He was absolutely confused, and kept on looking at the portrait in silence.

" Well, now, have you found it ? " I asked him. " Fedya, you silly, how could you believe an anonymous letter ? "

Fiodor instantly turned his face to me. " How do you know of the letter ? "

" How ? I myself sent it you ! "

" What do you mean ; you sent it me ? It is incredible ! "

" I'll prove it to you at once."

I went to the other table on which lay the copy of *The Otechestvennya Zapiski*, and got out several sheets of paper, on which I had practised my changed hand-writing.

Fiodor raised his hands in astonishment. " And did you yourself compose the letter ? "

" Not at all. I simply copied it from Sophie's novel. Surely you read it yesterday ? I thought you would guess at once."

" Well, how could I remember ! Anonymous letters are always in that style. I simply can't understand why you sent it me ? "

" I just wanted to have a lark," I explained.

" How could you play such a joke ? I have been in anguish for the last half hour."

" How could I know that you would be such an Othello, and get into such a rage without giving yourself time for a moment's thought ? "

" One does not think in such cases. Ah, well, it is clear that you have never experienced real love and real jealousy."

" As for real love, I experience it even now, and as for my not knowing ' real jealousy,' it is your own fault. Why aren't you unfaithful to me ? " I laughed, wishing to divert his mood. " Please, be unfaithful to me. Even then I would be kinder than you are. I would not touch you, but I would scratch out her eyes, the villainess . . . "

" Well, you are laughing, Anechka," Fiodor began apologetically. " But think what a misfortune might have happened : indeed, in my anger I could have strangled you. I may indeed say : God has taken pity on our little ones. And suppose I had not found those portraits, a grain of doubt as to your faithfulness would have remained in my mind for ever, and would have tortured me all my life. I implore you, do not play with such things : in a rage I am not responsible for my actions."

During the conversation I felt a slight awkwardness in moving my neck. I passed my handkerchief over it, and there was a line of blood on it. Evidently the

chain in being wrenched off by force had scratched
my skin. Seeing blood on my handkerchief, my
husband was in despair.

"My God," he exclaimed, "what have I done?
Anechka, my dear, forgive me. I have wounded you.
Does it pain you, tell me, does it pain you very much?"

I began to reassure him that there was no 'wound,'
but just a mere scratch which would disappear by the
morning. Fiodor was seriously upset, and, above all,
was ashamed of his fit of anger. The whole evening
was given up to his apologies and expressions of sympathy and tenderness. And I, too, was boundlessly
happy that my absurd joke had ended so happily. I
sincerely repented of having made Fiodor suffer, and I
promised myself never again to play such a joke, having
learnt from this experience to what a furious, almost
irresponsible state my dear husband was capable of
bring reduced in moments of jealousy.

I still preserve the locket and the anonymous letter
(of 18th May, 1876).

In the winter of 1876 the number of Fiodor's acquaintances in society had considerably increased. Everywhere he was very welcome ; for people valued not only his intellect and talent, but also his kind heart, so responsive to all human misery.

I did not go into society that winter. I used to get so tired during the day with my work on *The Journal of an Author*, with my household occupations and with looking after the children that in the evening I only wanted to rest, or to read a book ; and in society I should probably have cut a dull figure. Yet I did not regret my absence from society ; for ever since our return to Russia (in 1871) Fedya, concerned at my not going into society and thinking I might be bored at home, had got into the habit, which he kept up for the rest of his life, of telling me everything he had seen or heard or talked about on such occasions. And Fiodor's accounts were so fascinating and were related so well that they were quite a good substitute for society. I remember always waiting impatiently for his return home. He used to return at one or half past in the morning. Fresh tea was always waiting for him at that hour. He would change into his wide summer overcoat (which served him as a dressing-gown), drink a glass of hot tea and start telling me of the events of the previous night. Fiodor knew that I was interested in details, and therefore he did not slur over them, but told me of all his conversations, in answer to my constant questions : " And what did she say to you ? What did you reply to him ? "

When he used to return from one of these evenings,

Fiodor did not sit down to work ; but as he was in the habit of going to bed late (at five in the morning), we would pass the time in talking till five o'clock. At last Fiodor would make me go to bed, saying I should have a headache if I sat up later, and promising to finish the account the next day.

Sometimes Fiodor would boast to me of how he had scored in a literary or political discussion. At others he would tell me of some blunder he had committed, of how he had not recognised one or had cut another, and what a misunderstanding had arisen on that account ; and he would ask my opinion or advice how to put the blunder right. Sometimes he frankly complained of how certain people were unjust to him, and how they tried to insult him or to prick his *amour-propre*. I must say that men of his profession, even those who possessed intellect and talent, often did not spare him, and with petty pricks and insults tried to show how little his talent meant in their eyes. For instance, some of them would not speak at all to Fiodor of his latest work, as though not wishing to upset him by their poor opinion of it ; although they, of course, knew that he did not expect extravagant compliments from them, but wanted their sincere opinion as to how far he had succeeded in carrying through the idea of this or that novel. Again, if Fiodor asked a ' friend ' point-blank if he had read the last instalment of his new story (say, a month after its publication), the ' friend ' would answer that ' the young generation was fascinated by the novel, that it was passing from hand to hand and was highly praised ' ; although the speaker knew quite well that it was not the opinion of young people that was valuable to Fiodor, but the speaker's personal opinion, and that Fiodor would be pained that his ' friend ' was so little interested in his work that for a whole month he had not found the time to read it.

I remember, for instance, a case when a certain

author, meeting Fiodor in society, declared to him that he had at last managed to read *The Idiot* (which had appeared five years previously), and that he liked the novel, but found an inaccuracy in it.

" And what is the inaccuracy ? " Fiodor was intrigued, thinking that it was in the idea, or in the characters of the novel.

" I spent this summer in Pavlovsk," the author answered, " and in my walks with my daughters we have been looking for the fine summer house, in the style of a Swiss châlet, in which the heroine of the novel, Aglaia Epanchin, lived. If you don't mind my saying so, we found no house like that existing in Pavlovsk."

Another writer declared (on another occasion) that he had read twice with the greatest curiosity the Crown Prosecutor's speech (in *The Brothers Karamasov*), and the second time he read it with a watch in his hand.

" Why with a watch ? " my husband asked, surprised.

" In the novel you say that the speech lasted . . . minutes. I wanted to verify it. It turned out that it lasted only . . ."

Fiodor first thought that the Crown Prosecutor's speech had so much impressed the speaker that he wished to read it a second time. But the reason turned out to be such a petty one, that it could only have been mentioned with the object of insulting or wounding Fiodor. And such instances of the attitude of literary contemporaries to my husband were not few.

One afternoon in the early spring of 1878 our whole family was sitting peacefully at dinner. Having just come home from a long walk, Fiodor was in a very good mood and chatted merrily with the children. Suddenly there was a violent ring of the bell. Our maid ran to answer it, and through the half-closed door of the dining room we heard a woman's shrill voice say :

" Is he still alive ? "

Our maid, who seemed not to understand the question, did not answer.

" I ask you, is Dostoevsky still alive ? "

" Yes, he is alive," the puzzled maid replied.

I wanted to come out to her to learn what she wanted ; but Fiodor, who sat nearer to the door, jumped up and ran into the hall. A not very young lady quickly got up from her chair to meet him, and holding out her hands exclaimed :

" You are alive, Fiodor Mikhailovich ! How glad I am that you are alive ! "

" But, madam, what's the matter ? " Fiodor exclaimed in his surprise. " I am alive and intend to be alive for a long time."

" In Karkhov there were rumours," the agitated lady contined, " that your wife had deserted you, that owing to her unfaithfulness you had fallen ill and were alone, without help, and I immediately took the train and came here to look after you. I have come straight from the railway station ! "

Hearing these exclamations, I went out into the hall and found Fiodor in a perfect fury.

" Do you hear, Anya ? " he turned to me, " some

scoundrels have spread the rumour that you have deserted me. Well, how do you like that ? Well, what do you think of that ? "

" But be quiet, my dear, don't be agitated," I said, " it must be a misunderstanding. Please come away, you are in a draught," and I quietly directed Fiodor to the dining room. He went back ; but his indignant exclamations, which reached me from the dining room, continued for a long time. I entered into a conversation with the stranger, who turned out to be a teacher, a very kind but probably not very wise person. I think she was captivated by the idea of looking after the famous writer, deserted by his wicked wife, and of seeing him off to the better world, and then priding herself for the rest of her life on the fact that the writer had died in her arms. I was so very sorry for the poor stranger, who seemed to be seriously concerned, that, excusing myself for a minute, I went into the dining room to tell my husband that I wanted to ask her in to dine with us.

Fiodor waved his hands and whispered : " Call her, only let me be off first ! " and he jumped off his seat and rushed away to his room.

I returned to the lady and asked her to have dinner and a rest ; but, evidently upset by the reception my husband had given her, she refused, and only asked that our maid should help her to carry her large wicker basket to a cab. When she arrived our gardener had taken it in. I did not insist on her staying to dinner, but only asked her name and the hotel she proposed to stay at.

When I returned to my husband, I found him in great irritation.

" Just imagine it ! " he said, pacing the room in agitation. " What a vile rumour to invent ; you deserting me ! What a base calumny ! What enemy could have invented it ? "

The idea that people could spread calumnies about me was what struck my husband most in that incident. Seeing that such an unimportant thing had so much upset him, I suggested that he should write to his old friend, Professor A. N. Beketov, at Kharkov, and ask him what rumours were circulating there about us. My husband took the advice, wrote to Beketov the same day, and calmed down. Next day he asked me to pay a visit to the lady. But I could not find her at the hotel : she had left for Kharkov early that morning.

His attacks of epilepsy greatly weakened Fiodor's memory, and above all his memory for people's names and faces. He acquired a number of enemies through his not recognising the face of a person ; and even when told the name, he was often quite unable, without detailed questions, to make out who the speaker was. This annoyed people who, having forgotten or being unaware of his illness, considered him proud, and his forgetfulness a deliberate intention to offend. Once when we were paying a visit to the Maikovs, we met on the staircase F. N. Berg, the author, who was once a contributor to the *Vremya* (Dostoevsky's review), but whom my husband had forgotten. Berg greeted Fiodor very cordially ; but seeing that he was not recognised, he said :

"Fiodor Mikhailovich, you don't seem to recognise me ? "

"I am sorry. I don't."

"I am Berg."

"Berg ? " said Fiodor, looking at him enquiringly. (He told me later that at the moment the name Berg reminded him of the German, the Rostovs' son-in-law, in *War and Peace*).

"Berg, the poet," the man explained. "Do you really not recognise me ? "

"Berg, the poet ? " my husband repeated, "I am so glad, so glad ! "

But Berg, compelled to enter into such detailed explanations of his identity, remained deeply convinced that Fiodor had cut him, and all his life he remembered the ' insult.' And what a number of enemies, particularly literary ones, Fiodor acquired through his forgetfulness ! That forgetfulness put me, too, sometimes into a ridiculous position, and I had to apologise for him.

I remember the following comical instance. Three or four times a year my husband and I used to go to pay a visit to the family of my cousin Snitkin. We nearly always met there my godmother Alexandra P. I., whom I had stopped visiting after my marriage, because her husband, on account of his political views, did not hit it off with Fiodor. She was deeply hurt that my husband, after politely greeting her, never engaged in talk with her. She spoke of it to my relations, who repeated it to me. The next time we were to go to the Snitkins I asked my husband to talk to Alexandra P. I. and to be as polite to her as possible.

" Good, good," Fiodor promised, " only you must point out to me which one of the ladies is your godmother, and I shall be sure to find an interesting subject of conversation. You will be pleased with me ! "

When we arrived, I pointed out to Fiodor the lady who sat on the couch. He first looked attentively at her, then at me, then again at her ; but during the whole evening he never went up to her. When we came home I reproached him for refusing to do me such a slight favour.

" But, please tell me, Anya," Fiodor said, perplexed, " who is whose godmother ? Is she yours, or you hers ? I recently looked at you both ; but you differed so little one from the other that I was seized with doubt, and so as not to make a blunder, I decided not to go up at all."

The point is that the difference in age between me and my godmother was comparatively small (sixteen years); and as I always dressed very quietly, almost always in dark colours, and she loved to dress smartly, she looked younger than she actually was. That youthful appearance of her's perplexed my husband.

But the most curious thing about it was that a year later, at Christmas, knowing that I was bound to meet my godmother again at the Snitkins', I turned to Fiodor with the same request, trying my very best to explain to him the degree of our relationship. My husband seemed to listen to me very attentively, but he must have been thinking of something else, and promised me that this time he would talk to her. But he failed to keep his promise : last year's doubts recurred to him, and he could not solve the problem of ' who was whose godmother ' ; and to ask me of it in the presence of company he thought would be awkward.

Fiodor's forgetfulness of the names of persons with whom he was most intimate put him sometimes in an awkward position. I remember my husband going once to the Russian Consulate in Dresden to have my name certified on a power of attorney. (I could not go there myself because of illness.) Seeing from the window Fiodor hastily returning home, I got up to meet him. He came in agitated and asked me in a cross voice :

" Anya, what do they call you ? What is your name ? "

" Dostoevsky," I replied, surprised at such a queer question.

" I know that it is Dostoevsky, but what is your maiden name ? They asked me at the Consulate what your maiden name was, and I forgot it ; so I have to go back there again. The clerks, I believe, had a laugh at me for forgetting my wife's name. Do write it please on your card ; for I may forget it again."

FIODOR'S JEALOUSY
(1879–80)

In the years 1879 and 1880 Fiodor gave frequent readings for the benefit of various institutions, such, for instance, as the Literary Fund. I used to accompany him to those evenings in view of his weak health, and also because I wished to hear his truly artistic reading, and to be present at the rapturous ovations with which the public always received him.[1]

To my regret these excursions of mine into society were often darkened for me by Fiodor's sudden and groundless fits of jealousy, which at times put me in an absurd situation. I shall give here one instance.

At one of those literary soirées we arrived a little late, and all the others who were taking part in it were already there. When we came in they all greeted Fiodor cordially, and the men kissed my hand. That social custom (the kissing of a lady's hand) evidently produced an unpleasant impression on my husband. He returned the greetings in a dry manner, and walked away. I instantly realised what was the matter. After exchanging a few words with our acquaintances, I sat down close to my husband so as to drive away his bad humour. But I failed. To the few questions I put Fiodor made no reply at all, and then, glancing at me, he announced ' ferociously ' : " Go to him ! ! "

In surprise I asked : " To whom ? "

---

[1] I always took with me to these evenings the volume from which my husband was to read, along with Ems pastilles—a remedy for his cough—a spare handkerchief (in case he lost his), a plaid to wrap up his neck on his coming out into the cold air, and so on. Seeing me always so equipped, Fiodor used to call me his " faithful armour-bearer."

" You don't understand ? "

" No, I don't. To whom, then, am I to go ? " I asked, with a laugh.

" To the man who has just kissed your hand so *passionately*."

As all the men who were in the artists' room had kissed my hand as a matter of custom, I could not, of course, decide who was the person guilty of the crime imagined by my husband.

Although this conversation was conducted by Fiodor in half-tones, yet it was managed in such a way that those who sat near us heard it quite well. I felt very disconcerted, and, fearing a scene, I said :

" I see, Fiodor, you are not in the right mood, and don't want to speak to me. I had better go into the auditorium, and find my seat. Good-bye ! "

And I walked away. Not more than five minutes had passed, when Gaidebourov came up to me and said that Fiodor was asking for me. Thinking that my husband could not find in the volume the passage he was to read, I proceeded at once to the artists' room. My husband met me in a hostile mood.

" You could not resist ? You came to have a glance at him ? " he said.

" Yes, of course," I replied with a laugh, " but also to have a look at you, too."

" Do you want anything ? " I asked.

" No, I do not want anything," he replied.

" But did not you ask for me ? "

" I never thought of asking for you. Don't imagine it, please ! "

" Well, if you did not ask for me, then good-bye, I'll go."

In about ten minutes one of the stewards came up to me and said that Mr. Dostoevsky was enquiring where I was sitting, and therefore he thought my husband wished to see me. I said I had just been in the artists' room and I did not want to hinder my husband from concentrating all his attention on his forthcoming reading. And so I did not go. Then, during the first interval, the steward came up again with my husband's urgent request that I should come to him. I hastened to the room, came up to my dear husband and saw his troubled, apologetic face. He bent down to me and said hardly audibly :

" Forgive me, Anechka, and give me your hand for luck : it is my turn now ! "

I was so pleased that Fiodor had calmed down, and I only wondered which one of the company (it so happened that all the men were of a more than respectable age) my husband had suspected of having conceived a sudden love for me. Only his contemptuous words : " Look at that little Frenchie with his grimacing ! " gave me the hint that the object of Fiodor's jealous suspicions was this time his old school friend, D. V. Grigorovich (whose mother was a Frenchwoman).

When we returned home I lectured my husband on his groundless jealousy. Fiodor, as usual, asked to be forgiven, admitted he was to blame, vowed that it should never happen again, and was sincerely repentant. But he assured me that he could not overcome that sudden fit, and that for a whole hour he had been madly jealous and deeply unhappy.

Scenes of that kind were repeated at nearly every literary soirée : Fiodor would invariably send the stewards or his friends to see where I was sitting and to whom I was talking. He often appeared at the half opened door of the artists' room and looked for me in the direction of my seat. (Usually the artists' relations were given seats along the right wall, close to the platform.)

Coming on the platform and bowing to the applauding public Fiodor did not start reading at once, but first carefully examined all the ladies sitting along the right wall. In order that he should notice me the sooner, I either passed a white handkerchief over my face, or got up from my seat. Only on convincing himself that I was there, would Fiodor start reading. Acquaintances as well as the stewards noticed these ways of his, and questioned my husband about me, and slightly chaffed both him and myself. And this at times angered me a good deal. I got tired of it, and once as I was going with him to a literary soirée, I said :

" You know, my dear, if this time, too, you start looking out for me and trying to find me in the audience, I give you my word, I shall get up from my seat and walk clean out past the platform."

" And I shall jump down from the platform and run after you to see if anything has happened to you and where you are going ! "

Fiodor said this in the most serious tone of voice, and I am convinced that he was capable, in case I suddenly left, of making such a scandal.

The beginning of 1880 was marked by the starting of our new undertaking : " F. M. Dostoevsky—Bookseller (exclusively to the provinces)."

Although each year our financial affairs had been improving and most of our debts (which had burdened Fiodor since the sixties) had been paid, nevertheless, our material position was insecure : living was becoming dearer and more complicated, and we could not possibly manage to save up for " a rainy day." This made us very anxious ; moreover, Fiodor himself realised that it was getting more and more difficult for him to work. Again, his illness (emphysema) was growing on him, and there was the fear that, through his failing health, there might be a break in his work. For such a sad contingency we wished to have some fund of money or some subsidiary occupation which would bring us in an income. But the sphere of occupations for women is even now fairly limited, and at that time it was much more so.

I had been thinking for a long time what occupation I could engage in, which might be of some support to us. After long consideration and consultations with experts, I determined to start a business for selling books to the provinces ; moreover, owing to the several books we had ourselves published, I was to a certain extent acquainted with the book trade. The new undertaking had two advantages for me. The first, and most important, was that it did not necessitate my absence from the house, and that I could as usual look after my husband's health, after the children, and run the house and my affairs. The second advantage was that there was almost no need of any initial outlay. There was no need to pay rent for a shop or to buy stock ; for I could at first confine myself to the buying of those books for which I had got orders accompanied by cash. The only expense would consist in paying the trading licence and in employing an errand boy, who would buy the books, pack the parcels, and take them to the post office. This would come to two hundred and fifty or three hundred roubles a year, and it was worth while risking that amount. Of course, for the success of the business it would be necessary to place advertisements in the papers ; but for the start I relied on sending out a circular letter to the late subscribers to *The Journal of an Author*, and the following year I intended, by sharing expenses with the publisher of *Family Evenings*, to send out several thousand copies of a long advertisement. (I sent out that advertisement in the beginning of 1881, but it no longer affected the business.)

Of course, this book business could reckon on success only on condition that it was carried on under the name of F. M. Dostoevsky. So, having taken out a licence in the Court of Exchequer, Fiodor had to turn tradesman, a circumstance at which our newspaper enemies did not fail to poke fun. Those jokes did not in the least touch my husband's *amour-propre* ; for, having thoroughly gone into the matter, he approved of my idea and believed, as I did, that it would turn out a success.

My hopes of success were chiefly based on the calculation that the subscribers to *The Journal of an Author* during the years 1876 and 1877, accustomed as they were to its punctual handling by the publisher (the Dostoevskys), would regard with confidence a book-selling business, conducted by the same persons, and would order their books from us. These hopes were realised, and in two or three months' time a group of thirty former subscribers to *The Journal* were sending us monthly orders for books. I remember, for instance, the Bishop of Poltava giving every month an order for many expensive editions (for his own library and for presents). I also remember a certain engineer at Minsk, who used to give us large orders for books, and those not only in his special line. But besides the steady circle of customers, there appeared not a few persons who had noticed the newly started bookselling firm. Of course, there were also annoying customers, as, for instance, subscribers to newspapers, on which orders the firm made only about sixpence as commission. But more annoying still were those customers who used to ask for books which had long been out of print. After careful and conscientious searches their money had to be returned to them.

The bookselling took up very little of my time : I had only to keep the accounts, to enter the orders, and to make out the bills. The boy Peter, whom I engaged, had formerly worked at a bookseller's, and though only fifteen years old, he managed the buying and the delivery of books excellently.

Fiodor was much interested in the progress of the business, and at the end of each month I prepared for him an account of income and expenditure. Our profits were between eighty and ninety roubles a month during the winter, and from forty to fifty roubles during the summer.

On the whole, the first year, after deducting all expenses, brought us a net profit of eight hundred and eleven roubles, and that result Fiodor and I regarded as a good omen for the future.

The business might from the start have assumed much larger proportions. Scholastic institutions and certain Zemstvos applied to us to have books sent to them on credit ; but as we had to make a large outlay to get those books, we had to refuse such orders, in spite

of the large profit which might have been made in that
way.

Bookselling to the provinces is a very profitable
business, if it is carried on capably and punctually;
and during the last thirty years I have seen several
similar small businesses develop into big book-trading
firms. And I am perfectly convinced that if I had
carried on my bookselling activity, I should now own a
bookshop not inferior to that of the *Novoye Vremya*.
But I did not carry it on, for the simple reason that I
undertook to bring out a complete edition of my husband's works, a task which demanded all my powers and
all my time.

When, after Fiodor's death, I announced my intention
of closing down the book business, many people asked
me to hand it over to them; some even wished to buy
it from me, and offered me fifteen hundred roubles for
the good-will.

But I could not agree to this. To carry on a book
business associated with the name of F. M. Dostoevsky
was my own peculiar concern; for I considered that I
had a personal responsibility for the dignity of the firm.
And I was not sure how the person who bought the
business, or to whom I gave it as a gift, might regard that
question. If he proved incapable or unconscientious,
would not the name of Fiodor, so dear to me, be exposed
to criticism or contempt?

So, in the beginning of March, 1881, the bookselling
firm of F. M. Dostoevsky ceased to exist.

Still, I remember the short-lived business with
pleasant feelings; chiefly on account of the friendly
relations which were established between the customers
and the firm. Some customers were so naive as to
think that Dostoevsky himself was engaged in the sale
of books, and in their letters they addressed themselves
to him personally. Others, writing to the firm, asked
that their admiration of *The Brothers Karamasov* or of

other novels of his might be conveyed to him.   Others,
again, asked that, when the bills were sent in, they
should be accompanied by a few words about the health
of the " great writer," and expressed their best wishes
for him.   Some such naïve and enthusiastic letters
touched Fiodor very deeply, and he asked me to send
his greetings and compliments to those correspondents.
He had so often met with hostility from his literary and
other friends and from the critics, that he valued the
more such simple-hearted and at times naive expressions
of admiration for his talent, and the respect and
devotion paid him by strangers who sympathised with
his literary activities.

Fiodor was naturally a singularly hard-working man. It seems to me that even if he had been rich and had had no need to earn a living, he would not have remained idle, but would constantly have found subjects for unceasing literary activity.

By the beginning of 1881 our debts, which had tormented us for so long, had all been paid, and we had even about five thousand roubles owing to us from the *Russky Vestnik* (the payments due for *The Brothers Karamasov*). It would have seemed that there was no urgent need for Fiodor to set to work instantly again ; but he did not want to rest. He decided to restart *The Journal of an Author* ; for, during the last few troublous years, there had been accumulating in his mind certain anxious ideas about the political situation in Russia, and he could express them freely in his *Journal* only. Besides, the success of the only number of *The Journal of an Author* for 1880 gave us hope that the renewed publication would find a greater number of readers, and Fiodor set a very high value on the dissemination of his innermost ideas. He intended to carry on the publication of *The Journal* for two years, and then he meant to write the second part of *The Brothers Karamasov*, in which nearly all the characters would reappear, twenty years later, almost in our own time, during which interval they would have managed to achieve and to go through a good deal. The plan of the future novel, outlined by Fiodor in his conversations and in his notes, was extraordinarily interesting, and it is the greatest pity that it was not destined to be completed.

The subscription to *The Journal of an Author*, announced in the papers, went on successfully, and in the middle of January we had . . . subscribers.[1]

Fiodor had always had the good habit of not considering the subscription money as his own until the subscribers had been satisfied ; and accordingly he opened in the State Bank an account to which I paid in the monies received from subscribers. Owing to this circumstance I always had it in my power to refund the subscription money to the subscribers.

The first half of January Fiodor felt very well, went out a great deal and even agreed to take part in a theatrical performance which was to be produced at the house of Countess S. A. Tolstoy in the beginning of the following month. Several scenes from Count A. K. Tolstoy's trilogy were to be performed, and Fiodor chose the part of the ascetic monk in *The Death of Ivan the Terrible*.

During the last three years his attacks of epilepsy had ceased to torment him, and his healthy and cheerful manner gave us all the hope that he would get through the winter satisfactorily. In the middle of the month he began working on the January number of *The Journal of an Author*, in which issue he had wished to express his ideas and opinions on the ' Zemsky Sobor ' Constitution. The subject of his article being one which the censor might object to, Fiodor felt very anxious about it. But the newly-appointed President of the Censorship Board, N. S. Abasa, having learnt from Countess S. A. Tolstoy of this anxiety, asked her to tell Fiodor not to worry, as he himself would be the censor of the article. By 25th January the article was ready and sent off to the printers. So, to have *The Journal* ready for delivery on the last day of the month all that remained to be done was the passing of the article by

[1] Here is a lacuna in the text.

the censor, the final reading of the proofs, and the actual printing of the review.

January 25th was a Sunday, and we had many visitors. Professor C. F. Miller came to ask my husband to give a reading on 29th January, the anniversary of Pushkin's death, at a literary evening for the benefit of poor students. Not sure that his article in *The Journal* would pass the censor, in which case he might have to write a new article, Fiodor at first refused ; but finally he agreed. As all our visitors noticed, Fiodor was quite well and cheerful, and nothing foreboded what was to happen a few hours later.

On the morning of 26th January Fiodor got up as usual at one o'clock, and, when I came into his study, he told me that during the night the following circumstance had occurred. His penholder dropped on the floor and rolled down under the bookcase. Now he wanted the penholder ; for he used it not only for writing, but also for making his cigarettes. So in order to find it he shifted the bookcase, which was heavy. Owing to this effort, an artery in one of his lungs suddenly burst, and blood came from his throat. But as the hæmorrhage was only slight my husband paid no attention to it, and did not even trouble to wake me. As I listened to his account I became much alarmed, and without saying a word to him I sent our errand boy, Peter, to fetch Doctor I. von Bretzel, who always attended him. Unfortunately the doctor had already gone out, and would not be back before 5 o'clock.

Fiodor was perfectly calm. He talked and played with the children, [1] and then began reading the *Novoye Vremya*. About three o'clock a friend came to see us,

[1] *Aimée* (born 14th September, 1869. After the Russian Revolution she left Russia ; lives abroad ; in 1920 she published a book on her father). *Fiodor* (born 16th July, 1871 ; died in 1922 (?)). Their first child, *Sonia*, was born February, 1868, died May, 1868. Their last child, *Aliosha*, was born in August, 1875, and died on 16th May, 1878).

a very kind man whom Fiodor rather liked, but who had the fault of always entering into terrible discussions. They began talking of Fiodor's coming article in *The Journal.* The man began to argue some point ; Fiodor, who was somewhat upset by the hæmorrhage of the previous night, replied, and a heated discussion arose between them. My attempts to stop the argument failed ; although I told the visitor twice that Fiodor was not quite well and that it was bad for him to talk so much and so loudly. At last about five o'clock the visitor left, and we were on the point of having dinner, when all at once Fiodor sat down on his couch, and was silent for a couple of minutes. Then, to my horror, I suddenly noticed that his chin was covered with blood, which ran in a thin stream over his beard. I cried out, and the servants and children came running to my call. Fiodor, however, was not alarmed ; on the contrary he began asking me and the crying children to be quiet. He took the children to his writing table and showed them the number of the just-received *Dragon Fly*, with a cartoon of two fishermen, entangled in their nets, and struggling in the water. He even read the accompanying verses to the children, and did it so merrily that they calmed down. About an hour passed, and the doctor arrived. When he began examining and sounding the patient's chest, a new hæmorrhage occurred, and this time it was so violent that Fiodor lost consciousness. When he came to, his first words addressed to me were :

" Anya, I beg you, send immediately for a priest, I wish to make my confession and to receive the last sacrament."

Although the doctor began assuring us that there was no particular danger, yet to set the patient at ease, I did as he wished me. We lived near the Vladimir Church, and Father Megorsky, who was summoned, arrived in half an hour's time. Fiodor received him calmly and kindly and remained closeted with him for

some time. When the priest left, the children and I
went into the study and Fiodor blessed me and the
children and asked them to live in peace, to love one
another, and to love and cherish me. When the children
had left the room, Fiodor thanked me for the happiness
I had given him and asked me to forgive him if he had
ever caused me pain. I stood more dead than alive,
not having the strength to make any answer. The
doctor came in, settled Fiodor on the couch, and forbade
him the least movement or conversation. Then he
asked me to send immediately for two other doctors—
his friend Pfeirer and Professor Koshlakov (the latter
of whom my husband had often consulted). Koshlakov
understood from Doctor von Bretzel's note that the
patient was in a grave condition, and he arrived at
once. This time Fiodor was not subjected to an examination, and the Professor declared that, as so little
blood had been lost (two glasses during three hæmorr-
hages), a " stopper " might be formed, and then Fiodor
would be on the way to recovery. Von Bretzel spent
the night with Fiodor, who seemed to sleep quietly.
I, too, went to bed only in the morning.

The whole day of the 27th passed quietly. Fiodor
had no hæmorrhage, and had evidently calmed down.
He was cheerful, asked me to call in the children, and
even spoke to them, in a whisper. In the afternoon he
began to worry about *The Journal*. The foreman from
Souvorin's printing house brought the last galley, and
there were seven lines too many, which had to be struck
out. I suggested to my husband that I should do it, and
he agreed. I kept the foreman waiting for half an hour ;
but after two corrections which I showed to Fiodor, the
matter was settled. On learning from the printer that
galleys of the January number of *The Journal* had been
sent to the censor and passed by him, Fiodor felt greatly
relieved.

The news of Fiodor's grave illness spread through the

town, and from two o'clock till late at night the door bell kept on ringing, so that we had to tie it up. Friends and strangers kept on coming to inquire about Fiodor's health, and letters of sympathy and telegrams kept on being delivered.

According to the doctor's orders no one was to be admitted to the patient ; but I came out now and then for a couple of minutes to tell our friends of his condition. Fiodor was very pleased too by the general attention and sympathy, questioned me in a whisper, and even dictated me a few lines in reply to a kind letter. Professor Koshlakov arrived, and said that the patient's condition had considerably improved, and assured him that he would be up in a week's time and would be quite well in a fortnight. He ordered the patient to sleep as much as possible ; and, therefore, we all went early to bed. As I had spent the previous night without sleep, in a chair, I had a mattress brought in now and placed on the floor by the couch on which Fiodor lay, so that he could easily wake me at any moment. Tired as I was, I quickly fell asleep ; but I got up several times during the night, and, by the light of the night lamp, I saw my dear patient sleeping quietly. I awoke at 7 o'clock, and saw my husband looking in my direction.

" How do you feel, my dear ? " I asked him as I bent over him.

" Do you know, Anya," Fiodor said in a whisper, " I have been awake these three hours and thinking all the time ; and I have just realised clearly that I shall die to-day."

" My darling, why should you think so ? " I said in terrible anxiety. " You are better now, you have had no hæmorrhage, and probably all is going well, as Koshlakov said it would. For the love of Christ, do not torment yourself with doubts. You have still a long time to live, I assure you."

" No, I know, that I shall die to-day ! Light the candle, Anya, and give me the New Testament."

That copy of the New Testament was given to Fiodor as a present, in Tobolsk, at the time he was on the march to Siberia to serve his term of hard labour, by the wives of the Decembrists (Mesdames P. E. Annenkov and her daughter, Olga N. D. Muraviov-Apostol, Von-Visin). They entreated the prison inspector to allow them to see the political prisoners, with whom they spent an hour. They blessed them, crossed them, and gave each one of them a copy of the New Testament—the only book allowed in prison. Fiodor during the four years of his hard labour never once parted with the holy book. And all his life afterwards that book was always on his writing table. Very often, as he thought of something or doubted something, he would open the New Testament, and read the first lines on the opened left-hand page. This time, too, Fiodor wished to verify his doubts by means of the New Testament. He opened the holy book and asked me to read.

It opened on St. Matthew, Chapter III, 14.

" But John forbad him, saying, I have need to be baptised of thee, and comest thou to me ? And Jesus answering said unto him, ' Suffer it to be so now : for thus it becometh us to fulfil all righteousness.' "

" Do you see, Anya ? ' Suffer it to be so now,'[1] it means that I am to die," my husband said, and closed the book.

I could not restrain my tears. Fiodor began comforting me, saying kind and loving words and thanking me for the happy life he had enjoyed with me. He entrusted the children to me, and said that he believed in me and hoped I would always love and cherish them. Then he spoke words to me which not many a husband

---

[1] In the old Russian version the word " suffer " is translated " do not hold me back."

could have spoken to his wife after fourteen years of married life :

" Remember, Anya, I have always loved you ardently and have never been unfaithful to you even in my thoughts."

I was deeply moved by his dear words ; but I was also alarmed, fearing that the agitation might do him harm. I implored him not to think of death, nor to grieve us all by his doubts : I asked him to rest, to sleep. My husband did as I asked him. He stopped talking ; but his composed face clearly showed that the idea of death had not left him, and that the passing into the other world did not frighten him.

About ten o'clock in the morning Fiodor fell into a quiet sleep with his hand enclosed in mine. I sat without stirring, afraid to break his sleep. At eleven he suddenly woke, raised his head from the pillow, and blood began to flow from his mouth. I was in complete despair ; but I tried my best to preserve a cheerful air, assuring my husband that the flow of blood was very slight and that it would stop just as it did the previous day. To my reassuring words Fiodor shook his head sadly, as though perfectly convinced that his prediction of his death would be fulfilled that day.

In the afternoon relations, friends and strangers began calling again, and letters and telegrams kept on arriving. Pashal Issayev (Dostoevsky's stepson), to whom I had sent a letter the day before telling him of my husband's illness, also arrived. He insisted on coming up to the patient ; but the doctor would not allow this. Then he began peering through the chinks of the door into the patient's room. Fiodor noticed his peering, was upset by it, and said to me :

" Anya, don't let him in to me, he will upset me ! "

Issayev meanwhile got very excited, telling everyone who came to hear of Fiodor's condition, friends and strangers alike, that his ' father ' had made no will, and that a solicitor ought to be sent for, so that Dostoevsky might personally dispose of his estate. Professor Koshlakov, who had come to see the patient, learning from the stepson of his intention to fetch a solicitor, objected to it, and declared that Fiodor must not be disturbed, that such a business scene, which would demand his explanations and instructions, could only strengthen the patient's idea of his imminent death, and that the slightest agitation might kill him.

Indeed, there was no need for a will : the copyright of his works had been given me as a present by Fiodor as far back as 1873. Apart from the five thousand roubles, which were due to us from *The Russky Vestnik*, Fiodor had nothing, and surely that small sum belonged to us, that is, to my children and myself.

All day long I did not leave my husband for a single minute : he held my hand in his and kept on saying to me in a whisper : " . . . my poor . . . my dear . . . how I am leaving you . . . my poor . . . how hard life will be for you ! "

I reassured him and comforted him with the hope of his recovery ; but it was clear that he himself did not entertain that hope, and was tormented by the idea that he was leaving his family almost without means. Indeed, the four or five thousand roubles which *The Russky Vestnik* owed us were our sole resources.

Several times he whispered : " Call in the children ! " I called them in. My husband held out his lips to them and they kissed him ; and then, as requested by the doctors, they left at once, Fiodor's eyes following them with a sad glance. Two hours before his death, when the children came in again at his request, Fiodor told me to give his New Testament to our son Fedya.

During the day a great number of people called, but I could not go out to them. Apollon Maikov was admitted to Fiodor and talked with him for some time, Fiodor answering his greetings in a whisper. About seven o'clock many people were gathered in our drawing and dining rooms, waiting for Koshlakov, who used to call at that hour. Suddenly without any visible cause Fiodor gave a shiver, slightly raised himself on the couch, and a trickle of blood again coloured his face. We began giving him little pieces of ice ; but the hæmorrhage did not stop. At that moment A. Maikov and his wife came again, and the good Anna Ivanovna went off to fetch Doctor Tcherepnin. Fiodor lay unconscious. The children and I knelt by his side and wept, making the greatest effort not to cry aloud ; for the doctor said that the last sense to leave a man was that of hearing, and that any emotional disturbance would prolong the agonies and pains of the dying man. I held my husband's hands in mine and felt his pulse growing weaker and weaker. At 8.38 Fiodor passed into eternity.[1]

When the end came, my children and I gave way to our despair : we wept and cried, and kissed the face and hands of our dear deceased. All this I remember only vaguely ; but I was clearly conscious of this alone, that from that minute my personal life, full of boundless happiness, had come to an end, and that in my soul I should for ever remain alone. To me, who so ardently, so devotedly loved my husband, and was so proud of the love, friendship, and regard given me by this rare man, the loss was irreparable. During those truly terrible moments of parting it seemed to me that I should not survive the death of my husband, that my heart would immediately burst or that I should go mad.

Of course, nearly everyone has experienced in his life the loss of some one dear to him. But at such unforgettable moments most people support their sorrow in their own family, among their relations and intimate

---

[1] Someone present (I believe it was Markevich) fixed the exact time of Fiodor's death.

friends, and can express their feelings without having to restrain themselves. Such good fortune was not granted me : my dear husband died in the presence of a number of people—some deeply attached to him, and some quite indifferent both to him and to the disconsolate grief of his family. To increase my sorrow, among those present was also the author B. M. Markevich, who had never before visited our house, but who now came at the request of Countess S. A. Tolstoy to learn of Fiodor's condition. From my knowledge of Markevich I was sure that he would not be able to restrain himself from describing the last moments of my husband's life ; and I was deeply sorry that the death of my beloved husband did not occur in private, in the presence of those only who were devoted to him. My apprehensions came true. I learnt with grief the next day that Markevich had sent to *The Moskovskya Vedomosti* an " artistic " description of the sad event. In a few days I read the article itself, and a great deal in it I failed to recognise. I could not recognise myself in the words I was alleged to have said ; so little did they correspond to my character and my inner state during those unforgettable moments. . . .

But God in His mercy sent me also a comfort : at ten o'clock that sad night my brother Ivan arrived. He had come up from the country on some business to Moscow, and having completed it, it suddenly occurred to him to go to Petersburg to see us. True, he had read in the papers of Fiodor's illness ; but he attached no importance to it, thinking that it was just a violent attack of epilepsy. The train was late, and my brother stopped at a hotel and decided to call on us in the evening. When he drove up to the house he saw all the windows of our flat lit up, and two or three suspicious-looking fellows standing near the entrance. One of these fellows followed my brother to the staircase and whispered to him :

" Sir, do us the favour and see that the order is given to us, please."

" What do you mean, what order ? " my brother asked in bewilderment.

" We are from so and so, undertakers, and wish to get the order for the coffin."

" But who has died ? " my brother asked.

" A writing fellow, I can't remember the name. The house-porter told us."

My brother ran upstairs, entered the open hall, where there were several people. Leaving his coat there, he entered the study where Fiodor's body lay. . . .

On 30th January N. S. Abasa, Court Chamberlain, came to the afternoon Mass and brought me a letter from the Minister of Finance in which " in gratitude for services rendered by the deceased to Russian literature," I was informed that an annual pension of two thousand roubles had been conferred on me and my children by His Majesty. . . .

I must say that I remember with terror the two and a half days during which the body of my husband lay in the house. The most tormenting thing was that our flat was all the time packed with people. A dense stream of people, some coming through the front door, and others through the back, was continually passing through all our rooms, and coming to a stop in the study. At moments the air there got so heavy and so deprived of oxygen that the icon lamp and candles surrounding the catafalque went out. Strangers kept on coming not only during the day time but also during the night ; there were people who wanted to spend the night near Fiodor's coffin ; others wanted to read psalms for hours, and read them. . . .

Deputations kept on arriving . . . I had to come out to them, and the head of each deputation, having previously prepared his speech, began talking about the

importance of my husband to Russian literature, point-
ing out the high ideals he had preached, and saying
" What a great loss Russian literature had suffered by
his death." I listened to these speeches in silence,
thanked the speakers, shook hands with them, and went
back to my room. In a few minutes another deputation would arrive and wish to see me. And again I
listened to speeches about the importance of my
husband and of " the loss which Russia had suffered."
Having listened for three days to many speeches of
condolence, I was at last overcome with despair.

" Lord," I said to myself, " how they worry me !
What does it matter to me ' whom Russia has lost.'
Why don't you think whom I have lost ? I have lost
the best man in the whole world, the man who was my
joy, my pride, the happiness of my life, my sun, my
deity. Have compassion on *me*, pity *me*, and don't
talk to me of Russia's loss at this moment."

And when one of the members of the numerous
deputations expressed his pity for me, as distinct from
' Russia,' I was so deeply moved that I seized his hand
and kissed it. . . .

On Saturday, 31st January, Fiodor's body was
removed to the Alexandro-Nevsky Monastery. . . .
The funeral procession presented a majestic spectacle :
long rows of wreaths, carried on poles, numerous student
choirs, and a huge crowd of many tens of thousands of
people following the coffin. . . . All institutions,
societies and associations, each on its own initiative,
sent deputations with wreaths. All parties of all
schools united in the common feeling of grief at the death
of Dostoevsky, and in a sincere desire to honour his
memory.

The funeral procession left the house at 11 o'clock,
and it was after two o'clock when it reached the Alexandro-Nevsky Monastery. I walked with my son and
daughter, and all the time I was oppressed by sad

thoughts. " How shall I bring up my children without their father, without Fiodor, who loved them so well ? What a great responsibility rests now on me to the memory of my husband : shall I be able to fulfil my duties worthily ? " As I followed Fiodor's coffin, I made a vow—to live for our children ; I vowed to devote the rest of my life to the glorification of my husband's memory and to the spreading of his noble ideas. . . . Now, nearing the end of my life, I say, with my hand on my heart, that all the promises made by me in these painful hours I fulfilled to the utmost of my powers and ability.

PART II

DOSTOEVSKY AND TURGENEV

DOSTOEVSKY AND TURGENEV

(Letters relating to their quarrel)

DOSTOEVSKY'S famous letter to Maikov of 16th–28th August, 1867, published below, originally appeared in Russian in *The Biography and Letters of F. M. Dostoevsky*, Petersburg, 1883, with considerable omissions and the names of Turgenev and Goncharov left out. It was published in full in the September number of the *Russky Archiv* for 1902. Its history is as follows. A person who wished to remain unknown handed over a copy of Dostoevsky's letter to the Editor of the *Russky Archiv* with the request that it should be kept in the Tchertkov Library until 1890.

Turgenev, who learnt about the letter from his friend Annenkov by the end of 1867, wrote the following letter to Mr. Barteniev, the Editor of the *Russky Archiv* :

" The news has reached me that a letter signed by F. M. Dostoevsky, addressed to you, has been deposited in the Tchertkov Library, and that in that letter, which is not to be made public before 1890, disgusting and absurd opinions about Russia and Russians are attributed by him to me. According to the assurance of Mr. F. M. Dostoevsky, these opinions forming as it were my innermost conviction, were expressed by me in his presence at Baden, last summer, during the only visit with which he honoured me there. Without going into the question of how such an abuse of confidence can be justified, I find myself compelled to declare on my part that to express my innermost convictions to

Mr. Dostoevsky I should consider inappropriate, were it only because I regard him as a man, who, through morbid fits and other causes, is not in full possession of his mental powers. This opinion of mine, by the way, is shared by many others. I met Mr. Dostoevsky, as I have said, only once there. He sat with me not more than an hour and, having relieved his heart by a severe abuse of the Germans, of myself and of my last book, retired. I scarcely had time or the desire to reply to him : I repeat, I treated him as a sick person. Probably, to his deranged imagination there occurred those arguments which he had expected to hear from me, and so he wrote . . . a denunciation of me to posterity. Without a doubt, neither Mr. Dostoevsky nor myself is likely to attract the attention of our countrymen in 1890 ; and if we have not been completely forgotten then, we shall be judged not by one-sided fulminations, but by the results of our whole lives and activities. Still I thought it my duty to protest now against such a distortion of my views."

On 24th April, 1871, Turgenev gave the following account to Polonsky of Dostoevsky's visit : " He came to me not to pay back the money which he had borrowed from me but to condemn me for *Smoke*, which according to him should have been burnt by the common hangman. I listened, in silence, to all his philippic ; but what am I to learn afterwards ? That I am alleged to have expressed to him all sorts of criminal ideas, which he hastened to inform Barteniev of. (B. actually wrote me about it.) It would be calumny plain and simple if Dostoevsky had not been mad, of which I have not the slightest doubt. Perhaps all this was what he really imagined. But, Lord, how petty and unimportant it all is ! "

In connection with Dostoevsky's letter to Maikov, in which his dislike of Turgenev is expressed quite clearly, it may be appropriate to add that the character of Karmasinov,[1] the author, in *The Devils* (called *The Possessed* in the English translation) is a malicious portrait of Turgenev, as visualised and presented by Dostoevsky.

How did Turgenev regard this caricature ? According to the evidence of a reliable witness Turgenev, having perused the passage in *The Devils* with the description of Karmasinov, smiled good-naturedly and said that "it was done in a perfectly Aristophanic manner." But after a careful reading of the novel Turgenev wrote to his friend, Mme. M. A. Milyutin, on 3rd December, 1872 : " Dostoevsky has permitted himself a something worse than parody ; in the character of Karmasinov he has presented me as secretly sympathising with the party of Nechayev.[2] And the strange thing is that for the original of his parody he has taken the only story of mine which appeared in the review he once edited, a story for which he overwhelmed me with laudatory and grateful letters. I have preserved these letters. How amusing it would be to publish them now ! But he knows that I shall not do it. It only remains for me to regret that he employs his indubitable talent for the gratification of such unseemly feelings : evidently, he values his talent too little if he stoops to a lampoon."

What really upset Turgenev was that Dostoevsky, in the character of Verkhovensky *père*, had pilloried his late friend Granovsky. Yet when *The Devils* was bitterly attacked by the reviewers, Turgenev most generously defended the novel, and gave it high praise.

---

[1] The very name Karmasinov (from the French, *carmin, cramoisie*) is significant, as it alludes to Turgenev's predilection for radical views and his admiration of Western culture. The names given by Dostoevsky to his characters are indeed never casual. There is always a deep meaning hidden in them. Viacheslav Ivanov has made a special study of the subject, and it is curious that he derives Stavrogin's (*The Devils*) name from the Greek STAUROS, as indicating Stavrogin's " crusade."

[2] An extreme revolutionary.

DOSTOEVSKY IN A NEW LIGHT

One of Dostoevsky's " laudatory and grateful letters "
to Turgenev has recently been made public in Russia,[1]
and is here reproduced :—

Letter written by F. M. Dostoevsky to I. S. Turgenev.

" Petersburg, December 23rd, 1863.

" Kindest and much respected Ivan Sergueyevich,

P. A. Annenkov told my brother that you were not
going to publish your story, *Ghosts*, because there was
a good deal of the fantastic in it. This perplexes me
awfully. First of all I must frankly say that we, my
brother and myself, count on your story. It will
greatly help us with the first number of our *Review*,
which we are *starting afresh* and which we, therefore,
must try again to push to the front. I expressly warn
you of this in order that in the further reasons I adduce
you may not suspect me of speaking for my own
personal ends. I must add one more circumstance, for
the truth of which I give you my word of honour : it
is your story that we need much more than the flaunting
of your name on the cover of the *Review*.

" Now I shall say a few words about your story, as
it impressed me. Why do you think, Ivan Sergueyevich (if, indeed, you think so), that your *Ghosts* will
not suit the times and will not be understood ? On
the contrary, the mediocrities, who have for six years
been imitating the masters, have brought the realistic
to such a pitch of banality, that people would just be
delighted with a poetical work (a most poetical work).
Many will receive it with a certain perplexity, but with
a pleased perplexity,—such an effect will it have on all
those who understand, both of the old and of the new
generation. As regards those who understand nothing
—well, is it worth taking any notice of them ? You

---

[1] In *Pechati Revoluzia*, No. 6, 1924. The letter originally appeared
in the *Revue des Etudes Slaves* (1921, Paris).

F. M. DOSTOEVSKY in 1847, at the age of 26
(*From a pencil drawing* by K. A. Troutovsky)

[*face p. 200*

would not believe the way they regard literature. Circumscribed utilitarianism—that's all they demand. Write for them the most poetic work, they would put it aside and take the one in which a flogging is described. *Poetic truth* they regard as nonsense. They want only copies from actual facts. Our prose is terrifying. *Quakerism*! After that one should just ignore them. The healthy section of the public, which is awakening, longs for a bold adventure in art. And your *Ghosts* is a sufficiently courageous adventure, and it will serve as a splendid example (to all of us) if you, the first of us, were to embark on such an adventure. The form of *Ghosts* is bound to strike everybody. And its realistic side will afford occasion for all kinds of wonder (save the wonder of fools and of those who, apart from their *Quakerism, do not want* to understand anything). Yet I know of a certain Utilitarian (a Nihilist) who, although dissatisfied with your story, said that he could not tear himself away from it, and that it was bound to produce a strong impression. (We, indeed, have a great multitude of would-be Nihilists.) But the principal thing is to perceive the realistic side of the story. In my opinion there is too much of the realistic in *Ghosts*. The realistic in it is the *nostalgia of an educated and thinking person of our time*, a nostalgia fully realised. Of that nostalgia *Ghosts* is full. It is 'the string sounding in the mist,' and it is well that it sounds. *Ghosts* is like music. By the way, how do you regard music? As an enjoyment or as a real necessity? In my opinion it is the same as language, only it expresses what consciousness has *not yet* grasped (not the mind, but the whole consciousness), and therefore it brings *positive* good. Our utilitarians won't understand this; but those of them who love music *have not given it up*, but go on with it as ever before.

The form of your *Ghosts* is superb. If there is any-thing questionable about it, it could, of course, only be as regards its form.   And so the whole point will be in the question : Has the fantastic the right to exist in art ? Well, who answers such questions? If anything in *Ghosts* could be said to call at all for criticism it would be that the story is not *quite fully fantastic.* There ought to be more of this.   Then its *daring* would be greater still.   The creature appearing in your story is explained as a vampire.   I think the explanation is not needed.   Annenkov disagreed with me and argued that it contained allusions to the loss of blood, that is, of the vital energies, etc.   But I, too, disagree with him.   It is quite enough for me to realise thoroughly the nostalgia and the beautiful form in which it is presented, that is, the travailing going on in the whole of reality *without any relief.*   And the *tone* is good, the tone of gentle sadness, without any malice.   And then your pictures, the cliff and the other allusions to the elemental, as yet unsolved, idea (the same idea that exists in the whole of nature).   The idea, about which we cannot say whether it is ever going to solve human problems, but now it fills the heart with anguish and frightens it still more, and yet the heart cannot tear itself away from it.   No, that idea is quite timely and such fantastic works are *very definitely real. . . .*"

(The last page of the letter seems to be missing.)
Now we give the material passages of Dostoevsky's letter to Maikov :

" Geneva, 16th/28th August, 1867.

" What a long time I have kept silent and have refrained from answering your dear letter, my dear and unforgettable friend, Apollon Nicolayevich.   I call you *unforgettable friend*, and I feel in my heart that the name is right : you and I are such old and familiar friends that life, that has separated and even *parted* us at times, has not only not parted us but perhaps has even finally bound us closer together.

" If you say that you have felt my absence a little, then how much more have I felt yours. Apart from the conviction that has been daily reasserting itself in me of the similarity and closeness of our ideas and feelings—take into consideration also this that I, besides having lost you, have got into a foreign country, where there is not only no Russian face, no Russian books, no Russian ideas, nor interests, but no welcoming face. Indeed, I can't understand how a Russian living abroad, if only he has feeling and sense, does not see this and feel it with pain. Perhaps those foreign faces are welcoming to one another, but to us they do not seem like that. *Indeed, it is so* ! And how can one live one's life abroad ? Without one's country—one *suffers*, I swear ! It is right to go abroad for six months, for a year. But to go, like myself, without knowing or telling when I am to go back—it is very bad and hard. The mere idea is painful. And I need Russia, I need her for my *writing* and for my work (without mentioning the rest of life), and how badly I need her ! I am like a fish out of water ; I am losing my strength and chances. . . .

" You know how I left and for what reasons. The principal reasons were two. The first : to save not only my health, but my very life. My fits began to recur every week, and to feel and to be aware of the nervous and *cerebral* derangement was unendurable. My mind was indeed getting deranged—that is the truth.   I was conscious of it ; and my nervous derangement drove me at times to wild moments. The second reason or circumstance was : my creditors would not wait any longer, and by the time I was leaving, legal proceedings had already been instituted.

(There follows an account of his debts.)

"... I went away then ; but I left with death in my soul.   I did not believe in Europe ; that is, I believed that its moral influence would be a very bad one : alone, as I was, *without material*, and with a young creature who with naive joy aspired to share with me my wandering life !   And I did see that in that naïve joy there was a great deal of inexperience and feverishness, and that worried and tormented me.   I was afraid that Anna Gregorevna,[1] left with me alone, would tire of it.   And, we have, indeed, up till now been quite by *ourselves*.   I could not count on myself ;   my disposition is a morbid one, and I foresaw that she would be borne down by me.   (*N.B.*—True, Anna Gregorevna turned out to be stronger and deeper than I had known and thought her to be.   On many occasions she has simply been my guardian angel ;   but at the same time there is in her a great deal of the child and of the girl of twenty.   This is excellent and quite *natural* ;   but I hardly have the power or capacity to respond to it.   All this I was vaguely turning over in my mind at the time I went away, and although, as I say again, Anna Gregorevna has turned out stronger and better than I thought, yet I am still not easy in my mind.)   Finally, our scanty means gave me anxiety ;   we went away with not much money, and on an *advance* of three thousand roubles made by Katkov.   It is true, I had reckoned on getting to work immediately on leaving for abroad.   And what's the result ?   Nothing, or nearly nothing have I done up to now, and only now at last am I sitting down to work seriously.   True, as regards my having done *nothing*, I am *still* in doubt ;   for I have gone through and *thought out* a great deal.   But in written matter, in *black* and *white*, I haven't much to show, and surely the *black* and *white* is the conclusive thing ;   it is for that that money is paid.

---

[1] Dostoevsky's young wife.

" Having left as soon as we could tedious Berlin (where I stayed for one day, and where the tedious Germans managed nevertheless to upset my nerves to the point of anger, and where I went to a Russian vapour bath), we came to Dresden, took rooms and settled there for a time.

" The impression was a very queer one. At once the question presented itself to me : why am I in Dresden, just in Dresden of all places, and why was it worth while to leave everything in one place and to come to another ? But the answer was a clear one (my health, escape from the creditors, etc.). But what was indeed bad was that I realised too clearly that now, wherever I lived, it was all the same to me—in Dresden or anywhere else abroad, anywhere I should feel a cut off slice. I had meant to sit down to work at once ; but I felt that I positively was not in the right disposition, the mood was positively not for work. What did I do then ? I vegetated. I read, wrote a little, wore myself down with nostalgia, and then with the heat. The days passed monotonously by.

" I shall not describe my thoughts. Many impressions had accumulated. I had been reading Russian papers and releasing my soul. I felt at last, that I had accumulated material enough for a long article on the relations of Russia to Europe, and on the upper stratum of Russian society. But what is the use of talking about it? The Germans upset my nerves ; and our Russian life, the life of our upper stratum, and its belief in Europe and *civilisation* did the same. The event in Paris[1] upset me terribly. Fine Paris advocates shouting *Vive la Pologne* ! Bah, how filthy and, worst of all, how stupid and threadbare ! I have become still more convinced of my old idea : that it is rather to our advantage that Europe does not know us or knows us so badly.

---

[1] Beresovsky's attempt on the life of the Russian Tsar, Alexander II.

And those details of Beresovsky's trial! How stereotyped the whole beastly thing; but worst of all, worst of all how they still blabber away, how they still go on turning round and round on the same spot, always round and round the same spot.

Russia, too, is seen from here in greater perspective. The extraordinary fact of the soundness and unexpected maturity of the Russian people in confronting all our reforms (if you take only the reform in legal procedure)! And yet along with that comes the account of a big merchant having been flogged by a Captain of Police in the Orenburg District! One is aware of this: that the Russian people, thanks to its Benefactor and to his reforms, has at last gradually come into a position in which it is bound to learn efficiency, and self-knowledge. Therein is the whole point. I swear that the present, through its break with the past, and through its reforms is almost more important than the time of Peter the Great. And what about the roads?[1] Those to the south should be laid down as soon as possible, as soon as possible; therein is the whole point. By then and with the establishment of *just laws* all over the country, then, what a great renewal! (Of all that I think and dream here; and my heart is pulsating with it all.) Here I meet almost nobody, but one can't help unexpectedly coming across someone. In Germany I came across a Russian who resides permanently abroad; he goes to Russia every year, for a couple of weeks, in order to collect his revenue, and returns to Germany, where he has a wife and children—they have all become germanised. I asked him, by the way:

" ' What made you expatriate yourself? '

" Literally (and with the insolence of irritation) he replied :

" ' Here is civilisation, and there barbarism.' . . .

[1] The historical gravitation of Russia to the Black Sea and Constantinople is here hinted at.

" . . . That man belongs to the young progressives, though I think he keeps himself apart. Here abroad they turn into grumbling and whining curs.

" At last our loneliness in Dresden wore down both Anna Gregorevna and myself. . . . We decided to spend the winter somewhere in Switzerland or Italy. But money there was none. What money I had received was all gone. I wrote to Katkov, described to him the whole position, and asked him for another five hundred roubles *in advance*. What do you think : he sent them ! What a superb man he is ! He is a man with a heart ! We went to Switzerland. But here I shall begin to describe to you my villainies and shames.

" Dearest Apollon Nicolayevich, I feel I can consider you as my judge. You are a man with a heart, of which you had convinced me long ago ; in the end I always valued your judgment. To make a confession to you does not pain me. But I write for *yourself* alone. Do not deliver me to the judgment of others.

" Passing near Baden I took it into my head to have a look round there. A tempting idea plagued me : to risk ten louis d'or, and perhaps I might win at least two thousand francs, and that would be enough to live on for four months, for ourselves and for those in Petersburg. The wickedest thing about it, as I have found previously, is that I sometimes happened to win. And the worst of all is my rotten and too passionate nature. In everything and everywhere I go to the very last limit ; all my life long I have gone beyond the limit.

" The devil at once played a trick on me : in three days I won four thousand francs with extraordinary ease. Now I'll tell you how it all presented itself to me : on the one hand, that easy gain—with one *hundred francs* I made in three days four thousand ; on the other hand, my debts, the legal proceedings, the anxiety, the impossibility of returning to Russia ; and, finally, the third and chief reason—the game itself. You know how absorbing it is! No, I swear to you, it was not the mere money, although above all I needed money for its own sake. Anna Gregorevna implored me to be satisfied with the four thousand francs and to leave the town at once. What an easy and practicable chance of setting everything right! And the examples before my eyes? Not to speak of my own gains, I saw every day how others win twenty, or thirty thousand francs (one does not see those who lose). Are they holier than I am? I need money much more than they do. I risked more and lost. I began to lose my very last; in feverish agitation—I lost. I began to pawn our clothes. Anna Gregorevna has taken to the pawnshop *everything* of hers, her very last things. (What an angel! How she comforted me, how lonely she felt in damned Baden, in our two rooms over the smithy to which we had removed!) Then came the end, all was lost. (O, how mean the Germans are, how all and sundry are usurers, scoundrels and swindlers! Our landlady, seeing that we must receive money before we could leave, raised the rent!) Finally, it became necessary, to save ourselves, to go away from Baden. Again I wrote to Katkov, again I asked him for another five hundred roubles (without telling him of my circumstances; but, my letter coming as it did from Baden, he must have guessed something). Well, he did send the money! He did! Altogether I have now had *in advance* four thousand roubles from *The Russky Vestnik.*

" But to be done with Baden : in Baden, in that hell, we worried our lives out for seven weeks. At the very start, when I had just arrived there, I came across Goncharov at the tables, the very next day! How shy Goncharov was of me at first! That Civil or Actual State Councillor was also losing. But since it was impossible for either of us to hide away, and as moreover I play with too crude frankness, then he, too, ceased to fight shy of me. He played with feverish excitement (staking small sums, in silver), he played the whole fortnight he spent in Baden, and I believe he lost considerably. But may God keep him, the dear fellow. When I gambled away every penny (and he saw a lot of gold in my hands) he made me, at my request, a loan of sixty francs. He must have condemned me awfully : why have I lost everything, and not half, like himself !

" Goncharov was talking to me all the time about Turgenev ; so that, although I put off calling on the latter, I at last made up my mind to pay him a visit. I went to him one morning at twelve, and found him at lunch. I tell you frankly : even before I never liked that man personally. The worst of it is that as far back as 1857,[1] in Wiesbaden, I borrowed from him fifty thalers and have not paid them yet ! Also I dislike the aristocratic-pharisaic embrace with which he comes up to you, and puts up his cheek for you to kiss. That General's manner, too ! And above all his book *Smoke*[2] irritated me. He told me himself that the principal idea, the basic point of his book, is contained in the phrase : ' Were Russia to go under there would be no loss, or excitement among mankind.' He declared to me that that was his fundamental conviction concerning Russia. I found him terribly irritated by the failure of his *Smoke*. And I must admit I did not know all the details of the failure. You wrote me about Strakhov's article in the *Otechestvennya Zapiski* ; but I did not know that he had been everywhere attacked, and that (in Moscow, I believe) in a club names had been collected for a protest against the book. He himself

---

[1] The date is erroneous. Instead of 1857 it ought to be 1863, as can be gathered from what Dostoevsky says later in his letter about Turgenev : " His crawling before the Germans I had observed as long back as four years ago."

[2] *Smoke*, Turgenev's novel, appeared in *Russky Vestnik*, in the first three numbers of 1867.

told me so. I confess to you I could not possibly have imagined that a man could have shown all the wounds of his self-love so naïvely and clumsily as Turgenev did. And these men boast, by the way, of their being atheists! He declared to me that he was a complete atheist! But, goodness me! Theism has given us Christ, that is, such a high conception of man as cannot be apprehended without reverence, and one can't help believing that it is the eternal ideal of mankind. And what have they—the Turgenevs, Herzens, Outins, Chernyshevskys—given us? Instead of the highest divine beauty, at which they spit, all of them are so filthily egotistical, so shamelessly irritable, light-mindedly proud, that one simply can't make out what they hope for and who will follow them. Turgenev abused Russia and Russians disgustingly, terribly. But this is what I observed : all these little Liberals and Progressives, still pre-eminently of Belinsky's school, find it their principal pleasure and satisfaction to rail at Russia, the difference only being that the followers of Chernyshevsky revile Russia plainly, and frankly wish her to go under (above all, to go under!) But these offshoots add that they *love Russia*. And yet not only is everything that is in the least original in Russia hateful to them, so that they deny it and instantly delight to turn it into caricature ; but if you were at last to present to them actually a fact, which could neither be refuted nor caricatured, but with which even they could not fail to agree, then it seems to me that they would be tormentingly, achingly, desperately unhappy. I also noticed that Turgenev (just like all the others who have not been in Russia for a long time) decidedly knew no facts. (Although they read newspapers.) They have so palpably lost all sensitiveness about Russia, that they fail to understand ordinary facts, which even our Russian Nihilists no longer deny ; though they, too, caricature them in their own way.

By the way, he said that we ought to crawl before the Germans, that there was one inevitable road common to all—that was civilisation, and that all attempts at Russianism and independence were piggishness and stupidity. He said he was writing a long article against all Russophiles and Slavophiles. I advised him, for the sake of convenience, to write to Paris for a telescope. ' What for ? ' he asked. ' Russia is too far away from here,' I replied. ' Point your telescope on her and examine us, for otherwise it is difficult to see us.' He became terribly angry. Seeing him so irritated, I said to him with cleverly managed *naïveté :* ' I really did not expect that all those criticisms of you and the failure of *Smoke* would have irritated you so much. Goodness me, it is not worth it, just spit at it all.' ' But I'm not at all irritated. What makes you say it ? ' and he blushed.

" I turned the conversation and began talking about domestic and personal matters. Then I took my hat and somehow, without intending it at all, I casually blurted out to him all that had accumulated in my soul during the three months owing to the Germans. 'Do you know,' I went on, ' what scoundrels and swindlers one comes across here ? Indeed, the masses here are much worse and more dishonest than our people ; and that they are stupider than ours, there's no doubt at all about that. Well, now, you are talking about civilisation ; well, what has civilisation done for them, and in what can they boast themselves superior to us ? ' He went pale (literally, I am not exaggerating a bit, not a bit) and said to me : ' When you speak like that, you offend me personally. You know that I have settled down here finally, that I consider myself a German, and not a Russian, and am proud of it.' ' Although I read *Smoke*,' I replied, ' and have talked with you now for a whole hour, still I could not possibly have expected to hear you say that, and therefore excuse me for having offended you.'

" Then we said quite a polite good-bye to one another, and I promised myself never again to meet Turgenev. Next day, exactly at ten o'clock in the morning, he drove up to the house and left his card with the land-lady. But I had told him the day before that I did not receive anyone before twelve, and that we slept till eleven. I took his call at ten o'clock as an obvious hint that he did not want to meet me, and paid his call on me at ten just in order that I should take the hint. During the whole seven weeks I met him only once at the station. We glanced at one another, but neither he nor I bowed. Perhaps you will find something unpleasant in the maliciousness with which I describe Turgenev and the way in which we offended one another. But, I swear, I could not help it ; he offended me too much by his convictions. To me personally it makes no matter ; though with his ' General '-ship he is not very attractive. But I could not hear such abuse of Russia from a Russian traitor who might have been useful. His crawling before the Germans and his hatred of Russians I had observed long since, as far back as four years ago. But his present irritation and his raging and foaming at the mouth comes solely from the failure of *Smoke*, and from the fact that Russia has had the audacity to refuse to recognise him as a genius. . . . It is sheer self-love, and so the filthier !

" Now listen, my friend, to my plans. It was certainly base of me to have lost that money. But, compara-tively speaking, I have not lost much of my own money. Nevertheless, that money might have served me for two months to live on, even for four months, judging by the way we live. I have told you already : I cannot resist the tempting idea that I'm going to win. Had I originally lost the ten louis d'or, I would have immedi-ately given it up and gone away as I had intended. But the gain of four thousand francs ruined me. There was no possibility of holding out against the temptation of winning more (when it seemed so easy), and thereby of ridding myself of all those legal proceedings, and of rendering secure for a time myself and all mine ; Emily Fiodorovna,[1] Pasha[2] and the others. Still, all this does not justify me in the least ; for I was not alone. I was with a young, kind-hearted and excellent creature, who believes in me completely, whose defender and protector I am, and whom, therefore, I had no right to ruin, and so I ought not to have risked the slightest sum, however small. My future I regard as very grave. I can't return to Russia, for the reasons mentioned above. And above all there is the problem : What is going to happen to those who depend on my help ? All these thoughts are killing me. . . .

" I have only you ; you are my precious friend, my providence. Don't refuse to help me in the future. For in all these matters and little affairs I shall beseech you to interest yourself.

" You, probably, realise clearly the idea, the fundamental idea of all my hopes ; it is clear that the achievements and results I long for depend on *one condition* only ; namely, that *my novel is good*. With that, consequently, I have now to occupy myself with all my powers. Ah, my dear old fellow, it was hard, too hard on me to have adopted the presumptuous idea, three years ago, that I could pay all those debts,[3] and to have foolishly given all those bills ! Where could I get the necessary health and energy for it ? And if experience had already shown that I could have success, then on what a condition ? On the sole condition that every book of mine should be so successful as to arouse a

---

[1] His brother Michael's widow.
[2] His adopted son through his first marriage.
[3] The debts incurred by Dostoevsky's brother in connection with the publications of the reviews *Vremya* and *Epocha*, debts which Dostoevsky took over.

rather strong interest among the public ; otherwise all were hopeless.   But is that possible, can that be regarded as an arithmetical certainty? . . ."

(The letter ends with a request for a loan of money, and a statement of details which show Dostoevsky's difficult position.)

DOSTOEVSKY AND MLLE. SOUSLOV

Dostoevsky's daughter, Aimée, in her book on her father which originally appeared in German, in 1920, and was translated into English and published here a couple of years ago, has for the first time given a somewhat lurid account of her father's love affair with Mlle. Souslov— " Pauline," as Aimée Dostoevsky calls her. From Dostoevsky's letters to his brother Michael, as well as from Mlle. Souslov's diaries and letters, we learn many interesting details of their travels and adventures abroad in 1863, some time before the death of Dostoevsky's first wife, Marie Dmitrievna Issayev.

The following letter written by Dostoevsky to Mlle. Apollinaria Pankratievna Souslov was quite recently found among Golziev's papers in Moscow, and published in Russia.

'Dresden, April 23rd, 1867.
May 5th.

" Your letter, my precious friend, was handed over to me at Basunov's (the bookseller) very late, just before I left for abroad ; and as I was in an awful hurry, I could not manage to answer it. I left Petersburg on Good Friday (April 14th, I believe) ; my journey to Dresden took a fairly long time, with stops, and I have, therefore, only now found time to have a chat with you.

" And so, my dear, you know nothing about me, at any rate you knew nothing when you sent me your letter ? I married last February. According to my contract with Stelovsky (the publisher) I was bound to deliver to him by November 1st of last year a *new novel*, of not less than ten folios of ordinary print ; otherwise

215

I was liable to a heavy fine. Meanwhile I was writing a novel for the *Russsky Vestnik.*[1] I had written twenty-four folios, but there remained another twelve to be done. And then I had also to write the ten folios for Stelovsky. It was the fourth of October, and I had not yet begun. Milyukov advised me to engage a stenographer to whom I could dictate the novel, which would speed up the work four times. Olkhin, the professor of stenography, sent me his best pupil, a young lady, whom I engaged. And on October 4th we commenced work. My stenographer, Anna Gregorevna Snitkin, was a young and rather pretty girl of twenty, of a good family, who passed her school examinations with honours and has an extraordinarily kind and bright disposition. The work went off superbly. On November 28th my novel *The Gambler* (just published) was finished in twenty-four days. Towards its completion I noticed that my stenographer was sincerely fond of me, although she had never said a single word about it ; and I went on liking her more and more. As since my brother's death[2] I have grown terribly weary and find life a burden, I proposed to her. She agreed, and now we are married. The difference in years is terrible (she twenty and I forty-four), but I am becoming more and more convinced that she will be happy. She has a heart and she can love.

" Now about my position generally. You are partly aware that after the death of my brother I lost my health completely through the worry caused by his Review ;[3] but, exhausted in my struggle with the indifference of the public, I dropped it. Again, the three thousand roubles (which I received from the sale of my works to Stelovsky) I spent on the Review, on

---

[1] *Crime and Punishment*, published in Nos. 1, 2, 4, 6, 8, 11–12 of Katkov's review, *Russky Vestnik* for 1886.

[2] Michael Dostoevsky died 10th June, 1864.

[3] *Epocha* stopped publication in 1865.

my brother's family, and on paying the creditors. The result was that I piled up new debts in connection with the Review, which, together with my brother's unpaid debts, amounted to over fifteen thousand roubles. That was the state of my affairs when I left for abroad in 1865, having on me altogether forty Napoleons. Abroad I made up my mind that only by relying on myself should I be able to pay those 15,000 roubles. Besides, with the death of my brother, who was *everything* to me, I have become very sick of life. I still thought of finding a heart that would respond to mine, but I did not find it. Then I plunged into work and began writing a novel. Katkov paid me more than the others, and I gave him the novel. But thirty-seven folios of the novel and another ten folios for Stelovsky turned out to be too much for me, though I have completed both books. My epilepsy became aggravated disgustingly. But after all I diverted myself and also saved myself from prison. The novel (published in the Review and in book form) brought me as much as 14,000 roubles, on which I lived, and also paid back twelve thousand of my fifteen thousand debt. Now my debts are altogether about three thousand roubles. But these three thousand are the wickedest. The more you pay back, the more impatient and more stupid creditors become. Mark you, had I not taken over those debts, the creditors would not have received a penny. And they know it themselves ; for they had begged me to take them over *out of pity* to them, promising not to touch me. But the repayment of the 12,000 aroused the cupidity of those whose bills had not yet been paid. Now I shall have no money till the new year, and that only if I finish the work on which I am now engaged. But how am I going to finish it if they give me no peace ? That is why I went (with my wife) abroad. Again, by living abroad I expect my epilepsy to be relieved ; for in Petersburg, lately, it has become almost impossible for me to work. I could no longer work at night, for every time I had a fit. And so I want to recover my health and to finish my work. From Katkov I received money in advance. They gave it willingly. They pay excellently. From the very first I declared to Katkov that I was a Slavophile, and that I did not agree with certain views of his. This improved and smoothed our relations considerably. As a man, he is the noblest fellow on earth. I did not know him at all before. His immense self-love is awfully damaging to him. But who is without immense self-love ?

" During my last days in Petersburg I met Mme. Brylkin, and paid her a visit. We spoke a great deal about you. She is fond of you. She told me she was very sad about my being happy with another woman. I shall write to her. I like her.

" Your letter left a sad impression on me. You say that you are very sad. I have not known your life for the last year, and what has been in your heart ; but judging from all I know about you, it is difficult for you to be happy. Oh, my dear, I do not call you to cheap, *necessary* happiness. I respect you (and always respected you) for your exacting nature, and I indeed know that your heart can't help demanding life ; but you yourself consider people either infinitely glorious, or—at once —scoundrels and banal. I judge from facts. Draw the conclusion yourself.

" *Au revoir*, my eternal friend ! I am afraid this letter will not find you in Moscow. Know at any rate that from May 8th (old style) I shall be in Dresden (that is in any case ; I may stay on longer), and there-fore, if you wish to answer me, do so immediately on receipt of this letter. (*Poste restante*, Dostoevsky, Dresden, Sax.). My further addresses I will communi-cate to you. Good-bye, my friend. I press and kiss your hand.

Your F. DOSTOEVSKY."

218

DOSTOEVSKY AND MLLE. SOUSLOV

The following article, written by Leonid Grossman, which contains a good deal of new and valuable information relating to the character of Mlle. Souslov, has recently appeared in a Petersburg literary monthly.

" One of Dostoevsky's greatest infatuations goes back to the beginning of the sixties. The young girl Apollinaria Pankratievna Souslov left a most profound trace on the creative activity of Dostoevsky's later period.

" From Aimée Dostoevsky's book on her father we can gather only a few facts concerning ' Pauline.' She came to Petersburg from the provinces, and became a student at the University. Although in the beginning of the sixties Dostoevsky only rarely appeared at students' literary evenings, and was not at all so popular with the students and public as he was at the end of the seventies, we take it that Mlle. Souslov had made his acquaintance at one of those evenings. In the existing Dostoevsky archives Apollinaria's first love-letter to him is not to be found ; yet we can accept Aimée Dostoevsky's assurance that he had actually received such a letter, and that it moved him by its sincerity, *naïveté*, and romantic tone, the tone of a young girl dazed by the genius of the great writer, and expressing her admiration for him.

" At any rate, there is no doubt whatever that in 1863 the love affair between Dostoevsky and Apollinaria was at its height. That summer Dostoevsky travelled abroad in the company of Mlle. Souslov. In his letters to his brother he speaks quite frankly of the happiness of travelling with his beloved. It is true, however, that his habitual distrust and disposition to gloom, and, chiefly, his losses at roulette, clouded his first European tour in the company of his beloved.

" ' We have lots of adventures,' writes Dostoevsky to his brother, ' yet I feel awfully dissatisfied, in spite of A. S[ouslov]. Even happiness I take with pain ;

for I have separated myself from all those I have hitherto loved and suffered for many a time. And although I have given up everything for the sake of happiness, even matters in which I could be of use— my egotism and the thought of this are now poisoning my happiness (if indeed it exists at all).'

" Dostoevsky's companion suffered because of his gambling losses. She pawned her ring, she experienced together with him the anxieties of a sudden impecuniosity, and was afraid of being presented with the hotel bill, which could not be met. The history of their relations, evidently complicated by various love incidents, is quite clearly reflected in Dostoevsky's *The Gambler*. Mlle. Souslov's Diary makes it possible to re-establish the history of their personal relations, and it also throws much light on Dostoevsky's method of transforming the raw material of experience into a work of art.

" Dostoevsky's relations with Mlle. Souslov did not run smooth ; there seem to have been ruptures, reconciliations, violent misunderstandings and, withal, a constant mutual attraction. Their correspondence, too, seems to have been interrupted for long intervals, and yet it did not cease even after Dostoevsky's second marriage. On the 5th of May, 1867, that is, two months after his marriage to Anna Gregorevna Snitkin, Dostoevsky sent Mlle. Souslov a detailed letter about the change in his life.[1]

" From the *Diary* of Anna Gregorevna Dostoevsky we learn that she was extremely distressed by the frequent correspondence between her husband and Mlle. Souslov. This is how Mme. Dostoevsky describes the reading by her husband of a letter from Mlle. Souslov, received on May 27th, 1867, whilst they were staying abroad.

" ' All the time he was reading that letter I watched

---

[1] See Dostoevsky's letter to Mlle. Souslov.

the expression of his face. He read and re-read the first page for a long time, as if he could not make out what was written there ; then, at last, he read it through and blushed scarlet. His hands seemed to tremble. I pretended not to know whom the letter was from, and asked him what Sonechka [a relation of D.] was writing about. He said that the letter was not from Sonechka, and gave a bitter smile. I have never yet seen such a smile on his face. It was a smile either of contempt or of pity—indeed, I do not know ; but it was a pitiable, lost smile. Afterwards he became awfully distrait, and he hardly could make out what I was saying.'

" We are inclined to think that Apollinaria Souslov was the object of Dostoevsky's greatest passion. A woman of extremes, ever disposed to unbounded sensations, to psychological polarities, she demanded a great deal from life. Her inclination to divide people only into saints or villains is as characteristic of her passionate, emotional nature as her constant infatuations, her directness, imperiousness, resoluteness. Her heart, moved to noble impulses of pity and loving-kindness (as, for instance, her tears on hearing of the illness of Dostoevsky's brother), was no less inclined to blind, riotous impulses of passion and persecution. Her sensibility, evidently, did not exclude a certain veil of cynicism. These traits are established beyond doubt from the evidence of V. V. Rosanov, who married Mlle. Souslov the same year in which Dostoevsky died [1881]. It is, however, necessary to bear in mind that Rosanov's account relates to a ' Pauline ' no longer young (when he married her she was about forty-five) ; moreover, his characterisation of her is perhaps somewhat unfavourably biassed. Nevertheless, Rosanov's evidence is of great value, and it also coincides with other evidence from different sources.

" ' I married her,' says Rosanov, ' when I was an undergraduate at the University, a year before I took my degree. But after six years of married life she left me, having fallen in love with a young Jew.' Then, in his application to the Synod, Rosanov gives the following information about his first wife : ' Apollinaria, née Souslov, left her husband, V. V. Rosanov, in 1886, giving as a reason that her husband, in violation of his promise to her, continued to meet a certain young man, a Jew, Goldovsky, who looked after the distribution of Rosanov's books in the bookshops.' But, from all the evidence at hand, it seems that she, having fallen in love with that Goldovsky, but having met with no response on his part, persecuted him abominably, and by indescribable quarrels compelled her husband to break completely with the man. Goldovsky came of an excellent Jewish family, and was an excellent young man : Apollinaria herself had invited him to spend the summer with the Rosanovs. On the whole, this was one of Apollinaria's most absurd and monstrous actions.'

" Having settled as teacher at Eletz, Rosanov goes on to say, he asked his wife to return to him, in the hope that in a new place, amongst new people and new surroundings, they would settle down. But she refused. ' Thousands of husbands,' she replied, ' are in the same position as you (*i.e.*, deserted by their wives) and yet they do not whine—men aren't dogs.'

" Apollinaria's father, to whom Rosanov wrote asking him to use his influence with his daughter and to urge her to return to her husband, wrote to him as follows : ' The enemy of the human race [*i.e.*, his daughter] is settled here in my house, and I can no longer remain here myself.'

" A friend of Rosanov's told me the following : ' In the nineties Rosanov's life became very miserable owing to Apollinaria's flat refusal to divorce him. In 1902 the late Rosanov sent a friend of his to Sebastopol, where A. resided at that time, to plead with her and to persuade her to divorce him. Apollinaria was over sixty then ; she lived quite alone in her own house, on which was the inscription, ' Mrs. V. V. Rosanov's House.' The house was extraordinarily clean and tidy ; she herself produced on me the impression of an active and energetic woman. In her conversation with her husband's messenger she remained inflexible. No arguments could change her decision. Of Rosanov she spoke with extreme bitterness, and despite the messenger's persistence, refused to make any concession."

" In reply to some questions put to him about his first wife [Mlle. Souslov] by A. S. Volzhsky, a personal friend of his and a student of Dostoevsky's works, Rosanov wrote the following extremely valuable letter :

" ' I met Apollinaria for the first time in the house of my pupil, Mlle. A. M. Scheglov (I was seventeen, Mlle. Scheglov twenty or twenty-three, Apollinaria thirty-seven). Apollinaria was dressed all in black ; her face bore ' traces of former (remarkable) beauty ' ; she was a Russian *légitimiste* waiting for the triumph of the Bourbons in France, where she had left her *best* friends, for in Russia she had none. Here she loved only what was aristocratic. With the look of an ' experienced coquette,' she understood that she had ' hit ' me—she spoke coldly, indifferently. In a word, she was a kind of Catharine de Medici. Indeed, she looked like de Medici. A crime she would commit coldly, and would assassinate with the greatest indifference. . . . Generally speaking, A. was indeed superb. I know that people (and a friend of hers, Anna Osipovna G., fifteen years her senior) were absolutely charmed by her. I have never seen such a Russian woman. In the *style of her soul* she was a perfect Russian, and as a Russian she might have been a *raskolnik* of the ' Universal Harmony ' sect, or, better still, a ' Mother of God ' of the *Khlysts*' sect.'

" ' She had had a liaison with Dostoevsky, and lived

with him.   I once asked her, ' Why did you part from him ? '

" ' Because he did not want to divorce his [first] wife, who was consumptive and dying,' she said.

" ' But she was dying ? '

" ' Yes, she was.   She died six months later.   But I had by that time already ceased to love him,' she said.

" ' Why did you cease to love him ? '

" ' Because he did not want to divorce her.'   And then, after a silence, she added :

" ' I had given myself to him in love, without questioning, without reasoning.   And he, too, ought to have acted likewise.   He failed to do so, and I left him.'

" ' This is her ' style,' ; the conversation is almost literally correct.''

" Rosanov asserts that Apollinaria possessed an almost unique fascination, an imperious, captivating ' style ' of femininity.   Coldly sensuous, she remained a ' tormentor ' even in love, showing deviations from the normal, and perverse traits of a complicated character.   Looking back thirty years, Rosanov still remembered, with profound agitation and keenest admiration, the fascination of that strange woman—the Catharine de Medici or the *Khlysts'* Mother of God.

" Rosanov compares Apollinaria to Dostoevsky's heroines. ' Dounia, Raskolnikov's sister (in *Crime and Punishment*),' he says, ' and Aglaia (in *The Idiot*) are like her.   But as to Groushenka (of *The Brothers Karamasov*)—no, nothing of the kind.   Groushenka is an obscene Russian ; but in Apollinaria there was nothing coarse or obscene.'

" Rosanov thinks that the following fragment from Dostoevsky's *Humiliated and Insulted* characterises Apollinaria perfectly correctly.   The fragment is a description of a certain Countess, given by Prince Valkovsky to Ivan Petrovitch : ' She was a first-rate beauty,' says the Prince.   ' What a figure, what a bearing, what a gait ! Her glance was piercing, like that of an eagle, but ever stern and severe. She was majestic and inaccessible. She was reputed to be as cold as icy winter, and she frightened all away by her exalted, by her rigorous virtue. . . . She regarded everyone dispassionately, like an abbess of a mediæval monastery. . . . And, well? There never was such a voluptuous woman as she was. . . . My lady was so perverse that the Marquis de Sade could have taken lessons from her. . . . Yes, she was the devil incarnate, but an invincibly fascinating devil. . . .' In Rosanov's opinion this description is the best characterisation of Mlle. Souslov, although, in fact, it has no reference to her, for *Humiliated and Insulted* was written by Dostoevsky before he met Mlle. Souslov.

" Rosanov's letter throws a good deal of light on the character of Dostoevsky's love affair with Mlle. Souslov. The latter furnished Dostoevsky with certain characteristics for his ' proud girls ' and ' infernal women.' In almost all the novels of Dostoevsky's mature period there appears a new type and character of woman, undoubtedly revealed to him by his captivating and unique travelling companion of 1863."

TOLSTOY AND STRAKHOV ON DOSTOEVSKY

A Note on N. N. Strakhov

Nicolay Nicolayevich Strakhov (1828–1896) studied at the Faculty of Mathematics in the Petersburg University and took his degree in 1848. He then continued his studies at the Faculty of Natural Sciences and, after taking his degree in 1851, he became a teacher of Physics and Mathematics. For his research work in Zoology he was made Master of Zoology in 1857.

In 1861 he became principal collaborator with the brothers Dostoevsky on their Review " Vremya." There he wrote a series of articles which had a great success and were directed against the " Westerners." " Vremya " was suppressed by the Censor because of an article by Strakhov called " The Fatal Problem," which dealt with Russian–Polish relations in a spirit of opposition to the Government.

Strakhov made Tolstoy's personal acquaintance in 1871. After a series of brilliant articles on " War and Peace," he wrote to Tolstoy, asking him to collaborate in the review " Zarya." Tolstoy sent him a pressing invitation to come and stay with him at Yasnaya Polyana. In June, 1871, Strakhov went there, and subsequently he used to spend a month or more every summer with Tolstoy. Their friendship grew stronger and stronger, and there was complete frankness between them, as can be seen from the Russian volume of " The Correspondence between Tolstoy and Strakhov (1870–1894)," published by the Tolstoy Museum, Petersburg, 1914. This large volume of nearly five hundred pages contains over two hundred letters written by Strakhov.

TOLSTOY AND STRAKHOV

Of his letters to Strakhov Tolstoy wrote to P. A. Serguc-yenko (February 6th, 1906): " Apart from Alexandra Andreyevna Tolstoy I had two friends to whom I have written many letters, a circumstance which, I fancy, may interest those who are interested in my personality. These two are Strakhov and Prince Urusov."

Tolstoy had the highest opinion of Strakhov and said: " Strakhov is one of the best men I know."

The friendship between Tolstoy and Strakhov lasted for twenty years, until the death of the latter. And on Strakhov's part it was a thirty years' adoration of Tolstoy's genius, of his great spiritual and intellectual powers. In an article written on the death of Strakhov, in 1896, V. V. Rosanov says: " Strakhov's attachment to Tolstoy was most deep and mystical. He loved him as the incarnation of the highest and most profound aspirations of the human soul, as a special nerve in the huge body of mankind, in which we others form parts less understanding and significant. . . . He loved in him the dark abyss, the bottom of which no one could see, and from the depths of which still rise treasures innumerable. There is no doubt that Tolstoy never lost a better friend."

In another passage Rosanov says:

" Tolstoy—the man, the writer, the thinker—was to him [Strakhov] great and supreme ; he could not find words to express his reverence and love for him. . . . Once Strakhov discussed a writer, now dead, and condemned him severely, saying: ' He [that writer] was, as it were, deprived of the sense of smell for the pure and the impure: he lacked altogether the feeling for these matters. Of great talent, possessing a wonderful language, he treats of the highest matters and all of a sudden drifts into talking of the greatest abominations, without any awareness that it is a totally different thing. . . . Now, you take Tolstoy—in him that sense of pureness is wonderful. Whatever work of his you take, you see that the pure and the impure is never mixed up in his eyes, that he himself

ever sees and makes you feel the boundary that divides them.' And Rosanov goes on to say: " Strakhov said this in such a peculiar tone of voice that you could not help feeling that just in that was the centre of his affection for Tolstoy; that after long seeking, after studying him for a long time, he came to see in Tolstoy a man, on whose bosom he could lay his head without being scorched, soiled or losing his soul; hence his trust in him."

Strakhov's letters to Tolstoy are of great interest not only because they speak of the literary men and events of the time, of problems of life and belief, but because of their perfect frankness, utmost sincerity and touching intimacy.

Strakhov was one of the most distinguished Russian literary critics, a real scholar, a man of strict honour and integrity, ever helpful to others, and deeply respected by all.

His best known works include:

From the History of Russian Nihilism.
Essays on Pushkin and Other Poets.
The Struggles with the West in our Literature
    (3 Vols.).
Critical Essays (2 Vols.).
Reminiscences of Dostoevsky.
The World as a Whole.
Danilevsky's Life and Works.

And various scientific works, as well as a number of translations into Russian of works on philosophical scientific and literary subjects.

A number of Strakhov's letters to Tolstoy, contained in the Russian volume of their " Correspondence " (Petersburg, 1914), appeared serially in the monthly Review, " Sovzemenny Mir " for 1913.

TOLSTOY AND STRAKHOV

*A FEW EXTRACTS FROM LETTERS EXCHANGED
BETWEEN LEO NICOLAYEVICH TOLSTOY AND
N. N. STRAKHOV RELATING TO F. M. DOSTOEVSKY.*

Leo Tolstoy to N. Strakhov.

" September 26th, 1880.

" I cannot understand the life in Moscow of those people who don't understand it themselves. But the life of the majority—of the peasants, pilgrims, and any others who understand their life—I understand and love awfully. I continue working on the same thing, and, it seems to me, not uselessly. The other day I felt seedy, and read *The Dead House* [by Dostoevsky]. I had forgotten a great deal of it, I re-read it, and I do not know a better book in the whole new literature, including Pushkin. If you see Dostoevsky, tell him that I love him."

N. Strakhov to L. Tolstoy.

" November 2nd, 1880.

" I saw Dostoevsky and gave him your praise and love. He was very delighted, and I had to leave with him the sheet of your letter that contained such dear words. He was a little vexed by your disrespect to Pushkin expressed there (' a better book in the whole new literature, including Pushkin '). ' What, *including*? ' he asked. I said that you ever were, and now especially you have become, a great ' free-thinker.' "

N. Strakhov to L. Tolstoy.

" February 3rd, 1881.

" A feeling of profound emptiness, my dear Leo Nicolayevich, has not left me since the moment I learnt of Dostoevsky's death.[1] It is as though half

---

[1] Dostoevsky died on 28th January, 1881. Strakhov later on wrote his reminiscences of Dostoevsky, published in 1883, in the first volume of *F. M. Dostoevsky's Complete Works.*

Petersburg had sunk down or a half of literature had died. Although during recent years we did not agree, I now feel of what an importance he has been to me. In his presence I longed to be both wise and good, and the deep respect we felt for one another, in spite of silly misunderstandings, was to me, as I see, extremely dear. Ah, how sad! There is no desire to do anything, and the grave into which I shall have to lie down, seems to have come near and to be waiting. All is vanity, all is vanity!

" In one of our last meetings I told him that I was very surprised and glad at his activity. Indeed, he alone was equal (in his influence on readers) to several monthlies. He stood apart, amidst a literature almost entirely hostile, and boldly spoke of what had long been considered as *temptation* and *madness*. The spectacle was such that I was amazed, in spite of all my cooling-down to literature.

" But it seems that just this activity ruined him. The enthusiasm which was manifested each time he appeared in public became very sweet to him, and during recent times a week would not pass without his appearing before the public. He eclipsed Turgenev, and finally eclipsed himself. But he needed success; for he was a preacher, a publicist still more than an artist.

" His funeral was grand; I watched attentively and inquired—there was almost nothing assumed, formal, or done to order. From schools there came so many wreaths that they seemed to be brought by a general order; and yet it was all done out of genuine good will.

" His poor wife cannot be comforted, and I felt very sad that I could not say something to her. ' If only I had fervent belief!' . . . she said.

" Now I have been given a difficult task, compelled to it, and I had to promise to speak of Dostoevsky at the meeting of the Slav Charity Committee on February 14th. Fortunately a few ideas have occurred to me, and I shall try as simply and clearly as possible to do my duty to the living and to the dead. I crave your permission to refer to the letter in which you wrote about *The Dead House*. I began re-reading that book, and was surprised at its simplicity and sincerity, which I could not appreciate before. . . .

Leo Tolstoy to N. Strakhov.

" 1881.

" . . . How much I should like to be able to say all that I feel about Dostoevsky ! You, in describing your feelings, have expressed part of my own. I never saw the man and never had direct relations with him ; and suddenly, when he died, I realised that he was to me the man nearest, most dear and most needed. And it never entered my head to measure myself with him, never ! Everything he did (the good, the genuine writings) was such that the more he did it, the better for me. Art arouses envy in me, wisdom too ; but the work of the heart—only joy. I did consider him as my friend, and I thought that we should meet, only that there was no occasion yet, but that it would come. At first I felt lost ; but then it became clear to me how dear he was to me, and I wept, as I weep now. Recently, before his death I read his *Humiliated and Insulted*, and was deeply moved."

N. Strakhov to L. Tolstoy.

" November 28th, 1883.

" I shall write you, precious Leo Nicolayevich, only a short letter, although I have a most fertile theme. But I am seedy, and also it would take me too long to develop that theme. You must by now have received *Dostoevsky's Biography*[1]—I crave your attention and

---

[1] This refers to *Dostoevsky's Biography, Letters and Notes*, by O. M. Miller and N. N. Strakhov, published in Petersburg 1883. The *Biography* contains Strakhov's *Reminiscences of Dostoevsky*.

gracious favour—tell me what you think of it. And on this occasion I want to make a confession to you. All the time I was writing it I was in a struggle. I struggled with the disgust that kept rising in me, I tried to suppress that bad feeling in me. Do help me to find a way out of it! I cannot consider Dostoevsky either a good man or a happy man (which, in the main, coincide). He was spiteful, envious, lewd, and all his life he spent in such agitations as would have made him pitiable, and would have made him ridiculous, if he had not at the same time been so spiteful and so wise. He himself, like Rousseau, considered himself the best of men and the happiest. In connection with the *Biography* I vividly remembered all these traits. In Switzerland in my presence he so harassed a waiter that the latter took offence and spoke out: 'But surely I am a man!' I remember how astonished I was then that this had been said to the preacher of *humanity*, and that these words expressed the notion of free Switzerland about the *rights of man*.

" Such scenes happened continually; for he could not control his spite. Many times I disregarded his outbursts which, like a regular old hag, he would make unexpectedly and obliquely. But on a couple of occasions I happened to say very hurtful things to him. But, of course, as regards hurting others he had the superiority over ordinary people. And the worst of it was that he delighted in it, that in all his mean acts he never repented to the end. He was drawn to abominations, and he boasted of them. Viskovatov began telling me how Dostoevsky boasted that . . . in a bath with a little girl whom the governess had brought to him. Note, that for all his animal sensuality, he had no taste whatever, no feeling whatever, for the beauty and charm of woman. This is seen in his novels. The characters most resembling him are the hero of *Notes from the Underground*, Svidrigailov in *Crime and*

Punishment, and Stavrogin in *The Devils.* One scene from Stavrogin (rape, etc.) Katkov refused to publish, but Dostoevsky had read it here to many persons.[1]

" With such a nature he was very much disposed to sweet sentimentality, to lofty and humane dreamings ; and these dreamings are his bent, his literary muse and path. Essentially, indeed, all his novels are a self-justification ; they prove that there may live in man alongside with nobility all kinds of abominations.

" How it pains me that I cannot rid myself of these thoughts, that I cannot find a point of reconciliation ! But am I indignant with him ? Do I envy him ? Do I wish him ill? Not in the slightest. It makes me only cry as I think that this recollection which *might* have been serene simply oppresses me.

" I remember your words that those who know us too well naturally do not love us. But the converse also holds true. In the course of a long, intimate friendship one may get to know in a man one trait for which one could afterwards forgive him anything. *A stirring of true kindness, a spark of genuine sincere warmth,* even a single minute of real repentance could expiate anything. And if I remembered anything like that in Dostoevsky, I would forgive him and be glad for him. But mere exalting oneself into a fine man, mere heady and literary humanity—Lord, how disgusting it is !

" He was a truly unhappy and wicked man who imagined himself happy, a hero, and loved tenderly himself alone. . . .

" Here is a little commentary on my *Biography* ; I could write down and tell of this side, too, of Dostoevsky. Many cases come to my mind more vivid than those I have recorded, and the account would be a much more

---

[1] The scene referred to here is *Stavrogin's Confession,* translated by S. S. Koteliansky and Virginia Woolf, published by the Hogarth Press, 1922.

truthful one ; but let that truth perish, let us display only the bright side of life, as we are doing everywhere and in everything !"

L. Tolstoy to N. Strakhov.

" . . . I have read your book. Your letter had a very sad effect on me, disappointed me. But I understand you fully and, to my regret, I almost believe you. It seems to me that you have been a victim of a wrong, a false attitude towards Dostoevsky, of his exaggerated —not by you, but by all,—importance, and of a sort of stereotyped exaggeration, of the exaltation into prophet and saint of a man who has died in the most fervent process of a struggle between good and evil. He is moving, interesting, but to put on a pedestal, as an example to posterity, a man who is all struggle—you can't. From your book I have learnt for the first time the depth of his understanding. I have also read Pressensé's[1] book; but all his scholarship is wasted through a little trifle. There are beautiful horses, race-horses worth a thousand roubles. But suddenly you detect a kink, and that beauty and champion of a horse is worth nothing. The more I live the more do I value people without a kink. You say that you have made it up with Turgenev, and I have become very fond of him. And, this is amusing, just because he was without a kink and would take you there ; and here you have a race-horse, but it won't carry you anywhere. Lucky if it does not land you in a ditch ! Both Pressensé and Dostoevsky have a kink. In the case of the former all his scholarship, and in the case of the latter all his wisdom and heart, were just wasted ; Turgenev will outlive Dostoevsky, and not for his artistry, but because he was without a kink."

---

[1] Edmond de Pressensé (1824–91), French Protestant theologian ; author of several works, one of which is dealt with here.

MME. DOSTOEVSKY at work in the Dostoevsky room of the Moscow Historical Museum
(Taken during her last visit there)

[face p. 234

MME. DOSTOEVSKY'S ANSWER

N. Strakhov to L. Tolstoy.

"December 12th, 1883.

"Do tell me then, precious Leo Nicolayevich, your opinion of Turgenev. How I long to read something which approaches the underlying profundity of your writings. For what we others write is either a toy for ourselves or a comedy which we play for others. In my *Reminiscences* [of Dostoevsky] I laid stress on the literary side of the matter. I wanted to write a page from the history of literature ; but I could not completely overcome my indifference. Of Dostoevsky the man I tried to show only his good points ; but I did not attribute merits to him which he did not possess. My account of literary affairs probably interested you very little. May I then say straight out ? Your explanation also of Dostoevsky, although it made many things much clearer to me, is too lenient to him. How can a radical change take place in a man, when nothing can penetrate his soul beneath a certain depth ? I say *nothing*, in the exact sense of the word. For so his soul presents itself to me. . . ."

MME. DOSTOEVSKY'S ANSWER TO STRAKHOV.

My Answer to Strakhov[1]

Even now, in face of the approaching end of my life, I have to come forward in defence of the glorious memory of my unforgettable husband against the abominable calumny uttered by the man whom my husband, myself and all our family, considered for long years as our sincere friend. I speak of N. N. Strakhov's letter to Count Leo Tolstoy (of November 26th, 1883), published in the October number of *The Sovzemenny Mir*, 1913.

When in November, 1913, I returned to Petersburg from my summer holiday and met my friends and

---

[1] From Mme. Dostoevsky's *Reminiscences*.

acquaintances, I was somewhat surprised that nearly everyone was asking me if I had read Strakhov's letter to Count Tolstoy. To my question as to where it had been published, they said that it had appeared in a newspaper, but they did not remember in which. I attached no significance to such forgetfulness, and was not particularly interested in the news ; for, I thought, what but good could Strakhov have written about my husband, who always spoke of him as a distinguished writer, approved his work, and suggested ideas and themes for work to him. It was only afterwards that I realised that none of my " forgetful " friends and acquaintances had wished to distress me mortally, as our false friend had done with his letter. It was not until the summer of 1914, when I began looking through the numerous cuttings from newspapers and journals, supplied to me by an agency for the collection of the " Museum of F. M. Dostoevsky," at Moscow, that I read that unfortunate letter.

[Here Mme. Dostoevsky quotes Strakhov's letters and Tolstoy's replies, published in the previous article, " Leo Tolstoy and Strakhov on Dostoevsky."].

Strakhov's letter exasperated me to the depths of my soul. The man who had been coming to our house for years and who all that time had met with such a cordial reception from my husband, turned out to be a liar who permitted himself to utter abominable calumnies against his friend. I was ashamed for myself, for my trustfulness, for the fact that both my husband and myself had been so deceived in that unworthy man.

The passage in Strakhov's letter in which he says that " all the time he was writing (his *Reminiscences of Dostoevsky*) he struggled with the disgust that kept rising in him," simply amazed me. If Strakhov felt disgust at the work he had undertaken, and could not respect the man whom he had agreed to write about, why did he not refuse the task, as any self-respecting person would have done in his place ? Was it because he did not want to put me, the publisher, into an awkward position by forcing me to look for another biographer ? But O. F. Miller had agreed to write the biography, and I had also had in view other writers (Averkiev, Sluchevsky), who actually wrote it for the later editions.

Strakhov says in his letter that Dostoevsky was spiteful, and as proof he cites the silly incident of the waiter, whom my husband " harassed." My husband, on account of his illness, was sometimes irascible, and it is possible that he might have shouted at the waiter, who was slow in bringing the food (for in what else could the " harassing " of the waiter consist ?) ; surely that did not imply spite, but only impatience. And how unlikely is the servant's answer : "I, too, am a man." In Switzerland the common people are so rude that a servant, in answer to an insult, would not confine himself to piteous words, but would dare to answer with a twofold impudence, perfectly certain of his impunity.

I can't understand how Strakhov could bring himself to say that Dostoevsky was " spiteful " and " tenderly loved himself only." Strakhov, indeed, was himself witness of the terrible situation in which the brothers Dostoevsky had been put by the suppression of *Vremya*, due to the incapable article (" The Fatal Problem ") written by Strakhov himself. Had not Strakhov written that ambiguous article, the *Review* would have continued to exist and to bring profits even after Michael Dostoevsky's death ; my husband would not have been burdened by all the debts connected with the *Review* ; and he would not have had all his life long to torment himself so much in order to pay all the obligations of the *Review*, which he had taken on himself. It can in truth be said that Strakhov was the evil genius of my husband not only during his lifetime, but, as it has now turned out, even after his death.

Strakhov was also the eye-witness of how Dostoevsky had for a long time supported the family of his late brother Michael, his invalid brother Nicolay, and his stepson P. Issayev. A man with a spiteful heart, who loved himself alone, would not have taken on himself such onerous financial obligations, he would not have taken on himself the care of his relations. And, knowing as he did the tiniest details of Dostoevsky's life, to say about him that he was " spiteful " and " tenderly loved himself only " was on Strakhov's part a sheer act of bad faith.

On my part, having lived with my husband for the last fourteen years of his life, I consider it my duty to bear witness that Fiodor Dostoevsky was a man of boundless kindness. He displayed it not only towards his intimates, but towards all and sundry, of whose misfortune, failure, or misery he had come to hear. There was no need to ask—he himself came forward with his help. Having influential friends (K. P. Pobedonoszev, J. I. Filippov, I. A. Vishnegradsky), my husband used their influence in order to help people in misfortune. What a number of poor old men and women he succeeded in placing in almshouses ; what a number of children he placed in asylums ; for what a number of people he found work ! What a lot of manuscripts he had to read and to correct for others ; what a number of frank confessions he had to listen to ; and what a lot of advice he had to give in intimate matters ! He grudged neither his time, nor his efforts, provided he could render assistance to anyone. He also helped with money, and, if he had no ready cash, he would put his signature to a bill, and occasionally had to pay for it. Fiodor's kindness went at times against the interests of our family, and at times I was annoyed by his boundless kindness ; yet I could not help being enraptured, seeing what happiness it was to him to be able to do good.

Strakhov says that Dostoevsky was "envious." But whom did he envy? All who are interested in Russian literature know that Dostoevsky reverently worshipped Pushkin's genius, and the finest tribute paid to the great poet was Dostoevsky's speech in Moscow at the opening of the Pushkin Memorial.

It is difficult to admit that Dostoevsky envied the talent of Count L. Tolstoy, if one remembers what my husband wrote of him in *The Journal of an Author.* I take, for instance, *The Journal* for 1877. In the January number, writing of the hero of *Childhood and Youth*, Dostoevsky says that " it is an unusually serious psychological study of a child's soul, wonderfully executed." In the February number my husband calls Tolstoy " an artist of extraordinary eminence." In *The Journal* for July-August Dostoevsky says of *Anna Karenin* that " it is an achievement of special significance, which should answer for us to Europe, and which we can point out to Europe." And further : " the great scene in which the poet describes the mortal illness of the heroine, is marvellously delineated." In concluding the article my husband says : " such men as the author of *Anna Karenin* are the teachers of the public, our teachers, and we are only their pupils."

In the famous novelist Goncharov Dostoevsky valued a man not only of " great understanding," but also of high talent ; he loved him sincerely and called him his favourite writer.

My husband's early attitude to Turgenev was enthusiastic. In the letter to his brother of 16th November, 1845, Dostoevsky writes of Turgenev : " But, my dear brother, what a fine fellow he is ! I, too, have nearly fallen in love with him. A poet, a man of talent, an aristocrat, handsome, rich, sensible, highly educated, twenty-five years old—I do not know what nature has denied him. Finally, his character is absolutely straightforward, splendid and well schooled."

Later on Dostoevsky and Turgenev drifted apart because of their opposing convictions, but the latter in his letter of . . . .[1] In 1880, at the Pushkin festivities in Moscow, speaking of Pushkin's *Tatyana*, Dostoevsky said : " Such a beautiful type of Russian womanhood has scarcely been repeated in our literature—except perhaps in the character of Lisa in Turgenev's *Nest of Noblemen*."

Need I speak of Dostoevsky's attitude to the poet Nekrasov, who was always dear to him from youthful associations, and whom he called the great poet who had created the great " Vlas." The article on the death of Nekrasov, in which Dostoevsky says that " among the poets (that is, those who came with a new utterance) Nekrasov must be placed directly after Pushkin and Lermontov "—that article, according to the best authorities on Russian literature, might be considered as the finest eulogy of the dead poet.

Such were the relations of my husband to the talents and the works of our distinguished writers, and Strakhov's words that Dostoevsky was envious are a cruel injustice to him.

But a still more crying injustice was done to Dostoevsky by Strakhov when he said that my husband was " lewd," that " he was drawn to abominations, of which he boasted." As proof Strakhov mentions the scene from *The Devils* which " Katkov refused to publish, but which Dostoevsky had read here to many persons."

For the artistic characterisation of Stavrogin, Dostoevsky had to ascribe some unpardonable crime to the hero of the novel. That chapter of the novel Katkov actually refused to publish and asked the author to alter it. Dostoevsky was grieved by the refusal, and, wishing to verify the correctness of Katkov's opinion, he read that chapter to his friends K. P. Pobedonoszev, A. N. Maikov, N. Strakhov and others,

[1] Here is a lacuna in the text.

but not in order to boast, as Strakhov explains, but asking their opinion and, as it were, their judgment on him. However, when all of them found the passage "too realistic," my husband began thinking out a variant of the scene, so essential in his opinion, for the characterisation of Stavrogin. There were several variants, and among them was a scene in a bath (a true occurrence of which some one had told my husband). In that scene a "governess" appears, and, in view of this fact, those to whom my husband, wishing to know their view, related that variant (and Strakhov was among them), formed the opinion that this incident might prejudice Dostoevsky in the eyes of the reading public. The imputation of such a disgraceful act to a "governess" would be regarded as an insult to the so-called "woman's cause," just as the presentation of the student Raskolnikov in the rôle of a murderer, had been interpreted as though Dostoevsky had thereby imputed similar crimes to all our young generation of university students.

And it is this abominable action of Stavrogin's in that variant, that Strakhov, in his malice, does not hesitate to attribute to Dostoevsky himself, forgetting that the practise of such refined vice involves a great expense, and is only possible to very rich men, while my husband was all his life long pressed for money. Strakhov's reference to Professor P. A. Viskovatov is the more astonishing to me because the Professor had never been to our house. Dostoevsky had a very poor opinion of him, as can be seen from his account of a meeting with a Russian in Dresden, contained in his letter to Maikov.

On my part, I can bear witness that, in spite of the occasional extremely realistic descriptions of base actions committed by the heroes of his novels, my husband remained all his life free from "perversity." Thanks to his talent, a great artist has evidently no need to perform the crimes committed by his heroes ; otherwise it would be necessary to admit that Dostoevsky must himself have committed a murder, seeing how artistically he succeeded in depicting the murder of the two women by Raskolnikov.

I recall with profound gratitude the way Fiodor behaved himself, how he guarded me against reading immoral novels, and how he used to be indignant when, owing to my youth, I would repeat to him an indecent anecdote, which I had heard someone tell. In his talks my husband was always very discreet and did not allow himself cynical expressions. Probably, all those who remember him, can confirm this.

Having read Strakhov's calumnious letter I decided to enter a protest against it. But how was it to be done ? The time for refuting the letter had gone by : it had appeared in October, 1913, and I had only learnt of it almost a year later. And what does a refutation in the newspapers amount to ? It would be lost among the current news, forgotten ; and how many people would notice it at all ? I began asking the advice of friends and acquaintances, some of whom had known my late husband. Their opinions were divided. Some said that such abominable calumnies must be regarded with the contempt which they deserved. They said that Dostoevsky's significance in Russian and in world literature was so great that calumnies would not harm his glorious memory. They also pointed out that the publication of the letter had aroused no discussion in the press—so palpable was the calumny and so understandable the calumniator to the majority of writers. Others, on the contrary, said that I had to make my protest, remembering the saying " Calomniez, calomniez ; il en restera toujours quelquechose." They said, seeing that I, who had devoted my whole life to the service of my husband and to his memory, did not consider it necessary to refute a calumny, people might conclude that there was some truth in it. My silence might appear like a confirmation of the calumny.

Many others, exasperated by Strakhov's letter, held, however, that *my* reply alone would not be sufficient ; that Dostoevsky's friends and the people who remembered him with kindly feelings ought to protest against the calumnies uttered against him by Strakhov. Some of them took upon themselves the labour of composing a protest and of collecting signatures to it. Others again wished to express their indignation by individual letters. Many of my friends gave it as their opinion that, as a counterblast to the calumny, the protest ought to be supplemented by reminiscences, published in the journals at various times and depicting Dostoevsky as an extraordinarily kind and responsive man. Following the advice of my friends, I append the protest and the articles to my *Reminiscences*.[1]

I talked to many persons about the unfortunate letter, which has so much clouded my last years, and asked them what they thought had made Strakhov write it. The majority inclined to the view that it was *jalousie de métier*, so habitual in the literary world ; that probably Fiodor, through his frankness or perhaps quick temper, had offended Strakhov (the latter spoke of it), and he wished to avenge himself even though the offender was dead. But Strakhov dared not express his opinion in the press ; for he knew that he would raise against himself too many defenders of Dostoevsky's memory, and to quarrel with people was not in Strakhov's nature. One person, who had known Strakhov intimately, expressed the idea that by his letter he had wanted " to belittle, to degrade " Dostoevsky in Tolstoy's eyes. When I questioned that view, my interlocutor gave a rather original opinion of Strakhov.

" Who, after all, was Strakhov ? " he said. " He

---

[1] The protest and articles mentioned are not contained in the text of the published *Reminiscences*.

was a type, now extinct, of ' the noble hanger-on,' of whom there were many in former times. Remember, he used to stay for months with Tolstoy, Fet, Danilevsky, and in the winter went on fixed days to dine with friends, and carried rumours and gossip from one house to another. As a philosophical writer he was of little interest to people, but he was received everywhere as a desired guest, for he could always tell something new about Tolstoy, whose friend he considered himself to be. He valued that friendship very much and, having a high opinion of himself, it is possible that he considered himself as a support to Tolstoy. How great must have been Strakhov's resentment when Tolstoy, learning of Dostoevsky's death, had called the deceased his ' support,' and expressed sincere regret that he had not met him. It is possible that Tolstoy often admired Dostoevsky's talent and spoke of him, and this must have vexed Strakhov. So he decided, in order to stop that admiration, to raise a series of calumnies against Dostoevsky ; so that his glorious image might be dimmed in Tolstoy's eyes. It is possible that Strakhov also entertained the idea of revenging himself on Dostoevsky for some offence, which he had to put up with from the latter, by bringing him into contempt with posterity ; for, seeing the admiration in which his great friend Tolstoy was held, he could suppose that in the future Tolstoy's letters and those of his correspondents would be published, and then, even though it were years and years later, his evil purpose would be achieved."

Not sharing the particular opinion of my interlocutor, I shall finish this painful episode of my life with the words from Strakhov's letter : " there may live in man alongside with nobility all kinds of abominations."

APPENDIX

From Dostoevsky's Notebooks

(Variants and Notes relating to *The Devils* and *The Adolescent*)

A Note on " The Devils "

The Devils (called *The Possessed* in the existing English translation) is one of Dostoevsky's most important works.   In its prophetic previsions it almost exactly anticipates the sinister aspects of the Russian Revolution, and creates the prototypes of many of the leading actors of the Revolution.

To show how much Dostoevsky was preoccupied with his work on *The Devils* we give here a few passages from his letters relating to that novel.

" Do you remember, my friend Sonichka, writing me once about a novel of mine, and saying how surprised you were at my undertaking to complete such a work by a fixed date ?   But will you believe me now, that the work [*The Devils*] I am doing now for *The Russky Vestnik* represents a still more difficult problem ?   I condense into twenty-five folios what ought to occupy fifty at least.   I compress in order to finish it in time, and I cannot do otherwise, because I cannot write anything else now " . . . (May 7th, 1870).

" Did I tell you . . . how I had suddenly realised that I should not be able to send anything to *The Russky Vestnik* by the new year ?   They did not reply, they only stopped sending me money.   In the beginning of the year I wrote to Katkov to say that in June I should start sending him *The Devils*, so that, if they wished, they could publish it at the end of the year. Now listen . . . I worked to the verge of exhaustion, for I am not in Russia, and if my literary relations with the *Russky Vestnik* cease, I shall have nothing to live on (for it is difficult for me at this distance to establish relations with other journals). Besides, I worried and suffered from the mere idea that the *Russky Vestnik* might consider me a scoundrel, and yet they have always treated me superbly. The novel I was writing was long, quite original, but its idea was of a kind somewhat new to me. A very great deal of self-confidence was needed to cope with that idea. But I could not cope with it, and burst. My work proceeded drowsily, I felt there was a capital defect in the whole, but what the defect was, I could not guess. In July, after my last letter to you, I had a whole series of epileptic fits (week after week). They upset me so much that I could not think of the work for a whole month, and also it would have been unsafe. And then, a fortnight ago, having set myself to the work again, I suddenly saw at once where it limped and where my mistake was ; and at the same time a new plan of the novel came to me by inspiration in complete shape. I had to alter everything radically ; without hesitation I crossed out all I had written (about fifteen folios) and began again from the first page. My whole work for a whole year gone ! Oh, Sonichka ! If you knew how hard it is to be a writer—I mean, to endure that lot. Do you believe me, I know for certain that if I could have two or three years secure for this novel, just as Turgenev can, or Goncharov, or Tolstoy, I, too, would write such a work as would be talked of a hundred years hence ! I am not boasting ; ask your conscience and your recollections of me : am I a boaster ? The idea of the novel is so fine, so significant, that I myself bow to it. And what will come of it ? I know beforehand : I shall be writing the novel eight or nine months, I shall

condense it and spoil it. The writing of such a thing should not take less than two or three years. The details will perhaps come off well, the characters will be outlined only in the rough. There will be a lot of unsustained passages, superfluous amplifications. A multitude of beautiful things (I speak literally) will not get into the novel, for inspiration depends largely on time. And yet I am sitting down to write ! Is it not torture—consciously to attempt one's own life? "
. . . (17th August, 1870).

" To M. N. Katkov.   Dresden, 8th October, 1870.
" I sent to-day to the office of *The Russky Vestnik* only the first half of Part I of my novel, *The Devils*. But very soon I shall send you the second half of Part I. There will be three parts altogether, each about ten or twelve folios. There will be no delay now.
" If you decide to publish my work next year, then it seems to me necessary to tell you beforehand, if even in a few words, what strictly the novel is about.
" One of the biggest events of my novel will be the well-known Moscow murder of Ivanov by Nechayev. I hasten to add : I never knew either Nechayev or Ivanov, or the circumstances of the murder, nor do I know them now, except from the newspapers. And if I knew I would not copy them. I only take the accomplished fact. My imagination may differ in the highest degree from the actual event, and my Peter Verkhovensky may not at all be like Nechayev. But it seems to me that in my amazed mind there has been created by my imagination the person, the type that corresponds to that murder. Without a doubt it is not useless to exhibit such a person, but in himself he would not have tempted me. In my view, these pitiable monstrosities are not worthy of literature. To my own surprise, that character turns out half comical in my novel. And, therefore, notwithstanding the fact that

all that event occupies one of the foremost planes of
the novel, it is nevertheless only an accessory and setting
for the actions of another character, who might indeed
be called the chief character of the novel. That other
character (Nicolay Stavrogin) is also a sinister one,
also a villain. But it seems to me that he is a tragic
character, although many people, on reading the novel,
are bound to say : " What does it mean ? " I sat down
to a composition of that character because I had long
wished to draw him. In my opinion he is both a Russian
and typical character. I shall be very, very sad, if I
cannot manage him. Sadder still will it be if I hear the
verdict that he is a stilted character. I took him from
my heart. Certainly, it is a character, rarely appearing
in all its typicalness ; but it is a Russian character (of a
certain stratum of society). But defer your judgment
of me until the novel is finished. Something in me
tells me that I shall manage that character. I do not
explain it now in full : I am afraid of saying the wrong
thing. I shall observe this only : that character is
described by me in scenes, in action, and not in discussion
—therefore there is a hope of his turning out a person.

" For a long time I could not manage the opening of
the novel. I re-wrote it several times. It is true, with
that novel something has happened to me which never
happened before : for weeks I would stop working on
the opening and would write from the end. Apart
from this, I am afraid, the opening could have been
livelier. With the five and a half folios (which I send)
I have hardly set the plot going. Still the plot, the
action, will expand and develop unexpectedly. For
the further interest of the novel I answer. It seems to
me it is better as it stands.

" But not all the characters will be sinister ones.
There will also be attractive ones. I am rather afraid
that a good deal is beyond my strength. For the first
time, for instance, I want to touch on a class of people,

still very little touched on in literature. For the ideal of such a character I take Tikhon Zadonsky. Mine is also a bishop living in retirement at a monastery. With him I contrast the hero of my work and bring them together for a time. I am in some trepidation ; I have never tried it before, but of that life I know something. . . ."

FROM DOSTOEVSKY'S NOTEBOOKS.

I

A variant of a passage in " The Devils."[1]

" Will no one in the whole planet, having done with God and believing in self-will, dare to assert the whole of his self-will in its most complete manifestation ? It is like this, as though a poor man on suddenly receiving an inheritance should get frightened and not dare approach his millions, considering himself unworthy of it. I want to assert, even if I am the only one who dares, yet I will assert."

" Assert then."

" I have done with God, and therefore I myself am obliged to become God. I must shoot myself."

" Can that indeed be the reason ? You see, you are saying that I always agree with you. I can't refrain from saying that these problems are unprofitable to me. Why must you shoot yourself ? "

" Because the most complete manifestation of my self-will is the taking of my own life. I will enact the most complete manifestation."

" You had better kill someone else."

" That would mean the lowest manifestation of my

[1] From the manuscript of *The Devils*, Part III.

self-will—and that is like you. But I want the highest
—and that is like me. I am bound to do it."

" You are bound ? You did not make it clear, did
you ? "

" In order to assert myself completely. There is no
higher idea to me than the idea that there is no God.
If there is none, I do not see how mankind will go on
living, unless it is reborn in a different form and body.
History is on my side. Man has always invented God
in order to make it possible for him not to kill himself.
But I do not want to invent God, I know that He does
not exist, and I do not want to lie in my turn. I alone
on earth and in the history of the universe do not want
to invent God ; I will not submit. If He is not, then
I certainly am God ; for then there is none higher than
myself on the planet. There cannot be. Science is
on my side. I occupy and succeed to the former place
of God, and therefore I must kill myself ; for I cannot
be without God, nor can I be God myself, if I am not
going to manifest my fullest self-will. As to the former
God of complete unbelief . . . I will kill myself. Let
them learn."

" Who is to learn ? "

" All, all shall learn. There is nothing hidden
which shall not be revealed ; it is He who said so."

And he pointed to the image of the Saviour, before
which a lamp was burning.

" In Him then you believe ? You have even a lamp
burning ? "

" In Him ? Listen. Exactly in the same degree
do I not believe in the former God as He did believe.
There was a day on earth and in the middle of the earth
stood three crosses. One on the cross believed so much
that He said to the other for his belief : ' to-day thou
shalt be with me in paradise.' The day passed, both
died—and found neither paradise nor resurrection.
What was said on the cross turned out a lie. That man

was the highest product of the earth. The whole planet
with all that there is in it, with all that has been and
will be, is not worth a single word of that man ! Never
before nor after, never will there be anything like him,
this miracle—the miracle being that there never was
nor will there be anything like him. And now, if with
him a lie happened, if the laws of nature did not spare
even him, and caused even him to tell a lie, to believe
in a lie and to die for a lie--then the whole planet rests
on a lie and on mockery. Therefore the very law of
the planet is a lie, and the whole of life is the Devil's
farce, if there were a Devil. And if so, wherefore live ?
Answer if you are a man, if you are an honest man, if
you are serious and great. Suppose I alone say that
I am God. But if I am God, I wish to be like the former
God, I wish to judge the planet, to alter the revolting
lie of its law, and if that is impossible, then to destroy
it ! But since I do not know how to alter it, and
cannot destroy it, then I, God, wish to destroy myself.
Enough, it is time ! "

[Let me be the one who does not lie against all !
To invent a God for the fools and to deceive them all
their lives long in order to ride on their backs and in
order that my seat may be soft to sit on—I do not
want that.][1]

" But are you alone an atheist ? Are you the only
one who has realised that there is no God ? Are you
alone a suicide ? "

" I alone. I alone have realised it, only myself. I
do not understand, how one can realise that there is no
God and not kill himself instantly. Only a wretch who
is not worthy of being a man could realise that there is
no God, and not kill himself. One can't consent to ten
or fifteen years of life in order to be annihilated afterwards. And, besides, all those fifteen years to be
aware that there is no God, and to go on inventing Him

---

[1] The passage in brackets is crossed out in the MSS.

for fools ! To realise that there is no God, and not to realise that oneself is God, is impossible. And once having realised, manifest the attribute ! My attribute is self-will—I shall shoot myself in order to manifest my self-will. That is the only way in which I can assert my protest and my refusal to submit. My attribute is self-will."

He was as though in a fever, he no longer paced the room from one corner to another, but whirled, as it were, round and round. His face was unnaturally pale. P.'s [Peter Verkhovensky's] face expressed again an extraordinary agitation. He had moved to consult the clock on the wall, but restrained himself. " A document ! He must at any cost extract a document from Kirillov ! Otherwise he might go off his head and end in a delirium."

" Give me a pen ! " Kirillov cried out all at once and quite unexpectedly, stopping in the middle of the room in a sort of inspiration. " Dictate what you like, I'll sign anything ! I shall prove to you that, although I shall sign, yet all that is hidden shall be revealed [and the lie will become truth]. Dictate, speak out, I am not afraid. I shall say that I killed Shatov."

II

ORIGINAL NOTES FOR " THE DEVILS "

The Bishop and the Prince[1]

The Prince is leaving (after putting his question " Do you believe in God "). The Bishop calls him back.

" Tell me I entreat you, did you tell me the truth or was it a lie ? "

---

[1] *The Prince* subsequently became Nicolay Stavrogin.

The Prince looks at him : " Was it all a lie ? "

The Bishop glances at him, thinks for a while, and blesses him : " Go in peace."

After that, on the following day, arrives a note from the Prince. " What I told you was all a lie, and you can convince yourself that I am not lying now, even for this reason that I am writing you not from fear of being exposed, for you will not tell it to anyone, but merely from my desire to render my unworthy behaviour to you less offensive. I was a bit out of my mind ; I suffer from a certain illness ; do forgive me and pray for me. Your son Stavrogin."

The Bishop writes to him the same evening : " And I implore you to put off your great deed for some time, as I advised you. For I see that you will not be equal to it. First strengthen yourself, master yourself, summon up all your power and perseverance, and then, if you can, do it. For the deed is very great."

Then, in the course of the novel, the Prince betrays himself again (and writes of this in his note from the station, from Uri) [in Switzerland], which makes it clear to the reader that he had actually committed the crime and had not lied to Tikhon. " Let Tikhon pray for me," he writes.

The Prince speaks to Shatov of the happiness of communion with nature. (To describe the elation that precedes an epileptic fit.) Götter Griechenlands, and what God says to man.

The Prince speaks to Shatov of the Apocalypse, of the name of the Beast, of the wounded head.

The whole difference between the Prince and Shatov lies in their convictions, in that Shatov is still walking outside the locked door, while the Prince has already arrived at all the conclusions, and as his *principal idea* he accepts *Orthodoxy* as the chief basis of the new civilisation from the East. The Bishop, while recognising the Prince's conceptions of Orthodoxy, does not harass him with the obligation of self-resurrection, of self-perfection, that is, with the obligation of the practical duty of Orthodoxy.

And it results in the Prince startling Shatov with the idea of Orthodoxy, that is, with the catechism of a new faith, which every new man is bound to accept at whatever cost. And the Bishop says that a catechism of a *new faith* is all right, but faith without deeds is dead, and he demands not the highest deed (the highest classicism), but one more difficult still—the works of Orthodoxy, as if he said : " Well now, *barin*, are you capable of this ? " And the Prince admits that he is a *barin* ; he assures them that he has lied and takes back his words ; as a result—Uri.[1]

The Prince and the Bishop. The *idea*. *The Bishop* argues that there is no need for a jump, but that one must first restore the man in oneself (by long labour and then make a jump).

The Prince : " And if suddenly it turns out imposs-ible ? "

The Bishop : " Impossible ? Then instead of the work of angels it will be that of the devils."

The Prince : " Ah, I knew it myself."

In the Prince's note about the rape there is this passage :

" . . . All this I have done, as a *barin*, as an idler, uprooted from the soil. Although I do admit that the chief cause lay in my evil will, and not merely in my surroundings. Of course, nobody commits such crimes. But all those who are uprooted from the soil do the same, although in a pettier, shallower manner. Many men, too, take no heed of their abominations, and consider themselves honest. . . . "

The Bishop says that he had better cross out the

---

[1] Stavrogin (originally *The Prince*) ends by going to Uri in Switzer-land and taking his life there.

passage.   The Prince, as if hurt, says : " I am not an author."

The Prince's main idea, which has struck Shatov, and which he has quite passionately adopted, is the following : the point is not industries, but morality, not the economic, but the *moral regeneration of Russia.*

For a fantastic page.   The Prince and Shatov.

The Prince : " All this is mere words—one must act."

Shatov : " Do what ? "

The Prince : " What the others do—build ourselves, build the kingdom of Christ.   We derive our faith from politics.   The Slavophiles with their icons,—but we must act through Orthodox discipline and humility ; no slaves, all are free.   Christianity permeating the lands of freedom with blessings.   The Pope as Anti-Christ.   Not in economics, but in moral regeneration is strength.   Complete power is needed to fulfil the whole idea."

" We Russians bring to the world the renewal of the ideal which it has lost ; the beast with the wounded head, the millennium.   Imagine that all are Christs, will there be poor people then ?   I know Herzen—it is a farce."

Shatov : " If so, one must become a monk."

The Prince : " Why ? Proclaim Christ in the Russian land and proclaim Him through yourself. Great deeds are needed.   A great deed must be accomplished.   One must be great in order to go against common sense."

Shatov : " They say : In Science is power."

The Prince : " Science gives no moral satisfaction ; it does not supply an answer to the chief problems. A great deed is wanted.   Let the Russian power show that it can perform it.   By deeds you will conquer the world."

Shatov gets into a strange reverie. " You know it is all fantasy," he said. " It is either bookish, or religious mania. . . . Just summon all to perform a great deed ! "

The Prince: " Why all ? Can't you conceive, how powerful one man can be ? Let there appear one, and all will follow him. There is needed self-accusation and deeds. An ideal is needed ; otherwise you will not find Orthodoxy, and there will be nothing."

The Prince is seeking for a deed, for active work, for the proclamation to the world of the Russian power. His idea is genuine Orthodoxy, active (for who believes now ?). Moral power before economic. (*N.B.*—He does not believe in God, but keeps in his mind Tikhon's deed) : " Do you know how strong one man can be ? " On the whole, to have in view that the Prince is as fascinating as the devil, and his terrible passions struggle with his idea of a deed. And along with that, unbelief and torture. The growth of faith. The idea of a deed prevails. Faith gets the upper hand, but the devils, too, believe and tremble. " It is too late," says the Prince, and runs to Uri, and then he hangs himself.

[Another variant.] Or like this : The Prince comes to Shatov, " What about Orthodoxy ? " he asks. Shatov begins to explain. The Prince agrees (and confirms it even from the Apocalypse). Shatov sees that their convictions are alike.

" How could that have come about ? " Shatov asks.

" But you are repeating the old ideas of the Slavophiles," the Prince says.

Shatov explains the difference : " The idea of the Slavophiles was an aristocratic game, an icon, (Kireyevsky), they can never believe directly."

The Prince agrees : " If they do not believe directly and completely, then they believe in nothing at all, and then it is better to wipe out everything, as Nechayev says."

" What do you mean by ' wiping out ' ? "

The Prince explains ; the philosophy of digestion ;[1] the question of time ; gradual extinction. " You see, there is this difference between us and the Slavophiles, that we attribute such an importance to the question and regard it as a *sine qua non*. Orthodoxy and Russia. We think that Orthodoxy and nothing else preserves the image of Christ, and we consider Russia as the standard-bearer of Orthodoxy. On the other hand, I think that Christianity contains all the solutions of all human problems. The child, the millennium, the Apocalypse, the wounded beast.

The Prince: " The whole question then is, can one believe ? "

Shatov: " Do you not believe then ? "

The Prince: " You see, either faith is everything or nothing ! We realise the importance of saving the world by Orthodoxy ; and so the whole question is, can one believe in Orthodoxy, throwing aside all philosophy of digestion ? If one can believe, then all is saved ; if not, then it is better to wipe out everything."

Shatov: " Indeed, do you not believe ? "

The Prince: " What do you want me for, I ask you ? I simply came to ask you, if you believed. I was curious to know."

Shatov: " I . . . think I believe."

The Prince: " It means then that you do not."

Shatov: " That comes from my being detached from the people."

The Prince: " But that again is a question of time. Even if you were not detached from the people now, you would still fail to believe a hundred years hence."

Shatov: " Tell me frankly : Do you indeed not believe ? "

---

[1] The materialistic conception.

The Prince: " I shall be polite and answer you. No, I do not believe. And look here, Shatov, let us try never to meet again. Tell me, I demand an answer, I speak earnestly. I am not speaking about the slap in the face you gave me."

The Prince and Tikhon.

Tikhon: " People should be happy on earth."

The Prince: " Mine is an idle mind and I am bored. I know that one could be happy on earth (and should), and that there is a something, in which there is happiness ; but I do not know what it is. No, I am not one of the disillusioned ones, I think. I am one of the depraved and idle. . . . I want to test my strength," and he tells him of the little girl (whom he had raped).

Tikhon: " Many are those who love, but very few who believe. What is a lover ? He who wishes, who would wish to believe. Only perfect love coincides with perfect belief. It is indifference that does not believe at all ; most complete atheism stands perhaps nearer to faith than anything else."

The most important scene takes place at Tikhon's. The Prince confesses to him that he has a furious passionate love for a certain woman. " I received a message that she would come to me. I shall *not be able to resist* ; the mere idea plunges me into a frenzy of passion."

Tikhon, saying good-bye to him : " I am terrified for you."

The Prince: " Leave it to me . . . ."

Tikhon: " I am terrified, because you are so very near a crime."

Tikhon: " I imagine it like this : Your soul will wander and see its sin, not as it sees it now, but the whole sin ; and your soul will see God opening his arms to it Then it will rebel and will itself demand punishment, and it will be seeking punishment ; but it will be answered with love ; and therein is its hell. The consciousness of love unrequited must be most terrible, and just therein is hell."

The Prince : " I do not believe in God. How can you say that God will forgive me ? "

Tikhon : " Oh, I do not understand it myself. Sin is infinite, but God, too, is infinite in his wisdom."

His wife lies in bed and Shatov paces his little chamber saying : " How good it is to live quietly, to love, to have children."

The Prince : " They are all against Christ (Renan and Granovsky) and they consider him an ordinary man ; they criticise his teaching as not valid for our times. But there is no teaching there, there are only accidental words ; the chief thing is the image of Christ, from whom comes all teaching. (On the other hand, mark the vanity and moral state of those critics. Now, how can they criticise Christ ?) From Christ comes the idea that the paramount achievement and goal of mankind is the result of the morality it has acquired. Imagine all to be Christs—would there be possible the present instability of ideas, the perplexities, pauperism ? "

Now examine civilisation : the first problem is the definition of happiness ? The problem is not only not solved by civilisation, but is made still more entangled.

(*For the characterisation of the Prince.*) Certain sinners (and they say also devils) can arrive at belief, and therefore understand and see clearly what they believe in.

The Prince confesses to Shatov his dastardly attack on the little girl (rape). He writes his confession, wishes to publish it, and shows it to Shatov, asking his

advice. He says he wants people to spit in his face.
But after that he gets to hate Shatov, and is glad that
he has been killed.

(*Nechayev—partly also Petrashevsky.*)

The Prince understands that he could save himself
by enthusiasm (for instance, by monastic life, by the
self-sacrifice of confession) ; but for enthusiasm he lacks
the moral sense (partly through unbelief), partly
through the riotous instincts of the flesh. *And unto
the angel of the church in Sardis write!* In a mood of
bitter irony at his incapacity for achieving self-mastery,
he marries. From a passion for tormenting he rapes
the little girl. A passion for racking his conscience.
Lisa's is a passionate nature. Having possessed her,
he kills the lame girl. After the murder of Shatov he
gets a fit of madness (there may be speeches) and
hangs himself. Nostalgia. But the principal thing is,
after all, his unbelief. Horror of himself, for instance,
because of his consciousness of the pleasure he takes in
the suffering of others.

The Prince says to Tikhon frankly, that at times he
suffers profoundly from compunctions of conscience.
At times those compunctions turn into pleasure (pins
under the little girl's finger nails).

The Prince quite believes in the anti-Christ and in
salvation by Orthodoxy. But as he conscientiously
believes that his belief is insufficient, he utters the
formula : " If I believe not sufficiently, then I believe
in nothing ! "

Tikhon answers him on this point : " Yes, it so
happens with certain people who insist vehemently
and demand a good deal. Others are satisfied even with
little faith and manage to live even on a rocking ground,
provided it does not rock too violently.'

The aesthetic principle depends on religion.

Tikhon. His main idea. The only freedom is to
conquer oneself. Slave and freeman.

All comes from my not knowing what is better : pins under the finger nails, or Christ.

At the very last meeting, between Granovsky and Nechayev in the country, Granovsky suddenly cries out in despair :

" Oh, good heavens ! If you have doomed the whole world to destruction, if you are so much convinced of the necessity of overthrowing and destroying, then won't you find a tear, even a grain of pity and sorrow for all that you destroy ? Why are you so calm, why are you so inhuman and so unfeeling ? Why don't you cry ? Are you a stone or a man, for I can't make out things at all ? "

The Holy Spirit is the direct understanding of beauty, the prophetic consciousness of harmony, and therefore the undeviating aspiration towards it.

Stepan Trofimovich says of God : " Give me God ! This alone, my recognition that there is a being superior to me, reconciles me to life and prevents me from falling into despair (and a smaller man it prevents from falling into depravity and coarseness).
The Prince's idea (in his meeting with Shatov) of the immense importance of Orthodoxy and of its new phase. The influence of Pius' Œcumenical Council. (*To express my whole opinion of Orthodoxy, as the completest and most genuine expression of Russia. This opinion to be expressed in the most outspoken fashion*).
The future war on account of the two religions (France and Russia). . . . Russia and Europe, indirectly perhaps, will be convinced that they are fighting not for religion, yet it shall be for religion. The spirit of the war and of its necessity will arise on account of religion as a new ideal.

(1870) Shatov is a restless product of books, who has come into collision with actuality, who has come to believe passionately, but does not know what to do. There is much beauty in his personality.

The great writer (Turgenev) says : " As to God, I do not believe in him."

Granovsky says of the great writer : " He screamed, ' Oh, my mother,' when something went wrong with the railway engine."

A Fragment from the Manuscript of " The Adolescent."

If I were to compose an opera, you know, I should take the subject of Faust. I love that theme very much. Gounod does it well ; but I would compose a scene in the cathedral. You know, a Gothic cathedral, the interior, choirs, hymns, enter Gretchen, and you know, mediæval choirs, as in Meyerbeer's, in whose *Robert* you can hear the tenth century ; it gets you into the tenth century.

Editor's Note : (In Versilov's speech, " One can't love people " . . . after the phrase " who is only a wee bit not silly . . . whether he is honest or not, it does not matter," comes the following fragment which is not given in the published text).

" Without a doubt Christ could not love us such as we are. He suffered us. He forgave us ; but certainly he despised us. I at any rate cannot understand his image otherwise. To love one's neighbour and not to despise him is impossible." . . .

Editor's Note : (Page 31 of the MS. of *The Adolescent* contains the following monologue bearing on Leo Tolstoy and on his *War and Peace*. The monologue of the MS. which is not included in the published text of the novel, is crossed out by Dostoevsky's hand.)

He [Versilov] smiled and was silent for a while. He visibly grew sadder and sadder ; but at the same time, as he went on, a violent agitation seized him quite obviously.

" I have, my dear, one favourite Russian writer. He is a novelist ; but to me he is almost the historian of your nobility, or rather of the cultured stratum, which crowns the period of ' enlightenment ' in our history, as a contemporary Russian General, who is also an author, puts it. In that historian of your nobility I love above all that very same ' beauty,' for which you have been searching, as shown in the characters depicted by him. He takes a nobleman from his childhood and adolescence, he depicts him among his family, his first steps in life, his first joys, tears and all so . . . [words illegible] firmly and unerringly."

He is the psychologist of the nobleman's soul. But the principal point is that what he presents is incontestable, and you are bound to agree with him. You agree and envy. Oh, how great the envy ! There are children, who from their very childhood are offended by the unseemliness of their parents, of their environment, and who, above all, still in their childhood, begin to understand the disorderliness and casualness of the foundations of their whole life, the lack of established forms and family traditions. These must envy my writer, envy his heroes, and rather dislike them. (*There are such, and I have known them from childhood.*) Oh, they are not heroes ; they are lovely children, having excellent, fine fathers who eat at clubs, who entertain guests in their Moscow houses, whose elder sons are Hussars or University undergraduates, of the kind that keep their own horses. The writer presents them with all frankness. Often they personally are ridiculous and funny, often even nonentities ; but as a whole, as a class, they indisputably represent something accomplished. In the foundations of this higher stratum of

Russians there is already something stable and indisput-
able. In it every individual may have his weakness,
and even be very ridiculous ; but he is strong by the
whole achievement of the last two centuries, the roots
of which go even further down. And despite the
realism, the actuality, the ridiculous and the comic,
there is also here what is moving and pathetic. However good or bad in itself, there is here *an achieved
definite form* (order and honour), here rules have been
established, here is honour and duty of a kind. Oh,
they are not only in Moscow, and not in clubs only, and
not all of them are constantly entertaining guests. The
historian paints the largest (and most glorious) historical
picture of the cultured class. He takes that class
and shows it in the most glorious epoch of the country.
They die for their fatherland, they rush to battle either
as ardent young men or as adored Generals, who lead
the whole country into battle. Oh . . . [word
illegible] the impartiality, the reality of the pictures
give an amazing fascination to the description ; alongside with representatives of talent, honour and duty,
what a number of frank scoundrels, ridiculous nonentities and fools ! In his best types the historian represents
precisely, with subtlety and wit, the reincarnation . . .
of European ideas in the persons of the Russian nobility.
There are Free Masons there, there is the reincarnation
of Pushkin's Silvio, taken from Byron, there are there
the origins of the Decembrists. In his last works the
artist already takes the new times, the present. The
boy whom he describes as a child, has now grown up ;
he is a present-day landlord living on his estate, with
no serfs. He takes no part in the Zemstvo councils,
he does not go there—he is not yet prepared . . .
[words illegible], but a calm and perplexed melancholy
always envelopes his actions and his outlook on life . . ."

MME. DOSTOEVSKY'S MARGINALIA TO THE WORKS OF F. M. DOSTOEVSKY

Mme. Dostoevsky made the following marginal notes to the volumes of the complete edition of Dostoevsky's works, which she herself brought out in 1906. The notes here given are taken from the volumes, kept in the Moscow Historical Museum. The pages here cited are those of the original Russian edition of 1906.

CRIME AND PUNISHMENT

Page 99. ("On the V. Prospect.") During the first weeks of our married life, Dostoevsky took me once to the court-yard of a house, and showed me the stone, under which Raskolnikov had hidden the things he had stolen from the old money-lender. The courtyard was in Vosnessensky Prospect, near Maximilianov Lane. On the site of the yard now stand the huge offices of a German newspaper.

Page 119. ("What it means to order at Charmer's.") Charmer was a tailor, well-known then in Petersburg, from whom Dostoevsky used to order his clothes.

Page 389. ("A restless delirium seized her.") The death scene of the consumptive woman is probably taken from that of Dostoevsky's first wife, Marie Dmitrievna. And I must also say that in the character of Katerina Ivanovna there are presented many of Marie Dmitrievna's traits. As far as I could judge from the accounts given by Dostoevsky and his friends and relations, Marie Dmitrievna during the last two years of her life, was not quite normal. Doctor A. P. Ivanov [the husband of Dostoevsky's sister] who treated Marie, told me, for instance, in 1867, that Marie loved to wind up the clock, and would wind it up until the spring burst. She often complained to the doctor that there were many devils in her room. Doctor Ivanov would

open the window, drive the devils out with his handkerchief, and then the poor invalid would feel relieved.

Page 395. (" In the consciousness of death and in
the sensation of the presence of death . . .") These
were Dostoevsky's sensations in those cases when he
had to be present at the death of someone, or at a
service for the dead.

HUMILIATED AND INSULTED

Page 185. (" And it crossed my mind then : what
if you, for instance, were to fall ill and die . . .")
These were the feelings of Dostoevsky with regard to
those of whom he was fond. Such were his feelings to
me, as his letters to me show.

Page 309. (" At such an intense moment . . .")
Dostoevsky used to speak in this way of his state of
mind when he had to work intensely.

Page 5. (" I noticed that in a crowded house . . .")
Dostoevsky was ready to deny himself anything, provided he could have even two large rooms in his house.

THE ETERNAL HUSBAND

Page 334. (" Velchaninov complained of loss of
memory . . .") All this happened to Dostoevsky
personally. He used so completely to forget the faces
of the people he knew, that at times he did not even
recognise my brother, of whom he was sincerely fond.
His forgetfulness created for him many enemies, who
took his not recognising them as a personal slight. He
would forget the most recent happenings ; yet he
remembered circumstances of the past, and used to
surprise his relations by the clarity of his recollections.

Page 378. Dostoevsky was bad at distinguishing
colours.

Page 400. (" It was a bright evening, the sun was
setting . . .") Dostoevsky experienced a similar
sensation when in 1868 he came for the first time to
the cemetery to visit the grave of Sonia, our dead baby
child. " Sonia has sent me this peace," he said.

Page 408.   (Chapter XII.)   In the characters of the Zakhliobin family Dostoevsky described the family of his own sister, Mme. Vera Ivanov.   That family, at the time I made their acquaintance, consisted of three grown-up daughters, and they had many girl friends.

Page 410.   (" In the company of a clever and sharp girl friend, Marie . . . ")   In the character of Marie, Dostoevsky described Marie Ivanchin-Pisarov, a very charming and witty girl, and an intimate friend of the Ivanovs.

Page 421.   (" Velchaninov chose Glinka's romance " When in a happy hour . . . ")   Dostoevsky told me on several occasions of the extraordinary impression produced on him by that romance, as performed by Glinka himself, whom he had met in his youth.

Page 430.   (" A very young man entered the room . . . ")   In the character of the young man Dostoevsky described his stepson, Pasha Issayev.

THE DEVILS

Page 60.   (" The Lake of Geneva gives you toothache . . . ")   During the winter of 1867–68 Dostoevsky had frequent attacks of toothache (we spent the winter in Geneva, and the spring in Vevey), and he assured me that his teeth ached because of the proximity of the Lake of Geneva, and said that he had once read something about that peculiarity of the Lake.

Page 101.   (" I love tea at night . . . " he said.)   Dostoevsky loved very strong tea.   The samovar was on the dinner table from 12 p.m.   But especially did he love tea at night when he was working.

Page 116.   (" The literary undertaking was of such a kind . . . ")   Dostoevsky longed for a similar literary undertaking, and he was convinced that a book of that sort could be of great value and sell a very great number of copies.   He asked me to collaborate with him in classifying the cuttings.

Page 292. (" They came to see Semion Yakovlevich . . . ") Dostoevsky describes his visit to the well-known crazy man of Moscow, Ivan Yakovlevich Koreisha.

Page 520. (" There are seconds, there come five or six of them all at once. . . . ") Sensations, experienced by Dostoevsky, which he used to describe to me and our children.

Page 521, 522. (" Mme. Shatov in labour.") Dostoevsky describes his state of mind during the hours of my giving birth to our first child, Sonia.

Page 568. (" From the village house they were taken direct to a large hut. . . . ") Dostoevsky describes " Ustrika " village, on the bank of the Ilmen Lake, where we and all our family had to wait for a boat on our return in September from Staraia Roussa to Petersburg. We often had to wait at " Ustrika " for two days.

THE BROTHERS KARAMASOV

Page 22. (" Such recollections one can preserve in one's mind. . . . ") One of Dostoevsky's recollections dated back as early as his second year. He remembered how his mother took him to the village church, and how, while the communion was being administered, a dove came flying across the church from one window to the other.

Page 32. (" One of our contemporary monks was saving his soul on Mount Athos. . . . ") Dostoevsky refers to *The Pilgrimages of the Monk Parfeni*. He had that book in his library and used to re-read it at times.

Page 53. (" I am sorry for my little son, for Boriushka, he was only three years old. . . . ") Here are reflected Dostoevsky's impressions on the death of our son Aliosha, who died in 1878. He was two years and nine months old. That very same year Dostoevsky began writing his *Brothers Karamasov*.

Page 54–57. ("'Behold, mother,' said the old man, 'it is Rachel crying . . .'") Dostoevsky repeated these words to me on his return from the Optino Monastery. There he had had a conversation with the venerable Amvrosi, and told him of how we grieved over our boy who had died recently. Amvrosi promised Dostoevsky to mention Aliosha and my grief in his prayers, and to pray for us all. Dostoevsky was greatly struck by the old man, and deeply moved by his promise to pray for us.

Page 186. ("The whole of our town is intersected by little ditches . . .") Dostoevsky is describing Staraia Roussa, where we lived. The place in the novel where the boys' fight occurred, is quite familiar to the Dostoevsky family.

Page 196. ("Tchermashnya.") Tchermashnya is a small forest, part of the Darovoye estate, in the Tula province, belonging to the children of Vera Ivanov, Dostoevsky's sister.

Page 302–303. ("It is wonderful, my Fathers and Masters, that the faces being so unlike . . .") This was how Dostoevsky regarded his intimate friend, the young philosopher Vladimir Soloviov, who, in his spirituality, reminded him of Ivan Shidlovsky, the friend who had had such a beneficial influence on the author in his youth.

Page 308. ("I was eight years old when I had my first spiritual experience . . .") These are Dostoevsky's personal recollections of his childhood. I have heard him say so on several occasions.

Page 426. ("The Plotnikov's Shop.") Dostoevsky speaks of the shop belonging to Plotnikov in Staraia Roussa, where he himself used to buy sweets and comestibles.

Page 657. ("Details, chiefly, details. . . .") Dostoevsky's favourite expression when he was interested in anything.

The Life of a Great Sinner.

In the winter of 1869–1870 Fiodor Mikhailovich was engaged in composing the plan of a new novel which he meant to call *The Life of a Great Sinner*. My husband's idea was that the work should consist of five long books, each book forming an independent novel, to be published serially or in book form. In all the five novels Fiodor intended to deal with the important and tormenting problem of the existence of God, the problem which tormented him all his life long. The action of the first novel was to take place in the forties of the nineteenth century. The materials and the types of that period were so clear and familiar to Fiodor that he could have written that novel even while remaining abroad. That novel Fiodor thought of publishing in Strakhov's *Zarya*. But for the writing of the second novel, the action of which was to take place in a monastery, Fiodor considered it essential to return to Russia. In that second novel he intended to present the venerable Tikhon Zadonsky as the chief character; of course, under a different name. Fiodor placed great hopes on this projected work, and regarded it as the culmination of his literary activity. But this anticipation was realised only later on, for many characters of *The Life of a Great Sinner* were included afterwards in *The Brothers Karamasov*. But at that time (1869–1870) my husband did not succeed in realising his intention, for he was carried away by another theme. "On the thing which I am now writing for the *Russky Vestnik*," he writes to Strakhov, "I rely very much—not as a work of art, but as an expression of a tendency. I want to express certain ideas, if even my artistry perishes in the task ; for I am carried away by what has been accumulating in my mind and in my heart. Suppose it even turns out a mere pamphlet, yet I shall have spoken out my mind."

The Devils.

That was his novel, *The Devils*, which appeared in 1871. The arrival of my brother had a certain influence on its origin. The point is that Fiodor, who read various foreign papers (which printed a great deal of information, not allowed to be made public in Russia), came to the conclusion that very shortly political agitations were bound to take place in the Petrovsky Academy of Agriculture. Fearing that my brother, owing to his youth and unformed character, might take an active part in the movement, my husband advised my mother to invite him to spend the summer vacations with us in Dresden. This invitation Fiodor meant as a pleasure both to myself and to my mother, who had lived the last two years abroad, and missed her son very much. My brother accordingly came to us for the summer vacations. Fiodor, who was always fond of him, was interested in his studies, in his friends, and generally in the life and the movements among the students. My brother told him everything and with enthusiasm. It was then that Fiodor conceived the idea of describing in one of his novels the political movement of that period, and as one of his chief characters he took the student Ivanov (called Shatov in *The Devils*), who was subsequently killed by Nechayev. My brother spoke of Ivanov as of a man of good sense and of a strong character, who had radically changed his former convictions. And how very distressed my husband was when he afterwards learnt from the papers of the murder of Ivanov, for whom he had conceived a sincere sympathy. The Academy park and the grotto, where Ivanov's murder took place, was described by Fiodor from the account given by my brother.

Although the material for the new novel was taken from actual life, Fiodor found it extraordinarily difficult to write the novel. As usual he was dissatisfied with his work, he re-wrote it many times, and destroyed fifteen folios of one version of it. A novel with a tendency evidently was not in keeping with his creative activity.

In Fiodor's notebook, under the date of December 24th, 1877, there is the following entry.

Memento. For my whole life.

1. To write a Russian *Candide.*
2. To write a book on Jesus Christ.
3. To write my reminiscences.
4. To write a poem on the Commemoration of the Dead.

(All these, except my last novel and the intended publication of my *Journal of an Author*, will take me at least ten years of work, and I am fifty-six now.)

For Product Safety Concerns and Information please contact our EU
representative GPSR@taylorandfrancis.com
Taylor & Francis Verlag GmbH, Kaufingerstraße 24, 80331 München, Germany